AF342674

Peter Porter

A Bibliography 1954–1986

Compiled by John R. Kaiser

LONDON AND NEW YORK

First published 1990 by
Mansell Publishing Limited
A Cassell imprint
Artillery House, Artillery Row, London SW1P 1RT, England
125 East 23rd Street, Suite 300, New York 10010, USA

British Library Cataloguing in Publication Data
Kaiser, John R.
Peter Porter: a bibliography, 1954–1986.
1. Poetry in English. Porter, Peter, 1929–. Bibliographies
I. Title
016.821'914

ISBN 0–7201–2032–2

Library of Congress Cataloging-in-Publication Data

Kaiser, John R. (John Robert)
Peter Porter: a bibliography, 1954–1986/compiled by John R. Kaiser.
p. cm.
ISBN 0–7201–2032–2
1. Porter, Peter—Bibliography. I. Title.
Z8706.1.K35 1990
[PR9619.3.P57] 89–13943
016.821—dc20 CIP

Printed and bound in Great Britain by
Biddles Ltd, Guildford and King's Lynn.

Contents

For Laurent LeSage and Bernard Stone

Acknowledgements

A great many people have helped in the preparation of this bibliography and I am most grateful to all of them.

Above all, I am indebted to Peter Porter for his unfailing cooperation, generosity and enthusiasm. I also wish to acknowledge the special help and services of Bernard Stone of the Turret Bookshop, London, without whom this work could not have been completed.

Many individuals, acting in an official or personal capacity, and unknown persons representing institutions, have gone out of their way to be helpful and I should like to express my gratitude to them. Mr Jonathan Barker; Belwin-Mills Music Ltd, Croydon, England; Basil Blackwell Publishers Ltd, Oxford; Boosey & Hawkes Music Publishers Ltd, London; Ms Fleur Bowers; Mr Alan Brownjohn; Ms Katie Burgess; Ms Ruth Cavin; Mr Alan Clodd; Mr Simon Copley; Ms Karen Cozens; Mr Desmond Clarke; Mr Ken Davison; Edinburgh International Festival; Dr J. A. Edwards; Mr Peter Finch; Ms Clare Fletcher; Mr John Fuller; Dr Jack W. C. Hagstrom; Mrs Ingrid Harrison; Ms Josie Hilliger; Mr Simon Huntley; Ilkley Literature Festival; Mr Peter Jay; Mr Thomas Kabdebo; Keepsake Press, Richmond, Surrey; Mrs Margaret Leach; Mr T. R. Manderson; Mr Charles Mann; Mr Simon Mason; Ms Clare Moore; Ms Helen Owen; Mr James Price; Quartet Books, London; Ms Jean Richardson; Mr Bernard Roberts; Robson Books, London; Mr John Rolph; Mrs Rosita Rosenberg; Mr Alan Ross; Mr David Roy; Mrs Stella Saludes; Ms Rosalind Sanderson; Schott Music Publishers, London; Ms Karen Scott; Ms Leonie Scott-Matthews; Mr Peter Scupham; Ms Pam Smith; Mr Geoffrey Soar; The Stourton Press, London; the University of Queensland Press; Mr Michael Wace; Mr Sam Wannamaker; and Ms Joan Ward.

I should also like to thank The Pennsylvania State University and the University Libraries for granting me a Sabbatical during the Fall of 1984 when a large portion of the work for this bibliography was completed.

Introduction

Up until now, there has been no full-scale bibliography of the works of Peter Porter, one of the most important poets writing in English today. In 1983, his *Collected Poems* were published and it seems time to establish a beginning for an exhaustive bibliography of Porter's works.

Although this bibliography ends with 1986, Peter Porter has, of course, continued to write poems and criticism for various journals and newspapers. In 1987, he published *The Automatic Oracle* (Oxford University Press) for which he was awarded the prestigious Whitbread Literary Award for Poetry in 1988. In 1988 he also published *Mars* (Andre Deutsch) in collaboration with Arthur Boyd, as well as editing the *Complete Poems* (Bloodaxe) of Martin Bell. In 1989 two other Porter texts were published by Oxford University Press—*Possible Worlds* and *A Porter Selected*.

This bibliography is basically one of published or printed works by Peter Porter; the exception is the section on recordings. It does not include critical articles, books, dissertations on Peter Porter, nor a list of reviews of his writings; other exclusions are radio and television appearances, a listing of manuscripts, translations of Porter's work into foreign languages, and such miscellanies as blurbs on dust jackets and publicity releases which contain excerpts of Porter's writings.

Although the format and most of the procedures followed in this bibliography are conventional and will be obvious to the user upon examination of the listings themselves, a few comments may be useful. As much as possible, I have followed the format of the excellent work of Jack W. C. Hagstrom and George Bixby in their *Thom Gunn: A Bibliography 1940–1978* (London: Bertram Rota, 1979). Each section of the bibliography is preceded by a separate introduction.

All of my citations and descriptions have been based, wherever possible, on examination of the items themselves. Any item which I have not personally examined is annotated, before the description, by the statement 'Not Seen' in square brackets.

Notes that add details or explanations are used throughout the bibliography and are inserted at points where they seem most appropriate. Information included in notes is generally based on examination of the item itself, but a variety of other sources have been used.

I have made no attempt to trace in any systematic manner the printing history of a given poem or prose piece, but this can easily be done by consulting the index. I have made no attempt to identify textual revisions of poems; however, parts of poems published separately are noted and included in the index.

Square brackets surrounding any data indicate that the information given does not appear as such. Thus square brackets are used with page numbers, dates and in transcriptions of title pages and descriptions of dust wrappers and covers to describe publisher's logos, decorative devices, etc., that cannot be adequately transcribed *per se*.

Accepted practice is observed when transcribing upper and lower case letters. Unless there is an indication otherwise, the type is roman, and I have made no attempt to indicate either the size of upper and lower case letters or the amount of space between individual letters or words. In the descriptions of title pages and quasi-facsimile material all printing is in black; colored printing is indicated before the relevant letters or words. A vertical rule marks the end of each line, and any type variation or specific color that continues on the following line is indicated again at the beginning of that line.

Designation of colors is perhaps one of the most difficult undertakings that a bibliographer faces. In general, I have based my assignments on Professor G. Thomas Tanselle's article, 'A System of Color Identification for Bibliographical Description' (*Studies in Bibliography*, XX [1967], pp. 203–4) and the color numbers for all colors (with a few exceptions when a color could not be reasonably matched) except black, white, gold, and silver refer to the *ISCC–NBC* (Inter-Society Color Council National Bureau of Standards) *Color-Name Charts Illustrated with Centroid Colors* (*Supplement to NBS Circular 553*). I have not systematically attempted to distinguish among types of cloth or paper used for bindings and wrappers. Wove paper is distinguished from laid paper and, when identifiable, special papers are named. For dust wrappers and paper wrappers, the indicated color of the paper is that of the base (i.e. unprinted paper stock) and the color of the finished wrapper is given when it is not the same as the base color. The word 'shiny' has been used to describe the whole spectrum of coated papers and glossy printing.

The collation is given by signatures and by leaves for sewn books. Standard notations (numbers or letters) are used for signatures. In most cases, books are not actually signed on the sheets and therefore, the signature marks are enclosed in square brackets. Books described as having 'perfect bindings' are those in which all the pages have been cut and are held together by glue or some other adhesive material; since identifiable signatures are generally no longer present, only the total number of leaves is given.

The size of an individual leaf is given to the nearest tenth of a centimeter, height preceding width. This also applies to size descriptions of broadsheets, labels, etc.

In all sections and subsections all items are listed chronologically. In Section C, items within a given year are listed preferentially by season, month and specific date. When only the year of publication is known for any given item, it is placed at the end of the listing for the year in which it was published.

Prices of each item at the time of publication are given only for the country in which the book was published. The exception to this is for books where the publisher has indicated foreign prices.

Publication data are based on information supplied by publishers and supplemented, as required, from other sources. The phrase 'data unavailable from publisher' indicates that the publisher either could not locate or preferred not to reveal the information requested.

Unquestionably there are errors, omissions, and incorrect data in this book. My aim has been to be as thorough and accurate as is possible. Any additions and emendations would be welcome and should be sent to the publisher.

Abbreviations

Abbreviations for Peter Porter's principal works used in this bibliography are listed in alphabetical order below.

AM	After Martial
APF	A Porter Folio
ASOTM	A Share of the Market
CP	Collected Poems
ES	English Subtitles
FF	Fast Forward
LIACC	Living in a Calm Country
M	Machines
N	Narcissus
OBTB	Once Bitten, Twice Bitten
PAAM	Poems Ancient & Modern
PTTC	Preaching to the Converted
TAP	The Animal Program
TCOS	The Cost of Seriousness
TLOE	The Last of England
TROYFL	The Run of Your Father's Library

A

BOOKS, PAMPHLETS AND BROADSHEETS BY PETER PORTER

In this section all books, pamphlets and broadsheets by Peter Porter are listed in chronological order. Data on reprints and new editions are included. No attempt has been made to denote textual differences in a poem when it is reprinted in a subsequent volume.

A1 ONCE BITTEN, TWICE BITTEN 1961

a. First edition:

ONCE BITTEN, | TWICE BITTEN | poems by | PETER PORTER | [publisher's logo: a full-length view of a scorpion viewed from above] | SCORPION PRESS 1961

Collation: $[1\text{-}5]^6$ = 30 leaves; 21.6 x 13.6 cm.

Binding: The first issue of 309 copies were bound in medium purple (223) cloth; the second issue of 191 copies were bound in dark grayish green (151); both are lettered down the spine in gold: ONCE BITTEN TWICE BITTEN Peter Porter SCORPION PRESS: white wove paper; all edges trimmed; white wove endpapers; dust wrapper of yellowish green (89) wove paper printed in dark olive green (126).

Publication date: 24 February 1961

Price: 15s; 25s for the 25 signed and numbered copies of the edition.

Number of copies: 500

Pagination: Blank endpaper; [1] half-title; [2] blank; [3] title page; [4] First published in February 1961 by | Scorpion Press | 11 Rofant Road, Northwood, Middlesex | © 1961 Peter Porter | [5 lines of acknowledgements] | Printed by Villiers Publications Ltd., | Ingestre Road, London, N.W. 5; [5] For Jannice; [6] *The first 25 copies of this | edition are numbered and signed | by the author;* [7-8] CONTENTS: 9-57, text; [58-60] blank; blank endpaper.

Contents: A Giant Refreshed - Forefathers' View of Failure - Once Bitten, Twice Bitten; Once Shy, Twice Shy - Mr. Roberts - A Christmas Recalled - Sick-room at Home - All Other Time is Peace - Syrup of Figs Will Cast Out Fear - The Picture of Nobody - Conventions of Death - Metamorphosis - Death's Morning Shadows - Beast and the Beauty - Walking Home on St. Cecilia's Day - Reflections on my own Name - Changes Wrung - Tunes for the Fortunate - Lament for a Proprietor - What a Lying Lot the Writers are - John Marston Advises Anger - Sick Man's Jewel - Made in Heaven - Apophthegms come to the Party - A Moral Tale has a Moral End - South of the Duodenum - Death in the Pergola Tea-Rooms - Suicide Unmasked - Away, Musgrave, Away - Jack and Jill - The Smell on the Landing - Party Line - Euphoria Dies - For John Clare from London - A Vicious Vignette - All, all of a Piece Throughout - The Historians call up pain - Annotations of Auschwitz - Who Gets the Pope's Nose? - The Conservation of Energy - Too Worn to Wear - Nature Comes to Stay - Phar Lap in the Melbourne Museum - Tobias and the Angel.

A2 POEMS ANCIENT & MODERN 1964

a. First edition:

PETER PORTER | [decorative rule] | Poems | Ancient & Modern | [publisher's logo: a full-length view of a scorpion viewed from above] | SCORPION PRESS

Collation: $[1\text{-}8]^4 + [9]^2$ = 34 leaves; 21.5 x 14 cm.

Binding: Bound in blue (181) cloth and lettered down the spine in gold: Peter Porter POEMS ANCIENT & MODERN Scorpion Press; white wove paper; all edges trimmed; white wove endpapers; dust wrapper of very light blue (184) wove paper printed in black and red (11)

Publication date: 6 November 1964

Price: 21s

Number of copies: 510 (there was an initial binding of 300 copies and a second binding of 210 copies in February, 1965). In October 1967, 750 copies were issued, 500 with a changed spine plate, title page and verso for Walker and Company of New York (see A2b) and 250 for distribution in the United Kingdom.

Pagination: Blank endpaper; [1] half-title; [2] *By the same author:* | ONCE BITTEN TWICE BITTEN (1961); [3] title page; [4] First published in 1964 by | Scorpion Press | Manor House, Pakefield, Lowestoft, Suffolk | c 1964 Peter Porter | ACKNOWLEDGEMENTS | [7 lines] | Distributed by | Hugh Evelyn Ltd., 9 Fitzroy Square, London W. 1 | Printed by Villiers Publications Ltd, Ingestre Road, London NW5; [5] For | William Porter | and | Katherine Porter; [6] blank; [7] CONTENTS; [8] blank; 9-65, text; [66-68] blank; blank endpaper.

Contents: The Unicorn's Horn - Septimius Severus at the Vienna Gate - A Minor Lear - [untitled poem] "Stepping from a flat-bottomed boat" (first line) - Vienna - Sydney Cove, 1788 - Madame de Merteuil on 'The Loss of An Eye' - A Huddle of IQ's - The World of Simon Raven - The Frankenstein Report - Shames - The Sins of the Fathers - Requiem for Mrs. Hammelswang - Two Merits of Sunshine - The View from Misfortune's Back - An Anthropologist's Confession - Homage to Gaetano Donizetti - Happening at Sordid Creek - The Great Poet comes here in Winter - How to get a Girl Friend - Story from a Time of Disturbance - Nine Points of the Law - To Start a Controversy - Encounter in Antioch - Punic Problems - Changed from Martial's Epigrams - Blucher's Prospect - Shopping Scenes - Inspector Christopher Smart Calls.

Note: For "Changed from Martial's Epigrams," the sections give are: Book IV No. XLIV; Book IX No. LIV; Book XII No. XVII; Book XII No. XVIII.

b. First American edition:

PETER PORTER | [decorative rule] | Poems | Ancient & Modern | [publisher's logo: a large dot surrounded by a circle of W's] | WALKER AND COMPANY | NEW YORK

Collation: $[1\text{-}8]^4 + [9]^2$ = 34 leaves; 21.2 x 13.5 cm.

Binding: Same as A2a except for Walker and Company's logo at the base of the spine of the binding and the dust wrapper.

Publication date: October 1967

Price: $3.50

Number of copies: 500

Pagination: same as A2a except for page [4]: © 1964 Peter Porter | All rights reserved. No portion of this work may be reproduced | without permission except for brief passages for the purpose | of review | ACKNOWLEDGEMENTS | [7 lines same as A2a] | Library of Congress Catalog Card Number: 67-28524. | First published in the United States of America in 1967 by | Walker and Company, a division of Publications Development | Corporation. | Published simultaneously in Canada by The Ryerson Press,| Toronto. | Printed and manufactured in Great Britain.

Contents: Same as A2a.

Note: The Ryerson edition could not be located.

A3 WORDS WITHOUT MUSIC 1968

a. First edition:

[cover title] [in light orange (50)] PETER PORTER | Words without Music | Sycamore Broadsheet 4

Collation: Broadsheet: single sheet, printed on both sides, folded twice to make six unnumbered panels; 20.2 x 32.5 cm. (size of fully open sheet).

Binding: White wove paper, printed in black and light orange (50); all edged trimmed.

Publication date: 4 November 1968

Price: 6d

Number of copies: 450

Pagination: [upper panel, when closed] title page; [when sheet is fully open]: [left panel] 1: Paroles sans Chant; [center and right panel] 2: Rondo Burlesque; [verso of right panel] blank; [verso of central panel] [in light orange (50)] [seven lines of biographical information on Porter] | [single rule] | Sycamore Press, Benson Place, Oxford. Autumn 1968.

Contents: Paroles sans Chant and Rondo Burlesque.

A4 SOLEMN ADULTERY AT BREAKFAST CREEK 1968

a. First edition:

SOLEMN ADULTERY | AT | BREAKFAST CREEK | [fancy italics] AN AUSTRALIAN BALLAD | BY | PETER PORTER | [fancy italics] SET TO MUSIC | BY | MICHAEL JESSETT | WITH | [fancy italics] GUITAR ACCOMPANIMENT | AND EMBELLISHED WITH | [fancy italics] THREE LINOCUTS | BY | PAUL PETER PIECH | [decorative double rule] | PRODUCED BY | [fancy italics] THE KEEPSAKE PRESS | LONDON [decorative device] 1968

Collation: $[1]^8$ = 8 leaves; 20.2 x 14. cm.

Note: Copies have been examined where the paper wrapper measures between 21.6 and 14.5 and 20.5 x 14.5 cm.

Binding: Stitched into stiff light gray (264) wove paper wrappers folded to form double front and rear wrappers; on the front wrapper within a decorative rectangle printed in irregular hand-printed letters: SOLEMN | ADULTERY | at | BREAKFAST | CREEK; the rear wrapper is blank; very light greenish blue (171) semi-shiny wove paper: all edges trimmed.

Publication date: December 1968

Price: 7/6

Number of copies: 200

Pagination: [1-2] blank; [3] title page; [4] blank; [5-6: a single sheet folded vertically to make six unnumbered panels which measure 20.2 x 42 cm] [unfolded sheet]; [4] *Note;* [5a] blank; [5b] blank; [5c-5d: musical score with partial lyrics]; [6] blank; [7-11] text; [12-13] blank; [14] *Printed by Roy Lewis* | *THE KEEPSAKE PRESS* | *26 Sydney Road Richmond Surrey* | [short single rule] | *Copyright Peter Porter 1968* | *Music Copyright Michael Jessett* | [short single rule] | *Limited edition of 200 copies: No.....* | [holograph signature of Peter Porter]; [15-16] blank.

Note: Illustrations appear on pages [7], [9] and [10].

Contents: Solemn Adultery at Breakfast Creek

A5 A PORTER FOLIO 1969

a. First edition:

A | Porter Folio | new poems by | PETER PORTER | [publisher's logo: a full-length view of a scorpion viewed from above] | SCORPION PRESS

Collation: $[1\text{-}9]^4$ = 36 leaves; 20.9 x 14 cm.

Binding: Bound in black cloth and lettered down the spine in gold: Peter Porter A PORTER FOLIO Scorpion Press; white wove paper; all edges trimmed; white wove endpapers; dust wrapper of pale pink (7) wove paper printed in black, deep purplish pink (251) and medium gray (265).

Publication date: June 1969

Price: 25s

Number of copies: 1,000

Note: The publisher reports that there was an initial binding of 500 copies and a second binding of 500 copies in December 1969.

Pagination: blank endpaper; [1] half-title; [2] By the same author: | ONCE BITTEN TWICE BITTEN (1961) | POEMS ANCIENT & MODERN (1964); [3] title page; [4] First published in 1969 by | Scorpion Press | Manor House, Pakefield, Lowestoft, Suffolk | © 1969 Peter Porter | ACKNOWLEDGEMENTS | [10 lines] | Printed by Villiers Publications Ltd., | Ingestre Road, London, NW5; [5] Dedicated to George MacBeth; [6] blank; [7] CONTENTS: [8] blank; 9-70, text; [71-72] blank; blank endpaper.

Contents: The Last of the Dinosaurs - The Three Dreams - The Thirteen Couplets - My Late T'ang Phase - Fantasia on a Line of Stefan George - The Battle of Cannae - After the Temptation - Dorothy Osborne in the Country - A Hoplite's Helmet - St. John on Patmos - Approaches to a Line of Auden & Kallman - First Scene from Dostoyevsky - Second Scene from Dostoyevsky - The Shining God and the God of Correction - What the Guide Book Said - Seahorses - Competition is Healthy - Steps on the Way - The Next Hundred Years will be Religious - The Return of Inspector Christopher Smart - At the Theatre on St. Valentine's Eve - Moaning in Midstream - The Eclipse of Lady Silvertail - Futurity - Homily in the English Reading Rooms - Three Poems for Music - St. Cecilia's Day, 1710 - St. Cecilia's Day Epigrams - One Died in Metaphor and One in Song - Why We Get Drunk - Pig in the Middle - The Recipe - Five Generations - An Unimportant Tragedy - Fair Go For Anglo-Saxons - The Porter Song Book.

NOTE: The Three Dreams (pp. 10-11) is composed of: The Bird Dream, The Egg Dream and The Poem Dream; Fair Go For Anglo-Saxons (pp. 56-62) is composed of: (1) Provincial Messiah; (2) At the Trat'; (3) Sibylline

Stutterings; (4) Lines; (5) Twenty-four lines; (6) Festina Lente; (7) Porter's Metamorphoses and (8) Half-Mast Poems; The Porter Song Book (pp. 63-70) is composed of: (I) (Wir haven beide lange zeit geschwiegen); (II) Story from a Travel Book; (III) The Sanatorium; (IV) Clairvoyant; (V) Journal Entry; (VI) Genius Loci; (VII) In Hora Ultima; (VIII) The Visitation; (IX) Lyric found in a bottle; (X) Late Lyric; (XI) Poetry; (XII) White Wedding; (XIII) Untitled: "The mynah bird dips its beak" (first line); (XIV) From an Old Master; (XV) Quick Frozen Poem and (XVI) One. two..three...lyric.

A6 THE LAST OF ENGLAND 1970

a. First edition:

Peter Porter | THE LAST OF ENGLAND | LONDON | OXFORD UNIVERSITY PRESS | *New York Melbourne* | 1970

Collation: $[A]^8 - E^8$ = 40 leaves; 21.5 x 13.5 cm.

Binding: Glued into stiff white wove paper wrappers, the exterior of which is shiny, printed in black, white and deep purplish red (256) and lettered down the spine in black: PETER PORTER THE LAST OF ENGLAND OXFORD; two deep purplish red (256) bands wrap around the top and bottom of the front wrapper, the spine and the back wrapper; immediately below the top band and above the lower band is a black band; between the bands on the front wrapper is a black and white reproduction of the oil painting by Ford Maddox Brown of "The Last of England;" at the left-hand side of the front wrapper in black italics: *Peter Porter*| [black italics] *The Last of England*; on the lower left-hand side of the front wrapper in white italics: *The Choice of the Poetry Book Society*; on the back wrapper on a section in white between the two black bands lettered in black:[19 lines of text on the book and Porter] |75p net | 15s net IN UK | OXFORD UNIVERSITY PRESS | SBN 19 211295 3; white wove paper; all edges trimmed.

Publication date: 17 September 1970

Price: 75p or 15s

Number of copies: 3,500

Pagination: [i] half-title; [ii] blank; [iii] title page; [iv] *Oxford University Press, Ely House, London WI* | [4 lines of imprint information]| SBN 19 211295 3 | © *Oxford University Press 1970* | [7 lines of rights information] | PRINTED IN GREAT BRITAIN BY | THE BOWERING PRESS PLYMOUTH; [v] To | the memory of | my Mother | and | the decade of the Nineteen Thirties; [vi] ACKNOWLEDGEMENTS | [8 lines]; [vii] CONTENTS: 1-67, text; [68-72] blank.

Contents: The Last of England - The Civil War - Elegy - A Meredithian Treatment - Christenings - Short Story - Diana and Actaeon - Keeping in Touch - Job's Discounts - The Workers - The Widow's Story - Europe - There are too many of us - A Consumer's Report - Stroking the Chin - Sunday - On Stonebarrow Hill - Let me bore you with my slides - The Sadness of the Creatures - At Whitechurch Canonicorum - On this day I complete my fortieth year - The Sanitized Sonnets - Addendum to Quarles Emblems - More from Martial - Real People - Japanese Jokes - Applause for Death.

Note: For "More from Martial," the sections given are: I, XLIII; I, XXI; II, LII; II, LIX; II, LXX; III, XII; III, XXII; III, XXXV; IV, XVIII; V, X; VII, XVII

A7 EPIGRAMS BY MARTIAL 1971

a. First edition

EPIGRAMS BY MARTIAL

Collation: Broadsheet: single sheet; 37.5 x 28.3 cm.

Binding: Yellow white (92) laid paper, watermarked with a crown above Old-English lettering: Abbey Mills | Greenfield; all edged trimmed.

Publication date: 1971 (Details unavailable from publisher)

Price: Data unavailable from publisher.

Note: This broadsheet was one of a series issued only to series subscribers.

Number of copies: 1,000

Pagination: Printed on one side only: EPIGRAMS BY MARTIAL [long rule under the "ARTIAL" of MARTIAL forming the top side of a rectangle surrounding the two poems which make up the text; the rule ends under the letter "E" of EPIGRAMS] | text | [holograph signature in dark blue ink within the bottom rule of the rectangle] Peter Porter | [at the base of the broadsheet] English Verse by Peter Porter published by Poem-of-the-Month Club Ltd., 27 Brynmaer Road, S.W. 11. Printed by John Roberts Press Ltd. Copyright (1971) Poem-of-the-Month Club Ltd.

Contents: Epigrams by Martial, V XXXIV and IX XXXIII

A8 AFTER MARTIAL 1972

a. First edition

PETER PORTER | AFTER MARTIAL | London | OXFORD UNIVERSITY PRESS | 1972

Collation: $[A]^8 - D^8$ = 32 leaves; 21.6 x 13.9 cm.

Binding: Glued into stiff white wove paper wrappers, the exterior of which is shiny and printed in black, white and brilliant orange yellow (67) and lettered down the spine: [in white] PETER PORTER [in brilliant orange yellow (67)] AFTER MARTIAL [in black] OXFORD; the front wrapper, the spine and the rear wrapper consist of a black and white photograph of "A Saturnalia" by Ernesto Biondi from the National Gallery, Rome from the Mansell Collection; on the front wrapper at the top left-hand side: [in white italics] Peter Porter | [in brilliant orange yellow italics] After Martial; on the rear wrapper: [in white: 20 lines on the book and cover photograph]; | £1.00 net | In U.K. | OXFORD UNIVERSITY PRESS | ISBN 0 19 211814 5; white wove paper; all edges trimmed.

Publication date: 19 October 1972

Price: £1.00

Number of copies: 2,000-2,500

Note: Publisher's records are incomplete.

Pagination: [i] half-title; [ii] blank; [iii] title page; [iv] [5 lines of imprint information] | ISBN 0 19 211814 5 | © *Oxford University Press 1972* | [6 lines of rights information] | PRINTED IN GREAT BRITAIN | BY THE BOWERING PRESS PLYMOUTH; [v] For Julian Cooper; [vi] blank; [vii] CONTENTS: [viii] blank; [ix-xiv] INTRODUCTION; [xv] [5 lines of quotation in italics] | *From Burnaby's Preface to his translation of the Satyricon*; [xvi] blank; 1-42 text; 43-45 NOTES; [46] blank; 47-48, INDEX OF FIRST LINES.

Contents: Introduction, Poems, Notes, Index of First Lines.

Note: The poems are numbered in the following manner: II. lxxxvi; I. xliii; I. lxxi; II. xvii; II. lii; II. lix; II. lxx; III. xi & III. viii; III. xii; III. xxii; III. xxxv; IV. xviii; IV. xxi; IV. xliv; IV. xlix; V. x; V. xviii; V. xxxiv; V. lviii; VI. xix; VI. xxiii; VI.xxvi; VI. xxxix; VI. xl; VI. xlvii; VI. xlix; VI. lxvi; VII. xvii; VII. xix; VIII. xxix; VIII. lxviii; IX. xxxiii; IX. liv; X. xlvi; X. xlvii; X. lxvi; XI. xxx; XI. xlvii; XI. xcix; XI. civ; XII. xvi; XII. xvii; XII. xviii; XII. xxxi; XII. xxxiv; XII. lxxxv; XIV. xxxix

A9 PREACHING TO THE CONVERTED 1972

a. First edition:

Peter Porter | PREACHING TO THE | CONVERTED | LONDON | OXFORD UNIVERSITY PRESS | 1972

Collation: [A] - D^8 + E^4 = 72 leaves; 21.4 x 13.7 cm.

Binding: Glued into stiff white wove paper wrappers, the exterior of which is shiny, printed in black, white, deep yellow (85) and lettered down the spine: [in white] PETER PORTER [in deep yellow (85)] PREACHING TO THE CONVERTED [in white] OXFORD; on the front wrapper in the upper left-hand corner: [in white] Peter Porter | [in deep yellow (85)] Preaching | [in deep yellow (85)] to the Converted | [reproduction in black and white of a Bernini painting]; on the rear wrapper running down the left-hand side in white letters: [35 lines of text on Porter and the book | [in white] £1.00 net | in U.K. | OXFORD UNIVERSITY PRESS | ISBN 0 19 211821 8; on the right: [a reduction of the illustration on the front wrapper in black and white] | [in white] Cover photograph: Monument of Pope | [in white] Urban VIII by Bernini; white wove paper; all edges trimmed.

Publication date: 19 October 1972

Price: £1.00

Number of copies: 2,000

Pagination: [i] half-title; [ii] blank; [iii] title page; [iv] [5 lines of imprint information] | ISBN 0 19 211821 8 | [© *Oxford University Press 1972* | [5 lines of copyright information] | PRINTED IN GREAT BRITAIN | BY THE BOWERING PRESS PLYMOUTH; [v] For Jannice and for Jane; [vi] blank; [vii] CONTENTS: [viii] blank; [ix] ACKNOWLEDGEMENTS | [12 lines]; [x] blank; 1-61 text; [62] blank.

Contents: The Old Enemy - The King of the Cats is Dead - Preaching to the Converted - Timor Mortis - Fossil Gathering - May, 1945 - Evolution - Sex and the Over Forties - Notes to a Biographer - Story which should have happened - Seaside Resort - Dream Restaurant - An Open and Shut Case - Between Two Texts - Affair of the Heart - The School for Love - On the train between Wellington and Shrewsbury - In the Giving Vein - A Hint from Ariosto - The Dust - At Scavanger House - The King of Limmerick's Army - The Great Cow Journeys On - Delphi - Two Poems with French Titles - The Isle of Ink - Can you call it a Vocation? - Thomas Hardy at Westbourne Park Villas - Chorus at the end of the First Act - Tending Towards the Condition - The Tomb of Scarlatti - La Déploration sur la mort d'Igor Stravinsky - Postcard Poems.

Note: "Two Poems with French Titles" is made up of: "Le Theatre de bruit," and "Mort aux chats."

A10 JONAH 1973

a. First edition:

JONAH | [decorative device] | Arthur Boyd *and* Peter Porter | *Secker & Warburg* | LONDON

Collation: [1-8]^8 = 64 leaves; 23.5 x 15.5 cm.

Binding: Bound in textured brilliant bluish-green (159) cloth and lettered down the spine in gold: JONAH Arthur Boyd [vertical rule] Peter Porter [and across the base of the spine] S&W; white laid paper, all edges trimmed; medium brown (58) endpapers; top edges stained brilliant bluish-green (159); pictorial dust wrapper of white wove paper, of which the exterior is shiny, printed in white, very light bluish green (16), brilliant greenish blue (168), medium blue (182) and medium red (15).

Publication date: 22 October 1973

Price: £4.75

Number of copies: 2,000

Pagination: [1] half title; [2] blank; [3] title page; [4] First published in England 1973 by | Martin Secker & Warburg Limited | 14 Carlisle Street, London WIV6NN | Copyright © 1973 Arthur Boyd and Peter Porter | SBN: 436 37805 1 | Printed in Great Britain by | Westerham Press Ltd, Westerham, Kent; [5] Contents; [6] blank; [7-9] THE BOOK | OF THE PROPHET | JONAH; [10] blank; [11] Part One; 12-64 text; [66] blank; [67] Part Two; 69-[127] text; [128] blank.

Note: Illustrations by Arthur Boyd appear on pages [11], 14-42, 45, 47-48, 50-51, 53, 55, 57-61, 63, 65, 68-74, 76-107, 109-110, 112-113, 115-120, 122-126.

Contents: PART ONE: Prologue - God's Briefing - The Embarkation - Slumber Song - Recitative - Jonah and the Sailors - Jonah in the Sea - Whaleland Sonnet One - Whaleland Sonnet Two - Jonah's Prayer - Jonah's Journal - Jonah's Contract with the Whale - On the Beach - The Whale Sails Away - Hymn; PART TWO: Nineveh Central - Nineveh Garden City - Jonah's First Nineveh Sermon - Jonah's Second Nineveh Sermon - Jonah's Annoyance - Jonah asks to die - Death and Jonah talk - Jonah sets up his Booth outside the City - Jonah asks Advice of a Cat - Jonah composes a Prelude on 'All Men Must Die' - The Gourd - The Worm - The East Wind - God's Benediction - Epilogue.

A11 A SHARE OF THE MARKET 1973

a. First edition:

A SHARE | OF THE MARKET | by | PETER PORTER | ULSTERMAN PUBLICATIONS

Collation: $[1]^{8}$ = 8 leaves; 19.2 x 12.4 cm.

Binding: Stapled (twice) into medium greenish-yellow (102) wove paper wrappers; on the front wrapper within a single rectangular rule: [in black within the rule at the upper left-hand side] PETER PORTER [within and at the base of the rule on a base of black in medium greenish-yellow (102)] A | SHARE | OF | THE | MARKET | [outside the rule in black at the lower left-hand corner of the rectangle] Ulsterman Publications; inside the front wrapper at the lower left-hand side of the page in black: PRICE 10p; the rear wrapper is blank; on the inside of the back wrapper in black: ULSTERMAN PUBLICATIONS | [10 lines of publications followed by a single rule] | Available from: | FRANK ORMSBY 56 University Street, Belfast BT7 1HB; white wove paper; all edges trimmed.

Publication date: Data unavailable from publisher.

Price: 10p

Number of copies: Data unavailable from publisher.

Pagination: [1] title page; [2] A SHARE OF THE MARKET | is published, with the financial assistance of the | Arts Council for Northern Ireland, by: | ULSTERMAN PUBLICATIONS | (Editor: Frank Ormsby) | 56 University Street | Belfast, BT7 1HB. | Cover: John Middleton Copyright: PETER PORTER, 1973; 3-15 text; 16 [17 lines of biographical information on Peter Porter].

Contents: To Accompany a Sheaf of Verses - Two Old Ladies Locked in the Lavatory - Images, Images - James Joyce Sings 'Il Mio Tesoro' - A Share of the Market - The Magnificent Seven - Up at the House - My Next Oratorio - An American Military Cemetery in Tuscany.

A12 PETER PORTER READS FROM HIS OWN WORK 1974

a. First edition:

Poets on Record General Editor: Thomas W. Shapcott | PETER PORTER | reads from his own work | [decorative device] University of Queensland Press.

Collation: $[1]^{28}$ = 28 leaves; 20.3 x 20.3 cm.

Binding: Bound into thick, stiff cardboard wrappers with shiny white wove paper on the interior; on the exterior, the spine is quarter-bound with a black textured paper and the front and rear wrappers are covered with black shiny wove paper; on the front wrapper printed in white: POETS ON RECORD 12 | [black and white reproduction of a photograph of Porter seated in an armchair] | [in white] PETER PORTER; on the rear wrapper printed completely in white: [at the upper left-hand corner] University of Queensland Press | (Hard cover) ISBN 0 7022 0908 2 | (Paperback) ISBN 0 7022 0909 6 | About this series | [10 lines of text] *Already available* | [list of 12 names]; [to the right] About Peter Porter | [19 lines of text] | *Others in preparation include:* | [list of 6 names] | Low cost offprints of this text are available | in multiple copies for educational purposes; white wove paper; all edges trimmed; white wove endpapers.

Note: Both the issues are identical except that one is hardback, the other paper.

Publication date: 11 March 1974

Price: $4.50 for hardback and $.75 for the paperback

Number of copies: 1,541 copies in hardback and 1,000 copies in paperback

Pagination: Blank endpaper; [i] POETS ON RECORD 12 | PETER PORTER; [ii] blank; [iii] title page; [iv] Published by University of Queensland Press, | St. Lucia, Queensland, 1974 | The poems © Peter Porter | and Oxford University Press, 1961, 1970, 1972 | This compilation © University of Queensland Press, 1974 | The recording ℗ University of Queensland Press, 1974 | Printed by Lantern Lithographics Pty. Ltd., Brisbane | Hardbound edition bound by | Gibbs and Podlich Pty. Ltd., Brisbane. | [3 lines ISBN information] | Distributed in the United Kingdom, Europe, the Middle East, | Africa, and the Caribbean by Prentice-Hall International, | International Book Distributors Ltd., | 66 Wood Lane End, Hemel Hempstead, Herts., England | [8 lines of rights information] | NOTE | The accompanying record should be played at 45 r.p.m.; [v] Acknowledgements; [vi-vii] Contents; [viii] [Facsimile reproduction of Porter signature in black]; 1-16 Text; 17-18 "Notes"; 19-20 "Selected Bibliography"; blank endpaper.

Contents: "Notes," pp 17-18.

Note: The contents also include "Your Attention Please," "Phar Lap in the Melbourne Museum," "Once Bitten, Twice Bitten; Once Shy, Twice Shy," "Notes to a Biographer," "The Sadness of the Creatures," "Sex and the Over Forties," "Story Which Should Have Happened," and "Mort aux Chats," which were previously published.

Note: A 45 r.p.m. record is contained in an envelope pasted inside the front wrapper. (See E3.)

A13 THE LADY AND THE UNICORN 1975

a. First edition:

The Lady and the Unicorn | ARTHUR BOYD & PETER PORTER | *Secker & Warburg* | LONDON

Collation: $[1\text{-}4]^{8}$ = 32 leaves; 28.6 x 21.3 cm.

Binding: Bound in black cloth and lettered down the spine in gold: THE LADY AND THE UNICORN *Arthur Boyd and Peter Porter S&W;* white wove paper; all edges trimmed; white wove endpapers; top edges stained gray purplish red (262); dust wrapper of white wove paper, shiny on the exterior and printed in black and white.

Publication date: April 1975

Price: £7.50

Number of copies: 1,000

Pagination: blank endpaper; [1] half-title; [2] ALSO BY | ARTHUR BOYD *and* PETER PORTER | *Jonah*; [3] title page; [4] *First published in England 1975 by* | Martin Secker & Warburg Limited | 14 Carlisle Street, London WIV 6NN |SBN 436 37811 6 | Copyright © 1975 Arthur Boyd and Peter Porter | Set in 14 on 16 point Imprint | and printed in Great Britain by Westerham Press Limited; [5] This book is published with the help of a generous | grant from the Tolarno Galleries of Melbourne...[See Note below]; [6] blank; [7] CONTENTS: [8] blank; [9] half-title; [10-31] text; blank endpaper.

Contents: I Invocation - II The Unicorn and the Ark - III The Unicorn's Survival Litany - IV Christ names His Cross for the Unicorn - V The Unicorn in the Forest - VI Enter the Emperor - VII The Hunters set out to trap the Unicorn - VIII Te Deum of the Unicorn - IX The Unicorn sees the lady - X The Unicorn's Love Dance - The Lady's Acceptance - XI The Unicorn in Love - XII The Lady betrays the Unicorn - XIII The Hunters trap the Unicorn - XIV The Unicorn before the Emperor - XV The Unicorn's Prison Song - XVI The Unicorn and the Angel - XVII Death of the Unicorn - XVIII The Lady's Wedding - XIX The Lady's Bridal Night - XX Epilogue.

Note: On the square label (15.3 x 15.3 cm.) pasted on the inside of the front cover and printed in deep purplish red (256): This edition of | THE LADY AND THE UNICORN, | which will not be reprinted, is limited to | 1000 copies numbered from 1 to 1000 and | signed by the artist, the poet and the publishers. The | copies numbered 51 to 1000 are for sale. | This is copy number . . . .

Note: This edition, which will not be reprinted, is limited to|1000 copies numbered from 1 to 1000 and signed by the | artist and the poet...|[Paragraph] The copies numbered 1 to 250 are reserved for the |Tolarno Galleries, the artist, the poet and the publishers. | The 750 copies numbered 251 to 1000 are for sale. [p. 5]

A14 LIVING IN A CALM COUNTRY 1975

a. First edition:

Peter Porter | LIVING IN A CALM | COUNTRY | LONDON | OXFORD UNIVERSITY PRESS | NEW YORK TORONTO | 1975

Collation: [A]-C^{8}, D^{10} = 34 leaves; 21.5 x 13.7 cm.

Binding: Glued into stiff white wove paper wrappers, the exterior of which is shiny, printed in gray olive green (127) and lettered down the spine in dark olive green (126): PORTER LIVING IN A CALM COUNTRY OXFORD; printed in white and gray olive green (127) on the front wrapper is a detail of a painting by A. Baldovinetti; [printed on the upper right hand side of the front wrapper in light orange (52): Peter Porter | Living in | a Calm | Country; printed across the base of the front wrapper in light orange: Choice of the Poetry Book Society; on the rear wrapper at the top printed in light orange (52): Choice of the Poetry Book Society |[printed in dark olive green (126) and dark gray olive green (128) are 29 lines on the book and other publications by Porter] | [in dark olive green (126) italics] Cover illustration: A detail from L'Adorazione dei pastori by A. Baldovinetti | reproduced by courtesy of The Mansell Collection. | £1.50 net | in U.K. | OXFORD UNIVERSITY PRESS | ISBN 0 19 2118544; white wove paper; all edges trimmed.

Publication date: 2 October 1975

Price: £1.50

Number of copies: Data unavailable from publisher.

Pagination: [i] half title; [ii] blank; [iii] title page; [iv] [5 lines of imprint information] | [paste-over tab]: ISBN 0 19 211854 4 © *Oxford University Press 1975* | [five lines of right information] | PRINTED IN GREAT BRITAIN BY THE BOWERING PRESS PLYMOUTH; [v] In Memoriam S.J.H. (1933-1974); [vi] blank; [vii] CONTENTS; [viii] ACKNOWLEDGEMENTS | [13 lines]; 1-60 text.

Contents: At the Castle Hotel, Taunton - His and Hers - Anger - Living in a Calm Country - Ode to Afternoon - Good Vibes - Seaside Picnic - To Make it Real - The Story of my Conversion - Night Crossing - Family Album - An Australian Garden - On First Looking into Chapman's Hesiod - Frogs at Lago Di Bolsena - An American Military Cemetery in Tuscany - A Table of Coincidences - That Depression is an Abstract - The Storm - A Study of a Bird - Three Bagatelles - Studies From Lempriere - Dreamtime - Meanwhile - Down Cemetery Road - A Toccata of Muffat's - Cat's Fugue - The Settembrini Waltz - Print Out: Apocalypse - Baroque Quatrains dedicated to James Fenton - Epigrams of the Abbot Bū-Shou-Sē - Exit, Pursued by a Bear.

A15 ARIADNE ON NAXOS 1976

a. First edition

Ariadne on Naxos

Collation: Broadsheet: single sheet; 32.5 x 25.4 cm.

Binding: Yellow white (92) laid paper, watermarked in an italic script: "Artone Text"; all edges trimmed.

Note: The edition contained an undetermined number of copies printed in light gray (264) and brilliant orange yellow (67) laid paper, watermarked as above, but the bottom edge is deckled.

Publication date: 31 July 1976

Price: Data unavailable from publisher

Number of copies: 120

Pagination: Printed on two sides; front side: on the left-hand side of the sheet is an etching (28.5 x 13 cm.) in medium red (15) of a nude male with his right arm outstretched, standing behind a kneeling woman facing outwardly, with head lowered; on the right-hand side of the sheet: Ariadne on Naxos | *O Teseo mio* | [text of the poem] | PETER PORTER | [holograph signature in black ink] Peter Porter; on the verso of the sheet, centered in the lower half of the sheet in black letters: Illustration by Jahna Knyvett | Broadsheet Number Twenty | Printed in Canberra on the Open

Door Press, | A.D. Hope Building, A.N.U. A.C.T. 2601, | In a signed, numbered edition of 120. | 31st July 1976. | This is number...

Contents: Ariadne on Naxos

Uncollected

A16 THE COST OF SERIOUSNESS 1978

a. First edition:

PETER PORTER | *The Cost of Seriousness* | [publisher's logo with the dates 1478/1978] | OXFORD UNIVERSITY PRESS | OXFORD LONDON NEW YORK

Collation: [A] - D^8 = 32 leaves; 21.5 x 13.3 cm.

Binding: Glued into stiff white wove paper wrappers, the exterior of which is shiny, printed in white, very light greenish blue (171) and deep blue (179) and lettered down the spine: [in deep blue (179)] Porter [in white] The Cost of Seriousness [in deep blue (179)] Oxford; on the front wrapper is an illustration of the face of an angel in deep blue (179) and very light greenish blue (171); on the front wrapper in white letters: The Cost of | Seriousness | Peter Porter; on the rear wrapper in white letters: Poetry Book Society Choice | [next 33 lines in deep blue (179)] [25 lines of text on the book] | Cover illustration: Face of an Angel, from Holy Trinity | Church, Blythburgh, Suffolk. Photograph by J.W. Tubb. | *By the same author* | After Martial | Living in a Calm Country | [publisher's logo] | OXFORD UNIVERSITY PRESS | £2.50 net in UK ISBN 0 19 211880 3; white wove paper; all edges trimmed.

Publication date: 23 March 1978

Price: £2.50

Number of copies: 3,000

Pagination: [i] half title; [ii] blank; [iii] title page; [iv] [6 lines of imprint information] | © *Peter Porter 1978* | [9 lines of copyright restrictions] | [5 lines of British Library Cataloguing in Publication data] | PRINTED IN GREAT BRITAIN BY | THE BOWERING PRESS LTD, PLYMOUTH; [v] For Sally McInerney [vi] blank; [vii] CONTENTS; [viii] ACKNOWLEDGEMENTS [11 lines]; 1-55 text; [56] blank.

Contents: Old Fashioned Wedding - At Ramsholt - The Picture of Nobody - Waiting for Rain in Devon - The Orchid on the Rock - The Charnel House, St. Leonard's, Hythe - A Portrait by Giulio Romano - Poem Waiting to be Translated - The Lying Art - The Easiest Room in Hell - An Angel in Blythburgh Church - An Exequy - The Delegate - A Lecture by my Books -

Scream and Variations - 'In the New World Happiness is Allowed' - The Cost of Seriousness - Three Transportations - Evensong - To Venetia's Shores have Come - Looking at a Melozzo da Forli - The Painters' Banquet - 'Talking Shop' Tanka - Schumann Sings Schubert - Non Piangere, Liù - A Brahms Intermezzo - A Scarlatti Sonata - L'Incoronazione di Poppea - Roman Incident - Under New Management.

Note: "Three Transportations" is made up of the following poems: 1. "Gertrude Stein at Snail's Bay"; 2. "Piero di Cosimo on the Shoalhaven"; 3. "The Boccherini Music Camp."

A17 LES TRES RICHES HEURES 1978

a. First edition:

[cover title] [within a rectangle surrounded by a decorative floral rule] *KEEPSAKE POEM 36* | [single rule.] | Les Très | Riches Heures | [single rule.] | Poem by Peter Porter | *Drawing by John Piper* | [at the base of the front wrapper] 1978 | [single rule.] | The Keepsake Press.

Collation: Single sheet, printed on one side only, folded horizontally twice to make six unnumbered panels: 22.4 x 43.9 cm. (size of fully open sheet).

Binding: Glued into vivid orange (48) stiff wove paper wrapper; the rear wrapper is blank; printed in black inside the rear wrapper: [single rule.] | © Peter Porter 1978 | [single rule.] | Printed by The Keepsake Press | 26 Sydney Road, Richmond, Surrey TW9 1UB | [single rule.] | An edition of 180 copies | of which twelve copies are signed by the author and the artist | [single rule]; white wove paper; all edges trimmed.

Publication date: October 1978

Price £0.25; £1.00 for the signed copies

Number of copies: 180

Pagination: [upper panel when closed] blank; [when sheet is fully open]; [left and center panel: abstract illustration of a lion]; [right panel] text; [versos of right, center and upper panels] blank.

Contents: Les Très Riches Heures

Note: Issued in a plain white envelop of AVON parchment.

A18 STORY WHICH SHOULD HAVE HAPPENED

a. First edition:

Story Which Should Have Happened

Collation: Broadsheet: single sheet; 45.2 x 28 cm.

Binding: Light gray (264) laid paper; trimmed on the top and base and on the right hand side of the sheet; the left-hand side of the sheet is deckled.

Publication date: 1972 or before

Note: This poem was included in *Preaching to the Converted* published on 19 October 1972. In the Acknowledgements it is states: "One poem was a *Leeds New Poets Broadsheet*."

Price: Data unavailable from publisher

Number of copies: 50

Pagination: Printed on one side only: Peter Porter | STORY WHICH SHOULD HAVE HAPPENED | [text of poem] | [holograph signature in blue ink] Peter Porter | NEW POETS BROADSHEET 1 | Number of 50 signed, hand printed copies | The School of English Press, University of Leeds.

Contents: Story Which Should Have Happened.

A19 THE SHAPE OF POETRY AND THE SHAPE OF MUSIC 1980

a. First edition:

THE SHAPE OF POETRY | AND THE SHAPE OF MUSIC | PETER PORTER | 1980 | UNIVERSITY OF TASMANIA OCCASIONAL PAPER 28

Collation: $[1]^{12}$ = 12 leaves; 21.1 x 14.8 cm.

Binding: Stapled (twice) into stiff textured medium orange yellow (71) wove wrappers; lettered on the front wrapper in black: THE SHAPE OF POETRY | AND THE SHAPE OF MUSIC | Peter Porter [the title and author's name are bordered on the right hand side and partially underscored by a black curved line ( )] | UNIVERSITY OF TASMANIA | OCCASIONAL PAPER | 28 [these words are bordered above and on the right hand side by a black curved line ( )]; the rear wrapper is blank.

Publication date: December 1980

Price: $2.00

Number of copies: 200

Pagination: [i] title page; [ii] *Wholly set up and printed by the* | *Printing Section, University of Tasmania* | *December 1980.* | ISBN 0 85901 144 5 | *The Shape of Poetry and the Shape of Music* is the text of the second James | McAuley Memorial Lecture, delivered by Peter Porter in the University of | Tasmania on 17 April 1980. | Requests for copies of this publication should be addressed to Information | Services, University of Tasmania, Box 252C GPO Hobart, Tasmania 7001; 1-22 text.

Contents: The Shape of Poetry and the Shape of Music.

Note: This prose statement appears here for the first time in print.

A20 ENGLISH SUBTITLES 1981

a. First edition:

[decorative rule] | ENGLISH SUBTITLES | [decorative rule] | PETER PORTER | Oxford New York Toronto Melbourne | OXFORD UNIVERSITY PRESS | 1981

Collation: $[1\text{-}8]^4$ = 32 leaves; 21.5 x 13.5 cm.

Binding: Glued into stiff white wove paper wrappers, the exterior of which is shiny, printed in black, white, deep yellow (85) and medium olive brown (94) and lettered down the spine in black: Porter English Subtitles Oxford; on the front wrapper is a detail from a Fra Angelico painting; on the left-hand side at the base of the front wrapper printed in white: Peter Porter | [thick rule.] | English Subtitles; at the top of the rear wrapper in black letters: POETRY BOOK SOCIETY RECOMMENDATION | [16 lines of text on the book] *By the same author* | After Martial | Living in a Calm Country | The Cost of Seriousness | *Cover illustration: detail from the Deposition by Fra Angelico,* | *San Marco Museum, Florence. Photo: Phaidon, Oxford* | OXFORD UNIVERSITY PRESS | £3.50 net in UK ISBN 0 19 2119427; white wove paper; all edges trimmed.

Publication date: 19 March 1981

Price: £3.50

Number of copies: 3,000

Pagination: [i] half title; [ii] blank; [iii] title page; [iv] [8 lines of imprint information] | © *Peter Porter 1981* | [9 lines of rights information] | [6 lines of Cataloguing in Publication Data] | *Typeset in Great Britain by* | *King's English Typesetters Ltd., Cambridge* | *and printed by* | *Lowe & Brydone Printers Lts., Thetford, Norfolk;* [v] *For Anthony Thwaite;* [vi] *Acknowledgements* | [11 lines]; [vii-viii] *Contents;* 1-56 text.

Contents: English Subtitles - The Winter Capital - The Need for Foreplay - My Old Cat Dances - Visiting Cornish Churches - How Important is Sex? - The American Articulate - A Philosopher of Captions - Occam's Razor - Returning - Good Ghost, Gaunt Ghost - Bei Einer Trauung - Sonata Form: The Australian Magpie - All the Difference in the World - Myopia - What I Have Written I Have Written - The Killing Ground - The Imperfection of the World - The Future - The Story of Jason - Garden of Earthly Delights - Alcestis and the Poet - Addio Senza Rancor - Talking to You Afterwards - The Werther Level - The Unlucky Christ - Two for the Price of One - Lip Service - Pope's Carnations Knew Him - Nights at the Opera - About the New - About on the Serchio - For Sophonisba Anguisciola - Pienza Seen by Prudes - At Lake Massaciuccoli - The Unfortunate Isles - Landscape with Orpheus.

A21 THE ANIMAL PROGRAMME 1982

a. First edition:

The Animal Programme | Four Poems | PETER PORTER | Anvil Press Poetry

Collation: $[1]^4$ = 4 leaves; 17.7 x 13 cm.

Binding: Stapled (twice) into heavy dull medium gray (265) textured wove paper wrappers; white wove paper; all edged trimmed; dust wrapper of heavy dull light blue (181) textured wove paper printed on the front wrapper in black: The Animal Programme | Four Poems | PETER PORTER | Anvil Press Poetry.

Publication date: December 1982

Price: £4 for the signed copies; £1.25 for the unsigned copies.

Number of copies: 500

Pagination: [1] title page; [2] blank; [3-7] text; [8] holograph number in black ink] | Published in 1982 | by Anvil Press Poetry Ltd | 69 King George Street London SE10 8PX | ISBN 0 85646 108 3 | Copyright © Peter Porter 1982 | This edition is limited to five hundred | numbered copies of which nos. 1-250 are | signed by the poet. | Anvil Press Poetry acknowledges | the financial assistance of | The Arts Council of Great Britain | Printed in England by | Ithaca Press Ltd London SE1.

Note: For the signed copies, the holograph signature ("Peter Porter") of Peter Porter comes directly below the holograph number in black ink. The ISBN for the signed copies is 0 85646 107 5.

Contents: The Animal Programme - Doll's House - Caliban Impromptu - Matutinal.

A22 A CELEBRATORY ODE 1982

a. First edition:

[cover title] [reproduction of "Rich's Glory" within a rectangle (8.4 x 14.8 cm.) composed of a thin rule on the inside and a thick rule on the outside] | RICH'S GLORY *or his* Triumphal Entry *into* Covent Garden | 7th December 1732 | [within a rectangle (8.4 x 14.8 cm.) composed of two thin rules on the inside and a thick rule on the outside] A Celebratory Ode *by Peter Porter* | *upon the Occasion of* The Precise | 250th ANNIVERSARY | *of the* Opening of A THEATRE at | Covent Garden, 7th *December 1732*

Collation: Broadsheet: single sheet, printed on both sides, folded once to make four unnumbered pages; 29.6 x 39.9 cm. (size of fully opened sheet).

Binding: White laid paper, watermarked with a decorative fish and the initials "M" and "W"; printed in black; top and side edges trimmed; bottom edge deckled:

Publication date: 7 December 1982

Price: Issued free

Note: Issued with the program of the Royal Opera House (London) on Tuesday, December 7, 1982 for its 5th staged performance of "Semele" (Congreve and Handel).

Number of copies: 2,100

Pagination: [when folded] [1] title page; [2] *Part One* | [decorative device] THE ODE [decorative device]; [3] *Part Two* | [decorative device] ANTI-ODE [decorative device]; [4] [continuation of text of ANTI-ODE] | [decorative device in the form of a group of instruments] | *Published by The Friends of Covent Garden* | *and printed by the John Roberts Press* | *at Clerkenwell Green, London* | *in Bell type (1788) on paper* | *mould-made at Wells, Somerset.*

Contents: A Celebratory Ode

Note: This poem appears here for the first time in print. Uncollected.

A23 COLLECTED POEMS 1983

a. First edition:

COLLECTED POEMS | [decorative device] | PETER PORTER | Oxford New York Melbourne | OXFORD UNIVERSITY PRESS | 1983

Collation: $[1\text{-}11]^{16}$ = 176 leaves; 21.4 x 13.7 cm.

Binding: Bound in a textured strong red (12) cloth and lettered down the spine in gold within a rectangle composed of a thick and a think rule in gold: PETER PORTER [the "P" of Peter and the last "R" in Porter are oversized] COLLECTED POEMS | [within the rectangle but across the base of the spine: OXFORD; white wove paper; all edges trimmed; white wove endpapers; the dust wrapper is of white wove paper, of which the exterior is shiny, printed in black and brilliant orange yellow (67).

Publication date: 21 March 1983

Price: £12.50

Number of copies: 2,500

Pagination: blank endpaper; [i] half title; [ii] blank; [iii] title page; [iv] [9 lines of imprint information] | © *Peter Porter 1983* | [9 lines of copyright restrictions] | [6 lines of British Library Cataloguing in Publication Data] | *Printed in Great Britain* | *by Butler and Tanner Ltd., Frome, Somerset.;* [v] *Preface*; [vi] blank; vii-xiii *Contents*; [xiv] blank; [xv] *For my daughters, Katherine and Jane*; [xvi] blank; [1] COLLECTED POEMS; [2] blank; 3-335 text; [336] blank; blank endpaper.

Contents: *Once Bitten, Twice Bitten (1961):* A Giant Refreshed - Forefathers' View of Failure - Once Bitten, Twice Bitten; Once Shy, Twice Shy - Mr. Roberts - A Christmas Recalled - Sick-room at Home - All Other Time is Peace - Syrup of Figs will Cast Out Fear - The Picture of Nobody - Conventions of Death - Metamorphosis - Death's Morning Shadows - Beast and the Beauty - Walking Home on St Cecilia's Day - Reflection on my own Name - Changes Wrung - Tunes for the Fortunate - Lament for a Proprietor - What a Lying Lot the Writers Are - John Marston Advises Anger - Sick Man's Jewel - Made in Heaven - Apophthegms Come to the Party - A Moral Tale has a Moral End - South of the Duodenum - Death in the Pergola Tea-Rooms - Suicide Unmasked - Away, Musgrave, Away - Jack and Jill - The Smell on the Landing - Party Line - Euphoria Dies - For John Clare from London - A Vicious Vignette - All, All of a Piece Throughout - The Historians Call Up Pain - Annotations of Auschwitz - Who Gets the Pope's Nose? - The Conservation of Energy - Too Worn to Wear - Nature Comes to Stay - Phar Lap in the Melbourne Museum - Tobias and the Angel.

1962/3: Your Attention Please - Legend - Somme and Flanders - Soliloquy at Potsdam - Nine O'Clock Thoughts on the 73 Bus - Ghosts - Eat Early Earthapples - Reading MND in Form 4B.

Poems Ancient & Modern (1964): The Unicorn's Horn - Septimius Severus at the Vienna Gate - A Minor Lear - 'Stepping from a flat-bottomed boat' - Vienna - Sydney Cove, 1788 - Madame de Merteuil on 'The Loss of an Eye'- A Huddle of IQ's - The World of Simon Raven - The Frankenstein Report - The Sins of the Fathers - Requiem for Mrs. Hammelswang - Two Merits of Sunshine - The View from Misfortune's Back - An Anthropologist's Confession - Homage to Gaetano Donizetti - Happening at Sordid Creek - The Great

Poet Comes Here in Winter - How to Get a Girl Friend - Story from a Time of Disturbance - Nine Points of the Law - To Start a Controversy - Encounter in Antioch - Shopping Scenes - Inspector Christopher Smart Calls.

A Porter Folio (1969): The Last of the Dinosaurs - The Three Dreams - The Thirteen Couplets - My Late T'ang Phase - Fantasia on a Line of Stefan George - The Battle of Cannae - After the Temptation - Dorothy Osborne in the Country - A Hoplite's Helmet - St John on Patmos - Approaches to a Line of Auden & Kallman - First Scene from Dostoevsky - Second Scene from Dostoevsky - The Shining God and the God of Correction - What the Guide Book Said - Seahorses - Competition is Healthy - Steps on the Way - The Next Hundred Years will be Religious - The Return of Inspector Christopher Smart - At the Theatre on St Valentine's Eve - Moaning in Midstream - The Eclipse of Lady Silvertail - Futurity - Homily in the English Reading Rooms - Three Poems for Music - St Cecilia's Day, 1710 - St Cecilia's Day Epigrams - One Died in Metaphor and One in Song - Why We Get Drunk - Pig in the Middle - The Recipe - Fair Go for Anglo-Saxons - The Porter Song Book - Farewell to Theophrastus.

The Last of England (1970): The Last of England - Civil War - Elegy - A Meredithian Treatment - Christenings - Short Story - Diana and Actaeon - The Workers - The Widow's Story - Europe - There Are Too Many of Us - A Consumer's Report - Stroking the Chin - Sunday - On Stonebarrow Hill - Let Me Bore You with My Slides - The Sadness of the Creatures - At Whitechurch Canonicorum - On This Day I Complete My Fortieth Year - The Sanitized Sonnets - Real People - Japanese Jokes - Applause for Death.

Preaching to the Converted (1972): The Old Enemy - The King of the Cats is Dead - Preaching to the Converted - Timor Mortis - Fossil Gathering - May, 1945 - Evolution - Sex and the Over Forties - Notes to a Biographer - Story Which Should Have Happened - Seaside Resort - Dream Restaurant - An Open and Shut Case - Between Two Texts - Affair of the Heart - On the Train between Wellington and Shrewsbury - In the Giving Vein - A Hint from Ariosto - The Dust - At Scavanger House - The King of Limerick's Army - The Great Cow Journeys On - Delphi - Two Poems with French Titles: Le Théâtre de bruit and Mort aux Chats - The Isle of Ink - Can You Call It a Vocation? - Thomas Hardy at Westbourne Park Villas - Chorus at the End of the First Act - Tending towards the Condition - The Tomb of Scarlatti - La Déploration sur la Mort d'Igor Stravinsky.

Living in a Calm Country (1975): At the Castle Hotel, Taunton - His and Hers - Anger - Living in a Calm Country - Ode to Afternoon - Good Vibes - Seaside Picnic - To Make it Real - The Story of my Conversion - Night Crossing - Family Album - An Australian Garden - On First Looking into Chapman's Hesiod - Frogs at Lago di Bolsena - An American Military Cemetery in Tuscany - A Table of Coincidences - That Depression is an Abstract - The Storm - A Study of a Bird - Three Bagatelles - Studies from Lemprière - Dreamtime - Meanwhile - Down Cemetery Road - A Toccata of Muffat's - Cat's Fugue - The Settembrini Waltz - Print Out: Apocalypse - Baroque Quatrains dedicated to James Fenton - Exit, Pursued by a Bear.

The Cost of Seriousness (1978): Old-Fashioned Wedding - At Ramsholt - The Picture of Nobody - Waiting for Rain in Devon - The Orchid on the Rock - The Charnel House, St. Leonard's, Hythe - A Portrait by Giulio Romano - Poem Waiting to be Translated - The Lying Art - The Easiest Room in Hell - An Angel in Blythburg Church - An Exequy - The Delegate - A Lecture by my Books - Scream and Variations - 'In the New World Happiness is Allowed' - The Cost of Seriousness - Three Transportations - Evensong - To Venetia's Shores Have Come - Looking at a Melozzo da Forlì - The Painters' Banquet - 'Talking Shop' Tanka - Schumann Sings Schubert - Non Piangere, Liù - A Brahms Intermezzo - A Scarlatti Sonata - L'Incoronazione di Poppea - Roman Incident - Under New Management.

English Subtitles (1981): English Subtitles - The Winter Capital - The Need for Foreplay - My Old Cat Dances - Visiting Cornish Churches - How Important is Sex? - The American Articulate - A Philosopher of Captions - Occam's Razor - Returning - Good Ghost, Gaunt Ghost - Bei Einer Trauung - Sonata Form: The Australian Magpie - All the Difference in the World - Myopia - What I Have Written I Have Written - The Killing Ground - The Imperfection of the World - The Future - The Story of Jason - Garden of Earthly Delights - Alcestis and the Poet - Addio Senza Rancor - Talking to You Afterwards - The Werther Level - The Unlucky Christ - Two for the Price of One - Lip Service - Pope's Carnations Knew Him - Nights at the Opera - About the New - About on the Serchio - For Sophonisba Anguisciola - Pienza Seen by Prudes - At Lake Massaciuccoli - The Unfortunate Isles - Landscape with Orpheus.

After Martial (1972).

b. First paperbound edition:

COLLECTED POEMS | [decorative device] | PETER PORTER | Oxford New York| OXFORD UNIVERSITY PRESS | 1984

Collation: $[1\text{-}11]^{16}$ = 176 leaves; 19.6 x 12.8 cm.

Binding: Glued into stiff white card wrappers, shiny on the exterior, and printed down the spine in black on a rectangle of brilliant orange yellow (67) which is surrounded by a thin black line on the inside and a thick black line on the outside: PETER PORTER COLLECTED POEMS [across the base of the spine] OXFORD; on the front wrapper are lines formed by the words "COLLECTED POEMS"; on a brilliant orange yellow rectangle surrounded by a thin black rule on the inside and a thick black rule on the outside: PETER PORTER | [single rule] | COLLECTED POEMS | 'a collection of enormous power | and range of experience' | Malcolm Bradbury, Observer; on the rear wrapper: A Poetry Book Society Recommendation; eight | times chosen as Book of the Year; winner of the | Duff Cooper Memorial Prize for 1983. | [25 lines of various critical comments] | [to the right: ISBN 0-19-211965-6 [digital price sticker] | At the lower left-hand corner of the wrapper: Oxford University Press | £4.95 net in UK | Also available in hardback; white wove paper; all edges trimmed.

Publication date: 25 October 1984

Price: £4.95

Number of copies: Data unavailable from publisher

Pagination: Same as A23a except for the following on page [iv]; after the © Peter Porter 1983 : *First published 1983 by Oxford University Press* | *First issued in paperback 1984;* after the 9 lines of copyright restrictions and conditions of sale: *British Library Cataloguing in Publication Data* | *Porter, Peter* | *Collected poems. -(Contemporary poetry)*| I . *Title* II. *Series* | 821 PR9619.3.P57 | ISBN 0-19-211965-6 | *Library of Congress Cataloging in Publication Data* | *Porter, P.* | *Collected poems.* | *Includes index.* | I. *Title* | PR9619.3.P57A6 1984 821 84-7166| ISBN 0-19-211965-6 (*pbk.*) | *Printed in Great Britain by* | *J. W. Arrowsmith Ltd.* | *Bristol.*

Contents: Same as A23a

A24 THE RUN OF YOUR FATHER'S LIBRARY 1984

a. First edition:

[fancy letters] The Run of Your Father's | [fancy letters] Library | [fancy letters] Peter Porter | [fancy decorative rule] | [fancy letters] Albion Press | [fancy letters] University of Leeds | 1984

Collation: $[1]^8$ = 8 leaves; 24.3 x 17.5 cm.

Binding: Sewn into light gray (264) heavy wove paper wrappers and lettered on the front wrapper in fancy letters: The Run of Your Father's | Library | Peter Porter | [fancy decorative rule] | Albion Press; the rear wrapper is blank; white wove paper; all edges trimmed.

Publication date: May 1984

Price: Data unavailable from Publisher

Number of copies: 50 numbered copies signed by the author.

Pagination: [1-2] blank; [3] title page; [4] blank; [5-12] text; [13-14] blank; [15] No. [holograph numeral in blue ink] of fifty numbered copies signed by the author | [holograph signature of Peter Porter in blue ink] | Hand printed in 12 pt. Garamond on an 1857 Albion | by Gisli Ragnarsson and Zoë Schramm-Evans, | students of the Institute of Bibliography and Textual Criticism, School of English | University of Leeds, | Leeds LS2 9JT | November 1983-May 1984 © Peter Porter; [16] blank.

Contents: The Flock and the Star - The Decline of the North - 'Old and Ill and Terrified and Tight' - Analogue of Helen - Schein Und Sein - The Run of Your Father's Library.

Note: "The Run of Your Father's Library" appears here for the first time in print.

A25 FAST FORWARD 1984

a. First Edition:

FAST | FORWARD | [decorative device] | PETER PORTER | Oxford New York | OXFORD UNIVERSITY PRESS | 1984

Collation: $[1\text{-}2]^{16}$ = 32 leaves; 21.5 x 13.5 cm.

Binding: Glued into stiff white card wrappers, shiny on the exterior and printed down the spine in black: PETER PORTER FAST FORWARD OXFORD: on the front wrapper in white and various shades of blue and gray is a reproduction of a detail from Chalk Cliffs on the Island of Rugen, 1818, by Caspar David Friedrich. Stiftung Oskar Reinhard, Winterthur; at the top of the front wrapper printed in white on blocks of blackish blue (188) surrounded and separated by a white border: F A S T F O R W A R D; at the base of the wrapper in the same format as the letters at the top: P E T E R P O R T E R: on the rear wrapper in black: [28 lines on the text, critical quotes and information on the front wrapper illustration] | *Poetry Book Society Recommendation* | ISBN 0-19-211967 - 2 | [to the left at the base of the wrapper] OXFORD UNIVERSITY PRESS | £4.50 net in UK [to the right: electronic stamp] | 9 780192 119674; white wove paper; all edges trimmed.

Publication date: 25 October 1984

Price: £4.50

Number of copies: 3,000

Pagination: [1] half-title; [2] blank; [3] title page; [4] *Oxford University Press, Walton Street, Oxford OX2 6DP* | [7 lines of publisher locations] | *Oxford is a trade mark of Oxford University Press* | © *Peter Porter 1984* | [4 lines of rights information] | [5 lines on conditions of sale] | *British Library Cataloguing in Publication Data* | [5 lines] | Library of Congress Cataloguing in Publication Data | [5 lines] | *Printed in Great Britain by* | *J. W. Arrowsmith Ltd.,* | *Bristol;* [5] *For Clive James;* [6] ACKNOWLEDGEMENTS | [15 lines]; 7-8, CONTENTS; 9-62, text; [63-64] blank.

Contents: At the Porta Humana - Decline of the North - The Flock and the Star - The Missionary Position - Analogue of Helen - Jumping to Conclusions - Poem Employing Words from an Article on Combat Strategy - Cleaning the Picture at the Edges - Clipboard - The Arbitrary Abrolhos - Doll's House - Comedy Lies - Venetian Incident - Elegy and Fanfare - Where We Came In - Dejection: An Ode - Matutinal - Student Canteen - The Biographer Promenades - Marianne North's Submission - Cyprus, Aeschylus, Inanition - The Cats of Campagnatico - A Guide to the Gods - Santa Cecilia in Trastevere - Unfinished Requiems - Little Harmonic Labyrinth - To Himself - Dis Manibus - A Vein of Racine's - Going to Parties - The Hedonists Rehearse the Uprising - Fast Forward - Cities of Light.

A26 NARCISSUS 1984

a. First edition

ARTHUR BOYD AND | PETER PORTER | NARCISSUS | [mirrored image of the title in light gray (264)] | SECKER & WARBURG·LONDON

Collation: $[1\text{-}4]^8$ = 32 leaves; 28.7 x 21.5 cm.

Binding: Bound in black cloth and lettered down the spine in silver: NARCISSUS | Arthur Boyd and Peter Porter SECKER & WARBURG; white wove paper; all edges trimmed; endpapers of deep purplish red (259) wove paper; dust wrapper of white wove paper, shiny on the exterior, and printed in black.

Publication date: November 1984

Price: £25

Number of copies: 525

Pagination: [i] half-title; [ii] Also by Arthur Boyd and Peter Porter | *Jonah* | *The Lady and the Unicorn*; [iii] title page; [iv] First published in England 1984 by | Martin Secker & Warburg Limited | 54 Poland Street, London WIV 3DF | Copyright © 1984 Arthur Boyd and Peter Porter | *British Library Cataloguing in Publication Data* | [6 lines] | Printed in Great Britain by | Expression Printers Limited, London; [v] Contents; [vi] blank; 1-[55] text and illustrations; [56-58] blank.

Contents: I Introduction; II The Making of a Monster; III Narcissus Loses his Love; IV The Painters' Banquet; V Narcissus among the Anthropologists; VI Narcissus Laments Orpheus; VII By the Waterfall; VIII The Narcissus File; IX From the Autobiography of Narcissus; X Intermezzo; XI The Shadow of the Charnel; XII The Narcissus Emblems; XIII Echo's Moon-Calf; XIV At the Palace; XV Narcissus as Critic; XVI The Rainbow Maker; XVIII Narcissus's Revolutionary Sayings; XVIII Echo's Farewell; XIX The Burial of Narcissus; XX Postlude.

Note: On the label (15 x 15.2) pasted on the inside of the front cover and printed in deep purplish red: This edition of | NARCISSUS | which will not be reprinted, is limited to | 500 copies numbered 1 to 500 and signed by | the artist and poet. 25 additional copies, | numbered I to XXV and not for sale have | been produced for the use of the publisher.| The copies numbered 1 to 100 are reserved for | the artist and the poet. The copies numbered | 101 to 500 are for sale. | This is copy number... [holograph number in black ink] | [holograph signature of Arthur Boyd in black ink] | [holograph signature of Peter Porter in black ink].

A27 MACHINES 1986

a. First limited edition:

[Fancy letters in very pale blue (184) and white] MACHINES | [fancy letters in very pale blue (184) and white] PETER PORTER | [etching in black and white] | [in very pale blue] The Starwheel Press 1986.

Collation: $[1]^8$ = 8 leaves; 26.1 x 18.2 cm.

Binding: Sewn into textured, semi-heavy paper wrappers in pale blue (185); lettered on the front wrapper in dark blue (183) fancy letters: MACHINES | [decorative rule in dark blue] | [in fancy dark blue letters] PETER PORTER; the rear wrapper is blank; laid white Arches Rives paper watermarked ARCHES | FRANCE ∞ ; edges untrimmed; endpapers of light blue gray (190) laid paper, watermarked with a crown above Old English lettering: Abbey Mills.

Publication date: 17 July 1986

Price: £15.00

Number of copies: 50

Pagination: [1] title page; [2] blank; [3-4] text; [5] [Etching]; [6] blank; [7-8] text; [9] [Etching]; [10] blank; [11-12] text; [13] [Etching]; [14] blank; [15] text; [16] *Machines* is published by The Starwheel Press, Hitchin, | the letterpress by Mandeville: an edition of 50 copies on | Arches Rives paper with four etchings by George Szirtes. | Each copy is signed by both the author and the artist. | © Peter Porter and George Szirtes 1986 | Copy Number [holograph number in black ink] | [decorative rule] | Peter Porter [holograph in black ink] | George Szirtes [holograph in black ink].

Contents: Machines

Note: Poems numbered 1,2,3,4,6,7, and 9 are untitled; number 5 has the title "Memo to Pliny"; number 8 has the title "Keep It With Kodak"; number 10 has eight poems with the following titles: "Heavier-than-air Machine," "Dialysis," "Time Machine," "The God from the Machine," "Bag Woman," "Answering Service," "Word Processor," and "Agent Orange."

b. First edition (trade)

[In fancy black and white letters] MACHINES | [decorative rule] | [in black and white letters] PETER PORTER | [publisher's logo] | [in black and white letters] MANDEVILLE | [in black and white open numbers] 1986.

Collation: $[1]^{6}$ = 6 leaves; 25.6 x 17.6 cm.

Binding: Sewn into pale blue (185) textured semi-heavy laid paper wrappers and lettered on the front wrapper in fancy dark blue (183) open letters: MACHINES | [decorative rule in dark blue] | [in dark blue open letters] PETER PORTER; the rear wrapper is blank; white wove paper; all edges trimmed.

Publication date: 17 July 1986

Price: £1.50 .

Number of copies: 250

Pagination: [1] blank; [2] Etching in vivid purplish blue (184); [3] title page; [4] blank; [5-11] text; [12] 250 copies of this edition have been printed, of which 60 | have been signed by the author and the artist. | Illustrations by George Szirtes | Published by The Mandeville Press, 2 Taylor's Hill, | Hitchin, Hertfordshire | © Peter Porter and George Szirtes 1986 | ISBN 0 904533 91 3 | Copy Number | [decorative rule] | [holograph number in black ink] | George Szirtes [holograph in black ink]| Peter Porter [holograph in black ink] | [Etching in vivid purplish blue].

Contents: Same as A27a.

A28 WILLIAM BLAKE 1986

THE ILLUSTRATED POETS | William Blake | [line of decorative squares] | Selected and with an introduction | by Peter Porter | OXFORD UNIVERSITY PRESS | 1986.

Collation: $[1\text{-}4]^{16}$ = 64 leaves; 17 x 11 cm.

Binding: Bound in textured vivid dark red (17) paper-covered boards and lettered down the spine in gold: William Blake OXFORD; white wove paper; all edges trimmed; marbled end-papers in various shades of purple, red and green; dust wrapper of white wove paper, shiny on the exterior, printed in dark reddish orange (38), black and various shades of red, orange, yellow, and brown.

Publication date: 6 November 1986

Price: £4.95

Number of copies: 10,000

Contents: "Introduction," pp. 10-12

A29 CHRISTINA ROSSETTI 1986

THE ILLUSTRATED POETS | Christina Rossetti | [line of decorative squares] | Selected and with an introduction | by Peter Porter | OXFORD UNIVERSITY PRESS | 1986.

Collation: $[1\text{-}4]^{16}$ = 64 leaves; 17 x 11 cm.

Binding: Bound in textured dark green (146) paper-covered boards and lettered down the spine in gold: Christina Rossetti OXFORD; white wove paper; all edges trimmed; marbled end-papers in various shades of pink, brown and blue; dust wrapper of white wove paper, shiny on the exterior, printed in medium green (145) and various shades of blue, brown, yellow, green, pink and black.

Publication date: 6 November 1986

Price: £4.95

Number of copies: 7,000

Contents: "Introduction," pp. 10-12

B

BOOKS AND PAMPHLETS EDITED OR WITH CONTRIBUTIONS BY PETER PORTER

In this section, books and pamphlets in which a contribution by Peter Porter appears either for the first time in a book or for the first time in print are listed in chronological order. Any material which was previously unpublished is identified by a note.

B1 PENGUIN MODERN POETS 2 1962

Penguin Modern Poets | [horizontal rule] 2 [horizontal rule] | KINGSLEY AMIS | DOM MORAES | PETER PORTER | *Penguin Books.*

Collation: 64 leaves; 18.1 x 11.1 cm.

Binding: A perfect binding glued into stiff white wove paper wrappers, of which the exterior is shiny and printed in black, white and strong purplish pink (247) and lettered down the spine: [in white] PENGUIN MODERN POETS 2 [in strong purplish pink (247)] AMIS MORAES PORTER [across the base of the spine the publisher's logo: (a penguin) in black and white] | in white] D62; on the front wrapper at the upper left-hand corner in strong purplish pink (247): Kingsley Amis | Dom Moraes | Peter Porter; on the front wrapper at the upper right hand side in white letters: PENGUIN MODERN POETS 2 [and the publisher's logo (a penguin)]; also on the front wrapper, a feather in white; at the lower right-hand side of the front wrapper in strong purplish pink (247): 2'6; on the rear wrapper: [in strong purplish pink (247)] Published by Penguin Books | [in white - 11 lines on the series] | *For copyright reasons this edition* | *is not for sale in the U.S.A.;* on the lower half of the rear wrapper a feather in white; white wove paper; all edges trimmed.

Publication date: April 1962

Price: 2'6

Number of copies: Data unavailable from publisher

Contents: "Your Attention Please," pp. 108-109; "Somme and Flanders," p. 116; "Soliloquy at Potsdam," pp. 117-118; "Nine o'Clock Thoughts on the 73 Bus," p. 119; "Ghosts," pp. 120-122, all collected in CP; "Reading a Novel," pp. 110-111; "Two Polemical Sonnets," pp. 112-113; "A Mass for Money," p. 123

Note: "Your Attention Please," "A Mass for Money," "Reading a Novel," "Two Polemical Sonnets" and "Soliloquy at Potsdam" appear here for the first time in print.

Note: The contents also include "Annotations at Auschwitz," "Beast and the Beauty," "Death in the Pergola Tea-Rooms," "Death's Morning Shadows," "Forefathers' View of Failure," "The Historians Call Up Pain," "John Marston Advises Anger," "Lament for a Proprietor," "Made in Heaven," "Once Bitten, Twice Bitten, Once Shy, Twice Shy," "Party Line," "Phar Lap in the Melbourne Museum," "South of the Duodenum," "Too Worn to Wear," "What a Lying Lot the Writers Are," and "Who Gets the Pope's Nose?," which were previously collected.

B2 A GROUP ANTHOLOGY 1963

A Group Anthology | Edited by | EDWARD LUCIE-SMITH | and | PHILIP HOBS-BAUM | *London* | OXFORD UNIVERSITY PRESS | New York Toronto | 1963

Collation: A-I^8 = 72 leaves; 18.5 x 12.5 cm.

Binding: Bound in textured medium bluish green (124) cloth and lettered down the spine in gold on a black rectangle: A GROUP ANTHOLOGY [across the base of the spine] OXFORD; white wove paper; all edges trimmed; white wove endpapers; dust wrapper of white wove paper printed in dull very deep purplish red (257), white and strong orange (50).

Publication date: 2 May 1963

Price: 21s

Number of copies: 2,000

Contents: "An Experience," p. 91; "Eat Early Earth Aples," pp. 89-91, collected in CP.

Note: These poems appear here for the first time in print.

Note: The contents also include "Annotations at Auschwitz," "Ghosts," "The Historians Call Up Pain," "John Marston Advises Anges," and "Metamorphosis" which were previously collected

B3 FESTIVAL OF POETRY 1963

[title page printed across two consecutive pages] [within an irregular square of black printed in white at the top of the right-hand page] Festival | of Poetry | at the Royal | Court Theatre | [printed across the two pages] Festival of Poetry at The Royal Court Theatre 1963 | [printed across the two pages] 15-20 JULY The Poetry Book Society Limited | [on the right hand page in italics] *(founded 1954)* | *Board of* Joseph Compton CBE (Chairman) |*Management* P.F. du Sautoy | Roy Fuller John Hayward CBE | John Lehmann | Stephen Spender CBE | Professor Constantine Trypanis | [on the left-hand page] Director | Patric Dickinson [on the right-hand page] *Festival* John Lehmann *(Chairman)* | *Advisory* David Carver | *Committee* Roy Fuller | George MacBeth | Anthony Thwaite | *Secretary* Eric W. White | *Festival Assistant* Nathalie Balck-Foote

Collation: [1-2]^5 + [3]^4 + [4]^6 + [5]^4 + [6]^6 = 30 leaves; 20.3 x 13 cm.

Binding: Glued into stiff strong orange (50) wove paper pictorial wraps, printed in black and very reddish orange (34); printed on the front wrapper in black: Festival of | Poetry | 1963 | *Director* | Patric Dickinson | Souvenir | Programme | FIVE SHILLINGS; white and light yellowish brown (76) wove paper; all edges trimmed.

Publication date: 15 July 1963

Price: 5s

Number of copies: Data unavailable from publisher

Contents: "A Minor Lear," p. [38], collected in PAAM and CP.

Note: This poem appears here for the first time in print.

Note: Cover design by Sarah Hamilton

B4 15 POEMS FOR WILLIAM SHAKESPEARE 1964

a. First trade edition:

[Complete text of title page is enclosed within a double rule border *15 Poems* | *for William* | *Shakespeare* | [single rule] | *edited by* Eric W. White | *with an introduction by* | Patrick Garland | John Lehmann & William Plomer | [single rule] | 1964: *Stratford-upon-Avon* | The Trustees & Guardians | of Shakespeare's Birthplace

Collation: $[1]^{12}$ = 12 leaves; 25 x 15 cm.

Binding: Sewn into a light shade of light yellowish brown (76) wallet-edged wove paper wrapper; on the upper wrapper [ornamental floral border printed in very dark green (147) which serves as a border surrounding the title] [in decorative type] 15 | [in decorative type] POEMS | *for William* | *Shakespeare* | Edmund Blunden Dom Moraes | Charles Causley Peter Porter | Roy Fuller W.J. Snodgrass | Thom Gunn Stephen Spender | Randall Jarrell Derek Walcott | Thomas Kinsella Vernon Watkins | Laurie Lee David Wright | Hugh MacDiarmid | [thick ornamental border in very dark green (147)]; white wove paper; all edges trimmed.

Publication date: June 1964

Price: 3s 6d

Number of copies: 1,000

Contents: "Reading M.N.D. in Form 4B," p. 13, collected in CP.

Note: This poem appears here for the first time in print.

[Not Seen]

b. First limited edition:

[The transcription of the title page is identical to that of the first trade edition.]

Collation: $[1]^{12}$ = 12 leaves;

Binding: Bound in paper vellum covered boards stamped in gold on the upper cover: [portrait of William Shakespeare surrounded by a rule and then surrounded by] WILLIAM SHAKESPEARE STRATFORD UPON AVON | 1564 1964 | 15 POEMS | *for William* | *Shakespeare;* white wove paper; all edges trimmed; white wove endpapers; the verso of the title page carries a statement of limitation and the copy number.

Publication date: June 1964

Price: 10s 6 d

Number of copies: 100

Contents: Same as B4a

B5 POETS IN PUBLIC 1965

[cover title] UNDER THE PATRONAGE OF HER MAJESTY THE QUEEN | AND HER MAJESTY QUEEN ELIZABETH THE QUEEN MOTHER | *Edinburgh* | *International Festival* | *In association with the Corporation of the City of Edinburgh* | *the Scottish Committee of the Arts Council of Great Britain* | *and the British Council* | [ornamental device of harp, horns, branches in brilliant purplish blue (195)]| POETS IN PUBLIC | FREEMASONS' HALL | *Tuesday, 24th August 1965, at 11 a.m.* | *Wednesday, 25th August 1965, at 2:30 p.m.* | *Thursday, 26th August 1965, at 11 a.m.* | *Friday, 27th August 1965, at 8 p.m.*

Collation: $[1]^{16}$ = 16 leaves; 24.9 x 18.5 cm.

Binding: Stapled twice into stiff, shiny white wove paper and lettered on the front wrapper as above; on the rear wrapper lettered in black and within a black rectangle are 29 lines on the Festival Guild and the address | [in black] Printed by McFarlane & Erskine Ltd., Edinburgh; white wove paper; all edges trimmed.

Date of publication: 24 August 1965

Price: Data unavailable from publisher

Number of copies: "approximately" 1,500

Contents: "Lyric," p. 16., collected in APF and CP

Note: This poem appears here for the first time in print.

Note: This poem was retitled "Clairvoyant" in both APF and CP as part 4 of *The Porter Song Book*.

B6 VERSE AND VOICE 1965

Verse and Voice | A FESTIVAL OF POETRY | Poems and ballads of the Commonwealth | at the Royal Court Theatre | September 20 to 25 | Empire into Commonwealth | September 26 to October 2 | Commonwealth Poetry Today | a festival promoted by | The Poetry Book Society | Director of Poetry Productions: Douglas Cleverdon | Associate Director: Garry O'Connor | Stage Designer: Arthur Boyd | Folk Song Adviser: A.L. Lloyd

Collation: 59 single leaves; 20.2 x 12.5 cm.

Binding: A perfect binding glued into a stiff wove paper pictorial wrappers printed on the inside of the front and rear wrapper in gray greenish yellow (105) and on the exterior in brilliant purplish blue (195), very pale blue (184), strong yellowish pink (26) and deep purplish pink (248) and lettered on front wrapper in white: [at the upper left-hand corner] verse and | voice | [at the lower left-hand corner] a festival | of commonwealth | poetry | [and in black letters on the right-hand lower corner] 3s 6d; white and gray greenish yellow (105) wove paper; all edges trimmed.

Publication date: 20 September 1965

Price: 3s 6d

Number of copies: Data unavailable from publisher

Contents: "Five Generations," pp. 68-70, collected in APF.

Note: This poem appears here for the first time in print.

Note: Cover design by Arthur Boyd.

B7 MOMENTS OF TRUTH 1965

[decorative rule: hourglass alternating with abstract floral design] | Moments of Truth | Nineteen Short Poems | by Living Poets | [decorative rule as above] London | The Keepsake Press | 1965 | [decorative rule as above]

Collation: $[1]^{14}$ = 14 leaves; 17.2 x 10.9 cm.

Binding: Stapled twice into a light shade of light gray yellowish brown (79) stiff card wrapper printed in dark yellowish brown (78); on the right side of the upper wrapper: MOMENTS | OF TRUTH | George Barker | Martin Bell | John Betjeman | Edwin Brock | Robert Conquest | Gavin Ewart | Roy Fuller | Thom Gunn | Bernard Gutteridge | Francis Hope | Ted Hughes | Edward Lowbury | Kathleen Nott | Peter Porter | Peter Redgrove | James Reeves | Peter Russell | David Wevill | Hugo William; the left side of the upper wrapper and the entire rear wrapper have an applied serigraph of a wavy pattern in multiple shades of gray and purplish blue; white wove paper; issued unopened.

Note: In some issues, the top edges were trimmed and the others untrimmed.

Publication date: October 1965

Price: 5s

Number of copies: 328

Note: The colophon reads: *Of this edition* | each contributor receives 12 copies as keepsakes; 100 | are for sale.

Contents: "St. Cecilia's Day Epigram," p. 9, collected in APF and CP. As II under "Saint Cecilia's Day Epigrams."

B8 POETRY SUPPLEMENT 1965

[cover title] Poetry | Supplement | edited by | Francis Hope | for the | Poetry Book | Society | [publisher's logo: fancy letters 'P | BS' in a laurel wreath] | Christmas | 1965

Collation: $[1]^{8}$ = 8 leaves; 21.5 x 12.7 cm.

Binding: Stapled twice into yellowish white (92) wove paper wrappers lettered in black on the front wrapper as stated above; on the rear wrapper in black: PUBLISHED BY | THE POETRY BOOK SOCIETY LTD | 4 ST JAMES'S SQUARE | LONDON SWI | [on the left of the lower cover] *John Roberts Press Limited* | London; yellowish white (92) wove paper; all edges trimmed.

Publication date: December 1965

Price: Date unavailable from publisher

Number of copies: 2,000

Contents: "Provincial Messiah," p. [10], collected in APF and CP under the overall title of "Fair Go for Anglo-Saxons."

Note: This poem appears here for the first time in print.

B9 LONDON MAGAZINE POEMS 1961-66 1966

London Magazine Poems | 1961-66 | Selected by Hugo Williams, with an | introduction by Alan Ross | Allan Ross *London 1966*

Collation: $[A]^8 + B\text{-}O^8$ = 112 leaves; 18.3 x 9 cm.

Binding: Glued into stiff light gray yellowish brown (79) wove paper wrappers and lettered down the spine in gray olive green (127): LMe 6 London Magazine Poems 1961-66; lettered vertically on the front wrapper in gray olive green (127) in stenciled "Futura Black" style: London | Magazine | Poems | [across the front wrapper in gray olive green (127): London | Magazine | editions | 6/6 | [in gray olive green (127) "Futura Black" style numerals] 1961-66; on the rear wrapper lettered in gray olive green (127): London Magazine Poems | [21 lines of text describing the collection]; white wove paper; all edges trimmed.

Publication date: May 1966

Price: 6s 6d

Number of copies: 3,000

Contents: "In a Suffolk Garden," p. 140.

Note: The contents also contain "Happening at Sordid Creek," and "Homage to Gaetano Donizetti" which were previously collected.

B10 BOOKS PLAYS POEMS 1966

[cover title] [in decorative black letters] BOOKS PLAYS [in black and white striped letters] POEMS | [in white letters on a black banner] SUMMER 1966 | [7 people in black and white in various costumes] | [at the lower left hand corner] BBC RADIO FOR SCHOOLS.

Collation: $[1]^{18}$ = 18 leaves; 17.7 x 23,5 cm.

Binding: Stapled twice into white wove paper wrappers; front wrapper as above; on the rear wrapper are schedules of broadcasts from April 27th through June 29th and a paragraph of acknowledgements; white wove paper; all edges trimmed.

Publication date: Summer 1966

Price: 1s

Number of copies: Data unavailable from publisher

Contents: "Lyric" (The astronaut is weightless.), p. 32; "An Interview," pp. 34-35.

Note: These poems appear here for the first time in print.

Note: The contents also include "The View from Misfortune's Back," "Once Bitten, Twice Bitten; Once Shy, Twice Shy," and "Somme and Flanders" which were previously published.

B11 GRAFFITI 1966

GRAFFITI | Richard Freeman | illustrated by | Tony Evershed | [collage of 5 photographs of graffiti in black and white] | HUTCHINSON

Collation: $[1\text{-}2]^8 + [3\text{-}8]^{10} + [9]^4 + [10\text{-}11]^8$ = 96 leaves; 22.8 x 15 cm.

Binding: Bound in light grayish olive (109) cloth and lettered on the spine: [across the top of the spine in black] RICHARD | FREEMAN; [down the spine in vivid red (11)] GRAFFITI | [across the base of the spine in black] [publisher's logo] | HUTCHINSON; lettered on the front cover at the lower right-hand corner in black: GRAFFITI | Richard Freeman; white wove paper; all edges trimmed; light gray (264) endpapers; dust wrapper of white wove paper, of which the exterior is shiny and printed in black, vivid red (11) and medium yellow brown (77).

Publication date: October 1966

Price: 42/-

Number of copies: Data unavailable from publisher

Contents: "Lines," p. 19, collected in APF and CP.

Note: This poem appears here for the first time in print.

B12 TWELVE POETS 1967

[cover title] Twelve Poets | Edited by | Charles Osborne | for the | Poetry Book | Society | [publisher's logo: fancy letters 'P | BS' within a laurel wreath] | Christmas | 1967

Collation: $[1]^8$ = 8 leaves; 21.4 x 12.6 cm.

Binding: Stapled twice into yellowish white (92) wove paper wrappers and lettered in black on the front wrapper as stated above; on the rear wrapper in black: *The Poets* | [37 lines of biographical information on the poets] | *Printed by the John Roberts Press* | *and published by the Poetry Book Society at 4 St. James's Square, London S.W. 1.*; yellowish-white (92) wove paper; all edges trimmed.

Publication date: November 1967

Price: Data unavailable from publisher

Number of copies: 2,000

Contents: "The Widow's Story," pp. [4-5], collected in TLOE and CP.

Note: This poem appears here for the first time in print.

B13 FORUM ON POETRY 1967

Greater London Arts Association + Poets in Public | FORUM ON POETRY | "The people which ceases to care for its literary inheritance becomes barbaric; the people | which ceases to produce literature ceases to move in thought and sensibility. The poetry | of a people takes its life from the people's speech and in turn gives life to it; and represents | its highest point of consciousness, its greatest power and its most delicate sensibility." | T.S. Eliot: Introduction to the Use of Poetry and the Use of Criticism. 1933.

Collation: $[1]^{18}$ = 18 leaves; 19.1 x 21 cm.

Binding: Stapled twice and glued into stiff dark gray yellowish brown (81) wrappers and printed on the front wrapper in black: forum | on | poetry | [single rule] | Greater London Arts Association + Poets in Public | French Institute, South Kensington | 26th November 1967; rear wrapper blank; white wove paper; all edges trimmed.

Publication date: 26 November 1967

Price: Data unavailable from publisher

Number of copies: Data unavailable from publisher

Contents: "Futurity," [p. 27]. Collected in APF and CP.

B14 LETTERS POEMS AND DRAWINGS FOR VERNON SCANNELL 1967

[facsimile reproduction of hand-printed title page] Letters Poems and Drawings | for | Vernon Scannell | by. | Martin Bax 2. | Edwin Brock 3. | Nancy 4. | Prosper Dowden 5. | John 7. | Richard Freeman 8. Nancy 9. | Alan Brownjohn 10. | George MacBeth 12. | Jane 15. | Dannie Abse 16. | Peter Porter 18. | Mike Foreman | arranged the cover. | Toby drew it. | Privately published by the authors, 1967.

Collation: $[1]^{10}$ = 10 leaves; 21.5 x 16.5 cm.

Binding: Stapled twice into stiff card wrappers, of which the exterior is shiny, printed in black and white; the front wrapper consists of three juvenile drawings in three panels; the rear wrapper is plain white; white wove paper; all edges trimmed.

Publication date: 1967

Price: Not offered for sale.

Number of copies: 21

Contents: "Letter to Vernon" (poem), pp. 18-20.

Note: This poem appears here for the first time in print.

B15 THE VOICE OF LOVE 1968

Nicholas Maw | The Voice of Love | *Song Cycle* | Poems by | Peter Porter | Boosey & Hawkes | Music Publishers Limited | *London · Paris · Bonn · Johannesburg · Sydney · Toronto · New York*

Collation: $[1]^{24}$ = 24 leaves; 30.5 x 23.4 cm.

Binding: Stapled twice into heavy white wove paper wrappers and printed in strong red (12), black and white; lettered in white italics at the upper left-hand side of the front wrapper: Nicholas Maw | The Voice | of Love | [to the right of this is a reproduction in black and white of a portrait of Dorothy Osborne within a white oval]; [on the lower right-hand side of the front wrapper in white italics]: words by | Peter Porter | Boosey & Hawkes; [to the left of this is a reproduction in black and white of a portrait of William Temple within a white oval]; the rear wrapper in strong red is blank; white wove paper; all edges trimmed.

Publication date: 9 April 1968

Price: £1.00

Number of copies: 1,000; second printing, March 20, 1981, 559 copies

Contents: "The Voice of Love," pp. [2-3]; the text is also repeated with the score which appears on pp. 5-48.

Note: This poem appears here for the first time in print.

B16 BOOKS PLAYS POEMS 1968

[cover title] [in white] BOOKS | [in white] PLAYS | [in black] POEMS | BBC Radio for Schools | SUMMER TERM 1968

Collation: $[1]^{24}$ = 24 leaves; 17.7 x 23.6 cm.

Binding: Stapled twice into white wove paper wrappers; on the front cover: [a black and white photograph of a small boy swinging on a chain in a park]; on the rear wrapper: [to the left] *Acknowledgement is due to the following, continued* | [48 lines of acknowledgements] | BOOKS, PLAYS, POEMS | Summer 1968 P36 | [to the right] [black and white reproduction of the painting "Portrait of his Parents" by Otto Dix] | © British Broadcasting Corporation 1968 | Published by the British Broadcasting Corporation | 35 Marylebone High Street, London W.1 | Printed in England by Quicks the Printers, Clacton-on-Sea, | SBN 563 07673 9 price one shilling and sixpence; white wove paper; all edges trimmed.

Publication date: Summer 1968

Price: 1/6

Number of copies: Data unavailable from publisher

Contents: "Seahorses," and "A Hoplite's Helmet,", p. 13, both collected in APF and CP.

B17 ALLSORTS 1 1968

[white] A [black] LLSORTS1 | [black] A [white] L [black] LSORTS1 | [black] AL [white] L [black] SORTS1 | [black] ALL [white] S [black] ORTS1 | [black] ALLS [white] O [black] RTS1 | [black] ALLSO [white] R [black] TS1 | [black] ALLSOR [white] T [black] S1 | [black] ALLSORT [white] S [black] 1 | [black] ALLSORTS [white] 1 | *edited by Ann Thwaite* [sloping dash] Macmillan

Collation: $[A]^{16}$ + $B\text{-}D^{16}$ = 64 leaves; 26.3 x 18.6 cm.

Binding: Bound in paper-covered pictorial boards printed in strong purplish blue (96), strong blue (178), light reddish purple (240) strong purplish pink (247), brilliant yellowish green (130), gray reddish brown (39), medium reddish brown (43), light orange yellow (70), very light bluish green (162), medium reddish orange (37), black and white; lettered down the spine: [strong purplish blue (196)] allsorts | [black] edited by anne thwaite | [across the base of the spine in strong purplish blue (196)] MACMILLAN: [lettered across the front wrapper at the top in strong purplish blue (196): allsorts 1; white wove paper; all edges trimmed; white wove endpapers.

Publication date: 26 September 1968

Price: 18s

Number of copies: Data unavailable from publisher

Contents: "The Year I was Eight. The History Parade," pp. 31-37.

Note: This prose statement appears here for the first time in print.

B18 NEW POEMS 1967 1968

[decorative floral device] | NEW POEMS | 1967 | A P.E.N. Anthology | of Contemporary Poetry | [decorative floral device] | *Edited by* | HAROLD PINTER | JOHN FULLER | PETER REDGROVE | HUTCHINSON OF LONDON

Collation: $[A]^8 + B\text{-}F^8$ = 48 leaves; 19.9 x 13.2 cm.

Binding: Bound in imitation black cloth and lettered down the spine in gold: NEW POEMS 1967 [vertical rule] A P.E.N. ANTHOLOGY HUTCHINSON; white wove paper; all edges trimmed; white wove endpapers; dust wrapper, shiny on the exterior, of white wove paper printed in vivid red (11), black and medium gray (265).

Publication date: 14 October 1968.

Price: 25s

Number of copies: 1,750

Contents: "Fantasia on a Line of Stefan George," p. 62; "The Return of Inspector Christopher Smart," pp. 63-66, both collected in APF and CP.

B19 TIRADE 1968

TIRADE | [the rest of the title-page is lettered in facsimile of hand-printed letters] A Triptych for Medium Voice & Instrumental Ensemble | [Piano, Harp & 3 Percussion] | Poem by PETER PORTER don banks | [in four columns across the page are lists under the headings of "Abbreviations etc.," "Distribution of Percussion Instruments" (in three columns)] | [thin rule] | [thick rule] | Composer's Facsimile | [thick rule] | SCHOTT & CO. LTD. LONDON | 48 Great Marlborough Street London W1 | B. Schott's Sohne, Mainz - Editions by Max Eschig, Paris | Associated Music Publishers Inco., New York

Collation: $[1]^{16}$ = 16 leaves; 25 x 35 cm.

Binding: Stapled twice into stiff medium orange (53) wove paper wrappers and printed on the front wrapper in strong reddish brown (40): [upper right hand corner] DON BANKS | TIRADE (covering three quarters of the front wraper] | [lower left hand corner of the front wrapper] PLAYING SCORE | SCHOTT | EDITION 11073; on the rear wrapper in strong reddish brown (40): SCHOTT'S | Study and Miniature Scores | *Recent and forthcoming additions* | [three columns of information on the study and miniature scores] | SCHOTT & CO LTD 48 Great Marlborough Street London W1; white wove paper; all edges trimmed.

Publication date: 1968

Price: Data unavailable from publisher

Number of copies: Data unavailable from publisher

Note: Copies were available in 1984 at £2.15 and the publisher reported the price as £3.00 in 1985.

Contents: "Tirade," p. [1]; the text is also repeated with the score, pp. 4-30.

B20 UCL (University College of London) Poetry 1969

[cover title:] *UCL POETRY* | *1969* | *Edited by* | *Thomas Kabdebo* | *Introduced by* | *Margaret* | *Richards* | *London* | *Poetry* | *Workshop* | *Seminar*

Collation: $[1]^{40}$ = 40 leaves; 22.9 x 15 cm.

Binding: Stapled twice into stiff medium orange yellow (71) wove paper wrappers; title on front wrapper as above; on the rear wrapper in black italics: UCL Poetry 1969 | Edited by Thomas Kabdebo | Cover design by Sarah John | Published by | University College of London | Poetry Seminar

Workshop | 12, Gordon Street WC1 | Printed by Clarion Photographic Ltd | Price six shillings; white wove paper; all edges trimmed; text is photo-offset of typed manuscript.

Publication date: June 1969

Price: 6s

Number of copies: 500

Contents: "Nothing less than the whole of the Self. . . ," 55-57.

Note: This poem appears here for the first time in print.

B21 AUSTRALIAN POETRY 1969 1969

AUSTRALIAN | POETRY | 1969 | *Selected by* | VIVIAN SMITH | [publisher's logo: an exotic plant within an oval] | ANGUS AND ROBERTSON

Collation: $[A]^8 + B\text{-}F^8 + G^4 + H^8$ = 60 leaves; 18.9 x 12.2 cm.

Binding: Bound in textured grayish green (150) imitation cloth and lettered down the spine in gold: AUSTRALIAN POETRY 1969 Angus and Robertson; white wove paper; all edges trimmed; white wove endpapers.

Note: Dust wrapper not seen.

Publication date: 16 September 1969

Price: $2.50 (Australian dollars)

Number of copies: 1,500

Contents: "The Sadness of the Creatures," pp. 64-66, collected in TLOE and CP.

Note: The contents also include "Seahorses" and "The History of Music" (published as one of three poems entitled "Three Poems for Music") which were previously collected.

B22 BROADSHEET 10 1970

BROADSHEET TEN

Collation: Broadsheet; single sheet printed on both sides; 37.3 x 30.3 cm.

Binding: White wove paper, printed in black; all edges trimmed.

Note: Broadsheet 10 contains six sheets, double-sided print; three sides are in color, nine black and white, and issued in a grayish brown (90) envelope printed on both sides.

Publication date: March 1970

Price: 50p.

Number of copies: 1,000

Contents: "Dirtyram on the Bird of Heaven"

Note: This poem appears here for the first time in print

Note: This poem, which is printed in black on white paper, is located on the lower right-hand quarter of the broadsheet and is one of 17 poems on the broadsheet.

B23 BREAKTHROUGH 1970

Breakthrough | Poetry in Britain during the 1960's | [single rule] | Edited by R.B. Heath | [publisher's logo] | Hamish Hamilton | London

Collation: $[1\text{-}7]^{16}$ = 112 leaves; 19.3 x 12.6 cm.

Binding: Glued into stiff white shiny wove paper and lettered down the spine: [brilliant orange yellow (67) over deep reddish orange (36) letters] BREAKTHROUGH [very purplish blue (194) *R.B. Heath* [across the base of the spine in very purplish blue (194): publisher's logo]; on the front wrapper in brilliant orange yellow (67) over deep reddish orange (36) letters surrounded by a very purplish blue (194) device used to surround spoken words in cartoons: BREAKTHROUGH | [in very purplish blue (194) an illustration depicting the cover as if it were torn] | [in very purplish blue (194)] *Poetry in Britain* | during the | [in white over very purplish blue (194)] 60's | [in very purplish blue (194)] *R B Heath;* on the rear wrapper the title as depicted on the front wrapper | [double column listing the names of the 24 poets included in the volume printed in very purplish blue (194)] | [very purplish blue] HAMISH HAMILTON | [at the lower left hand corner of the rear wrapper in very purplish blue (194)] *Cover Design: Barrington Barber*

Publication date: April 1970

Price: 10s

Number of copies: Data unavailable from publisher

Contents: "A Consumer's Report," pp. 152-153, collected in TLOE and CP.

Note: The contents also include "Lyric," "Once Bitten, Twice Bitten; Once Shy, Twice Shy," "What a Lying Lot the Writers Are," "Somme and Flanders," "The View from Misfortune's Back," and "St Cecilia's Day, 1710" which were previously collected.

B24 A BRITISH FOLIO 1970

[folder title] UNICORN FOLIO | *Series Three Number Two* | A BRITISH FOLIO | [A unicorn head in silhouette printed in deep red (13) and white stripes]

Binding: A folder of stiff wove paper in light purplish blue (199) containing 14 separate sheets: contents, introduction, capsule biographies of the poets; 10 broadsheets, each a different color and size and by a different poet, a colophon; the folder (closed) measures 50.7 x 33.2 cm.

Publication date: 22 May 1970

Price: $5.00

Number of copies: 375

Contents: Diana and Actaeon, collected in TLOE and CP.

Note: Broadsheet; single sheet; 45 x 40.5 cm.; yellow white (92) laid paper; printed on one side only; trimmed on the top, bottom and left sides; right side has a deckled edge in brilliant yellow (83).

Note: The colophon reads: "Three hundred and seventy-five numbered | copies of this folio of British Poetry were | published as the tenth Unicorn Folio in a | series of twelve. Typography by Allan Bril- | liant. Printed by Noel Young. Bindery by | Donald Rojo. Copyright MCMLXX. Unicorn | Press books are published in Santa Barbara | by Alan Brillant [sic] and Teo Savory. | [fancy letters] No. [number written in white ink over a series of seven printed horizontal lines]"

B25 BROADSIDE EIGHT 1970

BROADSIDE EIGHT

Collation: Broadsheet; single sheet, printed on both sides; 41.7 x 33.5 cm.

Binding: White wove paper, printed in black, all edges trimmed.

Publication date: June 1970

Price: 1s

Number of copies: 1,000

Contents: Job's Discounts, collected in TLOE

Note: This poem appears here for the first time in print.

Note: Porter's poem, printed on the front side of the broadshee, is in the middle of the sheet on the left hand side and is one of 18 poems on the broadsheet.

B26 CONTEMPORARY POETS OF THE ENGLISH LANGUAGE 1970

CONTEMPORARY POETS | OF THE | ENGLISH | LANGUAGE | WITH A PREFACE BY | C.D. LEWIS | EDITOR | ROSALIE MURPHY | DEPUTY EDITOR | JAMES VINSON | ST JAMES PRESS | CHICAGO LONDON

Collation: $[1]^{10} + [2\text{-}39]^{16} + [40]^{14}$ = 632 leaves; 24.6 x 17.5 cm.

Binding: Bound in brownish black (65) cloth and lettered across the spine in gold: Contemporary | Poets | of the | English | Language | St. James Press; lettered in gold across the front cover: Contemporary | Poets | of the | English | Language; white wove paper; all edged trimmed; white wove endpapers; textured dust wrapper of gray yellowish brown (80) paper printed in gold.

Publication date: August 1970

Price: $25.00, £8.50

Number of copies: 3,000

Contents: [Prose statement on poetry], pp. 865-866.

Note: The book's title was changed to "CONTEMPORARY POETS" in a second printing (June 1973) and a third printing (March 1974). A second edition with a change of editors and design was published by St. James Press, London (June 1975) and St. Martin's Press, New York (August 1975); in this edition Porter's statement on poetry has been omitted.

B27 POETRY SUPPLEMENT 1970

[cover title] Poetry Supplement | Edited by | John Fuller | for the | Poetry Book | Society | Christmas | 1970

Collation: $[1]^{8}$ = 8 leaves; 21.4 x 12.7 cm.

Binding: Stapled twice into yellowish white (92) wove paper wrappers lettered in black on the front wrapper as stated above; on the rear wrapper: [12 lines of biographical information on two of the poets in the Supplement] | *Printed by John Roberts Press* | *and published by the Poetry Book Society at 105 Picadilly, London, WIVOAU;* yellowish white (92) wove paper; all edges trimmed.

Publication date: November 1970

Price: Data unavailable from publisher

Number of copies: 2,000

Contents: "Notes to a Biographer," pp. [9-10], collected in PTTC and CP.

Note: This poem appears here for the first time in print.

B28 VORTEX 1970

VORTEX | Edited and Managed by | Tim Collins | John Incledon | W. Scott McIntosh | Harold Ober | VORTEX is published yearly at one dollar per | copy. Send subscriptions to VORTEX, 84 Broad | Street, Hamilton, New York, 13346. Unsolicited | manuscripts, art and photography accompanied | by a stamped, self-addressed envelope, should | be sent to the above address. Payment upon ac- | ceptance will be in copies. | © VORTEX 1970 | No part of this magazine may be reproduced | without written consent of the editors.

Collation: $[1]^{67}$ = 67 leaves; 24.9 x 20 cm.

Binding: Stapled twice into heavy strong reddish orange (35) paper wrappers and lettered on the front wrapper: [in deep red (13)] VORTEX |[in black] Spring 1970 No. 4 | [in black] Michael Hamburger George | [black] MacBeth • Hugh MacDiarmid | [black] Peter Redgrove • Robert | [black] Conquest • Peter Porter | [black] John Hearne • James Tate • Frederick | [black] Busch • Harold Ober | One Dollar; on the lower right hand side of the front wrapper and in the center of the rear wrapper in black: details of the design of "The Vorticist" by Wyndham Lewis; white wove paper; all edges trimmed.

Publication date: Data unavailable from publisher

Price: $1.00

Number of copies: Data unavailable from publisher

Contents: "Kreuznaer's Inheritance," p. 101; "The Way We Think of It," p. 102; "In Place of Canto," pp. 104-106.

Note: "Kreuznaer's Inheritance," and "In Place of a Canto" appear here for the first time in print.

Note: The contents also include "Let Me Bore You With My Slides," and "A Meredithian Treatment" which were previously published.

B29 A CHOICE OF POPE'S VERSE 1971

a. First edition, hardcover issue:

[*A Choice of* | POPE'S VERSE | *Selected and with an Introduction* | *by* | PETER PORTER | FABER AND FABER | 3 Queen Square | London

Collation: $[A]^8$ + $B\text{-}K^8$ = 80 leaves; 19.9 x 13.2 cm.

Binding: Bound in textured light yellow brown (76) cloth and lettered down the spine in gold: *A Choice of POPE'S VERSE - edited by Peter Porter Faber;* dust wrapper of shiny yellowish white (92) wove paper printed in black and medium orange yellow (71); white wove paper; all edges trimmed; white wove endpapers.

Publication date: 12 July 1971

Price: £1.75

Number of copies: 1,000

Contents: "Introduction," pp. 9-39.

b. First edition, papercover issue:

[The transcription of the title page is identical with that of the hardcover issue.]

Collation: $[A]^8$ + $B\text{-}K^8$ = 80 leaves; 18.4 x 12.2

Binding: Glued into stiff white wove paper wrappers, of which the exterior is shiny and lettered down the spine: [in black] *A Choice of POPE'S VERSE Peter Porter* [in white letters on a medium orange yellow (71) rectangle] FABER; on the front wrapper in medium orange yellow (71) *A CHOICE OF* | [in black] *POPE'S* | [in black] *VERSE* | [a head-and-shoulders portrait of Pope in medium orange yellow (71) and white] | [in black] *Selected with an introduction by* | [in black] *PETER PORTER;* [running from top to bottom in white on a black band] *FABER paper covered EDITIONS*; on the rear wrapper printed in black: *Also in Faber Paper Covered Editions* | [list of 38 titles, followed by 4 lines of publisher information]; on the left-hand side of the cover running from bottom to top in white on a medium orange yellow (71) band: *FABER paper covered EDITIONS*; white wove paper; all edges trimmed.

Publication date: 12 July 1971

Price: 60p

Number of copies: 5,000

Contents: Same as B29a

B30 POET'S CHOICE 1971

POET'S | CHOICE | 1971 | [publisher's logo in strong reddish brown (40): an open book with blank pages backed by wavy lines within an oval] | Island Press | Sydney

Collation: $[1]^{10} + [2]^{8} + [3]^{10}$ = 28 leaves; 21.2 x 13.4 cm.

Binding: Glued into stiff very pale blue (184) wove paper wrappers and lettered down the spine in black: POET'S CHOICE 1971 ISLAND; front wrapper identical to title-page; on the rear wrapper in black: [11 lines listing contributors to the volume and that "Each copy numbered"] | [in black] Australian National Library Card No and | ISBN 0 909771 022 | Island Press, GPO Box 4430, Sydney 2001, Australia | $1.50; white wove paper; all edges trimmed; stiff very pale blue (184) endpapers.

Publication date: 1971

Price: $1.50 (Australian dollars)

Number of copies: 500

Contents: "Preaching to the Converted," pp. 17-18, collected in PTTC and CP.

Note: This poem appears here for the first time in print.

B31 POEMS FOR SHAKESPEARE 1972

a. First edition, limited hardcover issue

Poems for | *Shakespeare* | *Edited with an* | *Introduction by* | *Christopher Hampton* | The Globe Playhouse | Trust Publications | London 1972

Collation: $[1\text{-}4]^{8}$ = 32 leaves; 20.3 x 12.8 cm.

Binding: Quarter bound in deep orange yellow (42) leather and in textured light gray (264) cloth and lettered down the spine in gold: [vertical rule] | POEMS FOR SHAKESPEARE | [vertical rule]; on the front cover a stylized illustration of the Globe Theatre with a flag in gold; white wove paper; all edges trimmed and stained in gold leaf; issued without a dust wrapper in a slip case of textured light gray (264) cloth.

Publication date: 23 April 1972

Price: £30

Number of copies: 100

Note: On the verso of the title page is this statement: "A limited, numbered edition of 100 copies, signed by | the poets and specially bound, has been printed | (hors commerce) in advance of the first edition." The publisher reports that there were 120 copies printed for the limited edition.

Contents: "The Kleenex and the Myrtle," pp. 33-35

Note: This poem appears here for the first time in print.

b. First edition, papercover issue

[The transcription of the title page is identical with that of the limited hardcover issue.]

Collation: 32 leaves; 20.3 x 12.8

Binding: A perfect binding glued into stiff white wove paper wrappers, of which the exterior is shiny, and lettered down the spine in black; POEMS FOR SHAKESPEARE; on the front wrapper in black: Poems for | Shakespeare | [a waving banner in white and vivid reddish orange (34)] | [a drawing of a bust of Shakespeare in black and grayish green (150)]; on the rear wrapper in black at the upper right-hand corner: 30p | [in grayish green (150)] THE GLOBE PLAYHOUSE TRUST LTD. | [in vivid reddish orange (34)] A DECLARATION OF PURPOSE | [33 lines of text in black] | [in vivid reddish orange (34)] *Cover design by Nicholas Jenkins* | [a drawing of the Globe Playhouse and the publisher's name and address in six lines in grayish green (150)].

Publication date: 23 April 1972

Price: 30p

Number of copies: 1,000

Contents: Same as B32a

B32 NEW POEMS 1971-72 1972

[decorative floral device] | NEW POEMS | 1971-72 | A P.E.N. Anthology | of Contemporary Poetry | [decorative floral device] *Edited by* | PETER PORTER | HUTCHINSON OF LONDON

Collation: $[A]^8 + B\text{-}K^8 + L^4 + M^8$ = 92 leaves; 19.8 x 12.9 cm.

Binding: Bound in strong reddish orange (35) imitation cloth and lettered down the spine in gold: NEW POEMS 1971/72 [vertical rule] A P.E.N. ANTHOLOGY [across the base of the spine: publisher's logo] | HUTCHINSON; white wove paper; all edges trimmed; light gray (264) endpapers; dust wrapper of white wove paper, shiny on the exterior, printed in black, white and off strong red (12).

Publication date: 26 June 1972

Price: £2.00

Number of copies: 2,000

Contents: "Introduction," pp. [11-13].

B33 OPENING FESTIVAL 1972

[cover title] THE WARD FREMAN | SCHOOL | BUNTINGFORD, HERTS. | [school insignia in vivid purplish blue (194) with three diamonds (upper right-hand corner], a horizontal line (from top left to bottom right) and a cross (lower left-hand corner) in white] | [in white on a vivid purplish blue (194) scroll] LIBER PER LIBROS | OPENING FESTIVAL | SATURDAY, July 1st, 1972 | at 2:30 in the School.

Collation: $[1]^4$ = 4 leaves; 20.4 x 12.7 cm.

Binding: Stapled twice in white wove paper; all edges trimmed.

Publication date: 1 July 1972

Price: Issued free

Number of copies: Data unavailable from publisher

Contents: "The Assassin," [p.] 7. Uncollected

Note: This poem appears here for the first time in print.

B34 THIRTEEN POETS 1972

[cover title] Thirteen Poets | Edited by | Dannie Abse | for the | Poetry Book | Society | Christmas | 1972

Collation: $[1]^{10}$ = 10 leaves; 21.1 x 12.6 cm.

Binding: Stapled twice into yellowish white (92) wove paper wrappers lettered in black on the front wrapper as stated above; the rear wrapper is blank; yellowish white (92) wove paper; all edges trimmed.

Publication date: November 1972

Price: Data unavailable from publisher

Number of copies: 2,500

Contents: "A Lesson in Logic," p. [10].

B35 BRITISH POETRY 1972 1972

British Poetry | 1972 | [illustration of two ancient coins] | Edited by | Vern Rutsala

Collation: $[1]^{16}$ = 16 leaves; 21 x 14.5 cm.

Binding: Stapled twice into stiff off-white wove paper wrappers; on the front wrapper [printed in black] enclosed in a white rectangle in vivid reddish orange (34) letters: *British* | *Poetry* | 1972 | [illustration of a standing male figure in black and white] | [vivid reddish orange (34)] *Edited by* | VERN RUTSALA; on the rear wrapper printed in off-white at the lower left-hand corner printed in black: [illustration of the King and Queen chess figures viewed from the back] The Baleen Press, P.O. Box 13448, Phoenix, Arizona, 8500; white wove paper; all edges trimmed.

Publication date: Data unavailable from publisher

Note: The preface by Vern Rutsala is dated July 1972

Price: $1.95

Number of copies: Data unavailable from publisher.

Contents: "Up at the House," pp. 17-18, collected in ASOTM; "The Old Enemy," p. 18, collected in PTTC and CP; "Images, images," p. 19, collected by ASOTM.

Note: "Up at the House" and "Images, images" appear here for the first time in print.

B36 POET'S CHOICE 1972

[in strong reddish brown (40)] POET'S CHOICE | [in strong reddish brown (40)] 1972 | [in black] Island Press | [in black] SYDNEY

Collation: $[1\text{-}2]^{8} + [3]^{10}$ = 26 leaves; 21.3 x 13.4 cm.

Binding: Glued into stiff strong orange yellow (68) wove paper wrappers and lettered down the spine in black: POET'S CHOICE 1972 ISLAND; on the front wrapper in black: [a thin rule over a thick rule] | POET'S | CHOICE | 1972 | [a thick rule over a thin rule] | [publisher's logo: an open book with blank pages backed by wavy lines within an oval in black] | [in black] Island Press | [in black] SYDNEY; on the rear wrapper in black: [12 lines listing contributors to the volume and that "Each copy numbered"] | [in black] Australian National Library Card No and | ISBN 0 909771 03 0 | Island Press, GPO Box 4430, Sydney 2001, Australia; white wove paper; all edges trimmed; stiff strong orange yellow (68) endpapers.

Publication date: 1972

Price: $1.50 (Australian dollars]

Number of copies: 500

Contents: "Verticordia," pp. 20-21.

Note: This poem appears here for the first time in print.

B37 LEEDS ARTS FESTIVAL 1973

[cover title] [superimposed on a photograph in black and white of bare trees and a wheel barrow; entire front wrapper printed in strong reddish orange (35)] [within a square and a parallel rectangle] LEEDS | ARTS | FESTIVAL [festival logo: a dog viewed from the rear looking toward the reader] [to the right of the rectangle] POETRY | 10p | [below the square and rectangle] Yorkshire Arts Association Sponsored | NEW POETRY | BY | ADRIAN HENRI | D.J. ENRIGHT | JEFF NUTTALL | PETER PORTER | VERNON SCANNELL | ALSO | GEORGE MACBETH | JON SILKIN

Collation: $[1]^4$ = 4 leaves; 21.5 x 15 cm.

Binding: Stapled twice into stiff shiny white wove paper wrappers; front wrapper as above; rear wrapper contains the last page of the text ["Epilogue" by Adrian Henri]; shiny white wove paper; all edges trimmed.

Publication date: 4 February 1973

Price: 10p

Number of copies: Data unavailable from publisher

Contents: "My Next Oratorio," p. [5], collected in ASOTM

Note: The programme was held at the Leeds Playhouse on Sunday, 4 February 1973 from 2:45 P.M. until approximately 5:30 P.M.

B38 TRIBUTE TO WYSTAN HUGH AUDEN 1973

[folder title] TRIBUTE TO | WYSTAN HUGH AUDEN | POEMS BY | ALAN BROWN-JOHN | CHARLES CAUSLEY | KEVIN CROSSLEY-HOLLAND | D.J. ENRIGHT | ROY FULLER | JAMES KIRKUP | GEORGE MACBETH | PETER PORTER | PETER REDGROVE | JON SILKIN | COMMISSIONED BY THE | ILKLEY LITERATURE FESTIVAL | AND PRINTED IN FACSIMILE | BY THE SCOLAR PRESS | APRIL 1973

Note: The portfolio folder is of stiff dark greenish yellow (103), printed in black and is supported by a black plastic strip running along the left-hand side of the fold; the folder measures 35.7 x 26.7 (when folded) and contained the following items:

a. A Booklet

A TRIBUTE | TO | W.H. AUDEN | by | Alan Brownjohn | Charles Causley | Keven Crossley-Holland | D.J. Enright | Roy Fuller | James Kirkup | George MacBeth | Peter Porter | Peter Redgrove | Jon Silkin | FOR THE ILKLEY LITERATURE FESTIVAL | PRINTED BY THE SCOLAR PRESS | 1973

Collation: $[1]^{12}$ = 12 leaves; 33 x 22 cm.

Binding: Stapled twice into heavy gray greenish yellow (105) wove paper wrappers, and printed on the front wrapper in black: A Tribute | to | W.H. Auden; the rear wrapper is blank; heavy gray greenish yellow (105) paper; all edges trimmed.

Publication date: 23 April 1973

Price: £1.00

Number of copies: 250 (10 copies were signed by the contributors and Auden)

Contents: "It pleases well the damed in Hell | To bring another there. | The Rake's Progress, ACT III, Scene II," pp. [18-19]

Note: First line of the poem: "Behind the dark pilasters of the House of Disappointment,"

Note: This poem appears here for the first time in print.

b. Twenty-five leaves in facsimile of original holograph contributions by the poets

It pleases well the damned in Hell | To bring another there. | The Rake's Progress, Act III, Scene II

Collation: 2 single leaves (printed on one side only); 33.4 x 22.2 cm.

Binding: White laid paper watermarked with a decorative fleur-de-lis and in open fancy letters: "L'ALMATRUDE AMALFI"; all edges deckled.

Publication date: Same as B38a

Price: Same as B38a

Number of copies: Same as B38a

Contents: "It pleases well the damned in Hell To bring another there," pp. [18-19].

B39 THE GREEK ANTHOLOGY 1973

a. First edition

The Greek Anthology | *AND OTHER ANCIENT GREEK* | *EPIGRAMS* | *A selection in modern verse translations,* | *edited with an* | *introduction by Peter Jay* | *ALLEN LANE*

Collation: $[1\text{-}14]^{16}$ = 224 leaves; 19.3 x 12.9 cm.

Note: The leaves are signed on the appropriate pages as follows:

$[G.A.\text{-}1]^{4}$ + $G.A.\text{-}1*^{12}$ + $G.A.\text{-}2^{4}$ + $G.A.2*^{12}$ through $G.A.\text{-}14*^{12}$.

Binding: Bound in semi-shiny, textured medium brown (58) cloth and lettered across the spine in gold: [single rule] | *The* | *Greek* | *Anthology* | [single rule] | Edited by | PETER JAY | [penguin publisher's logo]; white wove paper; all edges trimmed; white wove endpapers; dust wrapper of white wove paper of which the exterior is shiny printed in black, white, vivid orange yellow (66) and deep orange yellow (72).

Publication date: April 1973

Price: £3.50

Number of copies: Data unavailable from publisher

Note: The publisher reported as of August 1985 the total sales were 719.

Contents: [Two poems by Nikarchos], 301, 302, pp. 155-156; [Three poems by Phanias], 305, 306, 307, pp. 157-158; [Anonymous Epigram], 318, p. 162; [Poems by Lucilius], 533, 535-45, pp. 249-253; 547, 549-554, pp. 254-256; 556-63, 565-71, 573, pp. 257-261; [Poems by Nikarchos], 574-584, pp. 262-265; [Anonymous Epigrams], 755, p. 326; [Anonymous Epigrams], 775 and 779, pp. 331-332.

b. First American edition 1973

The Greek Anthology | AND OTHER ANCIENT GREEK EPIGRAMS | *A selection in modern verse translations,* | *edited with an* | *introduction by Peter Jay* | NEW YORK OXFORD UNIVERSITY PRESS | 1973.

Collation: $[1\text{-}14]^{16}$ = 224 leaves; 19.3 x 12.9 cm.

Note: The leaves are signed on the appropriate pages as follows:

$[G.A.\text{-}1]^{4}$ + $G.A.\text{-}1*^{12}$ + $G.A.\text{-}2^{4}$ + $G.A.2*^{12}$ through $G.A.\text{-}14*^{12}$.

Binding: Bound in semi-shiny, textured medium brown (58) cloth and lettered across the spine in gold: [single rule] | *The* | *Greek* | *Anthology* | [single rule] | Edited by | PETER JAY | OXFORD; white wove paper; all edges trimmed; white wove endpapers; dust wrapper of white wove paper of which the exterior is shiny printed in black, white, vivid orange yellow (66) and deep orange yellow (72).

Publication date: Data unavailable from publisher

Price: $12.50

Number of copies: Data unavailable from publisher

Contents: Same as B39a

c. First English paperbound edition 1981

The Greek Anthology | AND OTHER ANCIENT | EPIGRAMS | *A selection in modern verse translations,* | *edited with an* | *introduction by Peter Jay* | [publisher's logo] | PENGUIN BOOKS.

Collation: 224 leaves; 18 x 11 cm.

Binding: A perfect binding glued into white card wrappers printed in white, black and strong yellowish-brown (74); printed on the spine in white: [across the top of the spine: publisher's logo] | [printed down the spine in white] THE GREEK ANTHOLOGY | [in two lines] ISBN 0 14 | 044.285 5; on the front wrapper: [in white] Penguin [publisher's logo] Classics | THE GREEK ANTHOLOGY | [in strong yellowish-brown (74) and black: a reproduction of a photograph of a cup by Peithinos, depicting Peleus embracing Thetis]; on the rear wrapper in white: Penguin [publisher's logo] Classics | THE GREEK ANTHOLOGY | EDITED BY PETER JAY | [22 lines on the text and the front cover illustration]; [at the left-hand bottom corner in white] United Kingdom £2.50 | Australia $7.95 (recommended) | Canada $5.95; [at the right hand bottom corner in white] Poetry | ISBN 0 14 | 044.285 5; white wove paper; all edges trimmed.

Publication date: Data unavailable from publisher

Price: £2.50

Number of copies: Data unavailable from publisher

Note: On the verso of one title page examined, there is the statement: "Published in Penguin Books 1981" and in another copy: "Published in Penguin Books 1981 Revised edition published in Penguin Books 1981." The publisher reports that the total number of copies printed was 22,500.

Contents: Same as B39a

B40 COLOUR ME CORNWALL 1973

[cover title] [fancy italics in brilliant greenish blue (168)] Colour me Cornwall | [in black] MUSIC WORKSHOP | STAGE ONE | SUMMER 1973.

Collation: $[1]^{12}$ = 12 leaves; 23.5 x 17.8 cm.

Binding: Stapled twice into white wove pictorial wrappers printed in black and brilliant greenish blue (168); front wrapper as above; on the rear wrapper in the lower left-hand corner in black: MUSIC WORKSHOP | STAGE ONE | P58 Summer 1973; at the lower right-hand corner in black: © British Broadcasting Corporation 1973 | First published 1973 | Published at the request of the School Broadcasting Council | for the United Kingdom | by the British Broadcasting Corporation, | 35 Marylebone High Street, London W1M 4AA. | Printed in England by Hollen Street Press, Ltd., Slough, Bucks. | ISBN 0 563 19912 1 price 5 1/2p.; white wove paper; all edges trimmed.

Date of publication: Summer, 1973; second printing, Summer 1976

Price: 5 1/2p

Number of copies: Data unavailable from publisher

Contents: Libretto by Peter Porter

B41 NEW POEMS 1972-73 1973

[decorative floral device] | NEW POEMS | 1972-73 | A P.E.N. Anthology | of Contemporary Poetry | [decorative floral design] | *Edited by* | DOUGLAS DUNN | HUTCHINSON OF LONDON

Collation: $[1\text{-}4]^{16} + [5]^{12} + [6]^{16}$ = 92 leaves; 19.5 x 12.5 cm.

Binding: Bound in strong red (12) imitation cloth and lettered down the spine in gold in two lines: NEW POEMS 1972-1973 [vertical rule] A P.E.N. ANTHOLOGY | Edited by Douglas Dunn [across the base of the spine: Publisher's logo] | HUTCHINSON; white wove paper; all edges trimmed; white wove endpapers; dust wrapper of strong orange yellowish (68) wove paper printed in black and light brown (57).

Publication date: 19 November 1973

Price: £2.00

Number of copies: 2,000

Contents: "Morning Song of a Court Dwarf," p. 127 and "Three Bagatelles," p. 128, both collected in LIACC and CP.

Note: The contents also include "An American Cemetery in Tuscany" which was previously collected.

B42 POET'S CHOICE 1973

POET'S CHOICE | 1973 | [publisher's logo: an open book with blank pages backed by wavy lines enclosed within an oval] | Island Press | SYDNEY

Collation: $[1\text{-}2]^{8} + [3]^{10}$ = 26 leaves; 20.9 x 13.2 cm.

Binding: Glued into stiff medium greenish yellow (102) wove paper wrappers and lettered down the spine in black: POET'S CHOICE 1973 ISLAND; on the front wrapper in black: [a thin rule over a thick rule] | POET'S CHOICE | 1973 | [a thick rule over a thin rule] | [publisher's logo: an open book with blank pages backed by wavy lines within an oval in black] | [in black] Island Press | [in black] SYDNEY; on the rear wrapper in black: [12 lines listing contributors to the volume and that "All copies numbered"] | ISBN 0 909771 06 5; white wove paper; all edges trimmed; stiff medium greenish yellow (102) endpapers.

Publication date: 1973

Price: $1.50 (Australian dollars)

Number of copies: 500

Contents: "The Hi-Fi Addict's Praise of Meat," p. 10.

Note: This poem appears here for the first time in print.

B43 TAMESIS 1973

Tamesis | Edited by Edward Chaney | Design and production by Robert Waller | Published by Reading University Students Union | © 1973 | Contributions from | O.S. Bradbury | Edward Chaney | Adrian Clarke | Kerry Downes | Chris Fowler | Josi de Gruyter | Dave Greenslade | Ron Knowles | Brian Patten | Peter Porter | Adrian Marshall | Christopher Salvesen | Michael Trevallion | Jeremy Wood | 15 pence

Collation: $[1]^{18}$ = 18 leaves; 19.5 x 21 cm.

Binding: Stapled twice and glued into stiff dark gray yellowish brown (81) wove paper wrappers and lettered on the front wrapper in gold: Tamesis; rear wrapper blank; light gray yellowish brown (79) heavy wove paper; all edges trimmed.

Publication date: 1973

Price: 15 pence

Number of copies: Data unavailable from publisher

Contents: "The number you first thought of," p. [12]; "The boy butler's sermon," p. [13] and "We northerners are really greek," p. [13]

Note: These poems appear here for the first time in print.

Note: The contents also include "The isle of ink" which was previously collected.

B44 POEMS FOR SHAKESPEARE / 3 1974

a. First edition, limited issue

Poems for Shakespeare/3 | Edited with a Foreword | by Anthony Thwaite | The Globe Playhouse Playhouse Trust | Publications London 1974

Collation: $[1\text{-}4]^{8}$ = 32 leaves; 22 x 14.7 cm.

Binding: Unbound; white wove paper; four signatures unopened

Note: On the verso of the title page this statement is given: "A limited numbered edition of 100 copies, signed by the poets and specially bound, has been printed (hors commerce) in advance of the first edition." A note from the publisher confirmed that the unbound sheets contained the signatures of the poets, but that the edition was never bound and offered for sale. This information was received in August, 1985.

Publication date: 23 April 1974 (proposed date: never offered for sale

Price: £35 (proposed price)

Number of copies: 100

Contents: "Exit, Pursued by a Bear," pp. 43-46, collected in LIACC and CP

Note: This poem appears here for the first time in print.

b. First edition, paperback issue

[The transcription of the title page is identical with that of the first edition, limited issue]

Collation: $[1\text{-}4]^{8}$ = 32 leaves: 20.4 x 13.4 cm.

Binding: Glued into stiff white card wrappers; on the front wrapper: [in medium reddish brown (43) and deep yellowish pink (27): a stylized illustration of the Globe Theatre with a flag] [in medium reddish brown (43)] Poems for Shakespeare/3 | [in medium reddish brown (43)] : portrait of Shakespeare]; on the rear wrapper in medium reddish brown (43) and deep yellowish pink (27)] at the lower left-hand corner: illustration of the Globe Theatre as on the front wrapper; white wove paper; all edges trimmed.

Publication date: 23 April 1974

Price: £1.25

Number of copies: 1,000

Contents: Same as B44a

B45 THE GROUP 1974

University of Reading | The Library | THE GROUP : AN EXHIBITION OF POETRY | 17 June to 10 December 1974

Collation: 27 leaves: 25.4 x 20.4 cm.

Binding: Stapled three places into stiff brilliant yellow (83) wove paper wrappers; on the front cover printed in black: The Group | An exhibition of poetry. | The Library, University of Reading. | 17 June-10 December 1974; text mimeographed on white wove paper; all edges trimmed.

Publication date: 17 June 1974

Price: 40p

Number of copies: 200

Contents: "The Donizetti Museum, Bergamo," pp. 48-49. Uncollected

Note: This poem appears here for the first time in print.

B46 THE ENGLISH POETS FROM CHAUCER TO EDWARD THOMAS 1974

THE ENGLISH POETS | from Chaucer to Edward Thomas | [decorative device: two cylindrical lines] | Peter Porter | and | Anthony Thwaite | Secker & Warburg | London

Collation: $[1\text{-}9]^{16} + [10]^{8} = [11]^{16}$ = 168 leaves; 23.3 x 15.4 cm.

Binding: Bound in deep red (16) cloth and lettered down the spine in gold in two lines: [a heavy and a thin vertical rule] | The English Poets | FROM CHAUCER TO EDWARD THOMAS [a thin, a heavy and a thin vertical rule] PORTER & THWAITE [a thin and a heavy vertical rule] [across the base of the spine] SECKER & | WARBURG; white wove paper; all edges trimmed; white wove endpapers; dust wrapper of white wove paper, shiny on the exterior, printed in deep gray reddish brown (47), white and very yellowish green (115).

Publication date: 29 July 1974

Price: £3.50

Number of copies: 3,500

Contents: "Introduction" (with Anthony Thwaite), pp. 1-4; "Anonymous medieval lyrics," pp. 17-28; "Christopher Marlowe (1564-1593) Thomas Nashe (1567-1601) William Shakespeare (1564-1616)," pp. 70-81; "Ben Johnson (?1573-1637) John Webster (?1580-1638) Cyril Tourneur (?1575-1626) Thomas Middleton (1570-1627) John Ford (?1586-1639)," pp. 82-94; "Thomas Campion (1567-1620) Sir Walter Raleigh (?1552-1618) Fulke Greville, Lord Brooke (1554-1628) John Donne (1572-1631)," pp. 95-107; "Robert Herrick (1591-1674) Richard Lovelace (1618-1657) Charles Cotton (1630-1687) Andrew Marvell (1621-1678) Samuel Butler (1612-1680) John Wilmot, Earl of Rochester (1647-1680)," pp. 130-143; "Jonathan Swift (1667-1745) Alexander Pope (1688-1744)," pp. 163-177; "Thomas Gray (1716-1771) Samuel Johnson (1709-1784) Christopher Smart (1722-1771) William Cowper (1731-1800)," pp. 178-190; "Robert Burns (1759-1796) George Crabbe (1754-1832) William Blake (1757-1827)," pp. 191-201; "Percy Bysshe Shelley (1792-1822) John Keats (1795-1821) John Clare (1793-1863)," pp. 211-224; "George Gordon, Lord Byron (1788-1824) Thomas Hood (1799-1845) Winthrop Mackworth Praed (1802-1839)," pp. 225-238; "Robert Browning (1812-1889) Eugene Lee-Hamilton (1845-1907)," pp. 249-260; "Dante Gabriel Rossetti (1928-1882)

Christina Rossetti (1830-1894) Algernon Charles Swinburne (1837-1909) Edward Lear (1812-1888) Lewis Carroll (Charles Lutwidge Dodgson) (1832-1898) Sir William Schwenck Gilbert (1836-1911)," pp. 271-282; "Ernest Dowson (1867-1900) Arthur Symons (1865-1945) William Ernest Henley (1849-1903) Rudyard Kipling (1865-1936)," pp. 293-303.

B47 ALLSORTS 6 1974

allsorts [the orts of allsorts overlays a large number in dark gray (266)] 6 | Edited by Ann Thwaite | [publisher's device] METHUEN CHILDREN'S BOOKS· LONDON

Collation: $[1\text{-}5]^{16}$ 80 leaves; 24.5 x 19 cm.

Binding: Bound in laminated pictorial boards in various shades of red, brown, yellow, blue, purple and pink; lettered down the spine in gray reddish orange (39): allsorts 6 | Edited by Ann Thwaite; lettered in gray reddish orange at the top of the front cover; allsorts 6; white wove paper; all edges trimmed

Publication date: September 1974

Price: £1.95

Number of copies: Data unavailable from publisher

Contents: "Katherine's and Jane's Poem About Rhyme," pp. [19]-[21]

Note: This poem appears here for the first time in print.

B48 LIVING IN LONDON 1974

LIVING IN LONDON | Paul Bailey. Alasdair Clayre. Michael Feld. Roy Fuller. | Jonathan Raban. Peter Vansittart. William Sansom. | Patrice Chaplin. Susan Hill. Angela Carter. Peter Porter. | Shiva Naipaul. Stephen Gardiner. Hugo Williams. | Reg Gadney. John Mellors. Gavin Ewart. | Edited by | ALAN ROSS | [publisher's device: L (leaf) M] | LONDON MAGAZINE EDITIONS

Collation: $[1\text{-}3]^{16} + [4]^{12} + [5]^{16}$ = 76 leaves; 21.5 x 15 cm.

Binding: Bound in medium yellowish green (136) imitation cloth covered boards and lettered down the spine in gold: LIVING IN LONDON [in two lines] Edited by | Alan Ross [across the base of the spine: publisher's logo]; white wove paper; all edges trimmed; white wove endpapers; pictorial dust wrapper of white wove paper, shiny on the exterior, printed in vivid yellowish green (115), deep yellowish green (118), medium purplish red (258) and white.

Publication date: October 1974

Price: £2.75

Number of copies: 2,000

Contents: Untitled essay (on living in London), pp. 88-95

B49 ROLOFF BENY IN ITALY 1974

[Within a white thin and a thick rule printed on gray reddish brown (46) wove paper] ROLOFF BENY | [decorative letters] IN ITALY | *Designed and photographed by Roloff Beny | with an epilogue by | Gore Vidal | Text and anthology by Anthony Thwaite | and Peter Porter | Historical notes on the plates by | Brian de Breffny | With 174 colour plates, 122 duotone plates | and 19 line illustrations and maps* | [publisher's logo] | THAMES AND HUDSON LONDON

Collation: $[1]^{7}$ + $[2]^{5}$ + $[3\text{-}4]^{4}$ + $[5]^{6}$ + $[6]^{4}$ + $[7]^{7}$ + $[8]^{8}$ + $[9]^{6}$ + $[10]^{4}$ + $[11]^{5}$ + $[12]^{8}$ + $[13]^{6}$ + $[14]^{4}$ + $[15]^{5}$ + $[16]^{4}$ + $[17]^{8}$ + $[18]^{6}$ + $[19]^{4}$ + $[20]^{7}$ + $[21]^{8}$ + $[22\text{-}23]^{10}$ + $[24]^{4}$ _ $[25]^{5}$ + $[26]^{8}$ + $[27]^{10}$ + $[28]^{4}$ + $[29]^{5}$ + $[30]^{8}$ + $[31]^{6}$ + $[32\text{-}33]^{10}$ = 210 leaves; 30.2 x 26 cm.

Binding: Bound in vivid orange (48) cloth and lettered in gold: [across the top of the spine] ROLOFF | BENY | [down the spine in open letters] IN ITALY | [across the base of the spine] THAMES | AND | HUDSON: on the front wrapper on a rectangle in gold within two rectangular rules in gold: [in vivid orange (48)] ROLOFF BENY | [in vivid orange (48) and gold] IN ITALY: off-white wove paper; all edges trimmed; gray reddish-brown (46) pictorial endpapers; shiny white wove pictorial dust wrapper in various colors with letters printed in gold and medium reddish purple (241).

Publication date: 14 October 1974; second printing, 7 March 1983

Price: £15

Number of copies: Data unavailable from publisher

Contents: "Book Four: Emilia, Tuscany, the Marches," pp. 219-296; "Book Five: Liguria, Lombardy, Piedmont," pp. 297-350; "Book Six: Venice, the Veneto, Friuli," pp. 351-407.

B50 PENTAMETERS ANTHOLOGY NO 2 1974

Pentameters | Anthology | No 2 | [single rule] | Edited by | Léonie Scott-Matthews | Guest edited by | Joaquina Gonzalez-Marina | Pentameters Press 1974

Collation: $[1]^{26}$ = 26 leaves; 20.5 x 14.5

Binding: Stapled twice into stiff white card wrappers and printed down the spine in black: Pentameters Anthology; on the front wrapper is an illustration in black and white of two faces, a line of row houses, a street lamp and a street; at the top of the illustration in white letters: Pentameters | Anthology; on the rear wrapper at the right-hand lower corner printed in black: 50p ISBN 0 9503729 0 0; white wove paper; all edges trimmed.

Publication date: November 1974

Price: 50p

Number of copies: 500-1,000

Note: The publisher reported that the number of copies printed was an approximate.

Contents: "For I have heard the heavens dropping" (First line), p. 11

Note: This poem appears here for the first time in print.

Note: The publisher reported that an error was made and that only one half of the poem was actually printed.

B51 POETRY SUPPLEMENT 1974

Poetry Supplement | COMPILED BY | PHILIP LARKIN | FOR THE | POETRY BOOK | SOCIETY | CHRISTMAS | 1974

Collation: $[1\text{-}3]^8$ = 24 leaves; 20.3 x 12.9 cm.

Binding: Glued into stiff light grayish red (18) wove paper wrappers; on the front wrapper at the top is the publisher's logo [fancy letters 'P | BS' in a laurel wreath] printed in black within a rectangle printed in medium greenish blue (173)] | [in black] POETRY | SUPPLEMENT | [in medium greenish blue (173)] COMPILED BY | [in black] PHILIP LARKIN | [in medium greenish blue (173)] for the POETRY | [in medium greenish blue (173)] BOOK SOCIETY | [in black] CHRISTMAS '74; on the rear wrapper at the lower left-hand corner in black: 40p; white wove paper; all edges trimmed.

Publication date: 1 December 1974

Price: 40p

Number of copies: 2,500

Note: B.C. Bloomfield states in *Philip Larkin. A Bibliography, 1933-1976* (London: Faber and Faber, 1979), p. 74 ". . . of | which 2,000 copies were distributed free to members of the Poetry | Book Society and the remaining 500 copies were put on sale at 40p."

Contents: "Halfway to a Heritage," p. [33]; "Personal," p. [34]

Note: These poems appear here for the first time in print.

B52 BOOKMARKS 1975

BOOKMARKS | [fancy letter] Q________________ | Edited and Introduced by | FREDERIC RAPHAEL | QUARTET BOOKS | LONDON

Collation: A perfect binding of 88 leaves; 17.8 x 11 cm.

Binding: Glued into stiff white card wrappers, of which the exterior is shiny, and lettered down the spine in black: BOOKMARKS Ed. FREDERIC RAPHAEL [across the base of the spine] [fancy] Q | *Quartet* | 0 704 | 31202 6; on the front wrapper [superimposed on a 32 line text printed in black from pages 1 and 2 of the Introduction is the end of a ribbon printed in vivid reddish orange (34); printed in white down the length of the ribbon: Kingsley Amis | Paul Bailey | David Benedictus | Melvyn Bragg | Brigid Brophy | David Caute | Maurice Cranston | Maureen Duffy | J.G. Farrell | John Fowles | Bamber Gascoigne | Brian Glanville | Patricia Highsmith | David Holbrook | Elizabeth Jane Howard | Edward Hyams | Francis King | Arthur Koestler | Olivia Manning | Iris Murdoch | Harold Pinter | Peter Porter | Frederic Raphael | Alan Sillitoe | Elizabeth Taylor | Hugh Thomas | Arnold Wesker | Raymond Williams; printed in black at the left-hand corner of the bottom of the wrapper: [fancy] Q | *Quartet* | [at the right-hand side at the bottom of the wrapper in black] Writers on their reading; printed on the rear wrapper in black: SOME OF OUR BEST WRITERS ARE 'READERS' | [20 lines of text] | Cover design by Paul May | LITERATURE | ISBN 0 704 31202 6 | United Kingdom 90p | Canada $3.50 | Australia* & New Zealand $2.75 | *Recommended price only; [on the right a vertical bar followed by]: [fancy] Q | *Quartet*; white wove paper; all edges trimmed.

Publication date: February 1975

Price: 90p

Number of copies: 4,000-6,000(?)

Note: The publisher's records are incomplete and these numbers are estimates.

Contents: "Neither my mother nor my father was a reader of books" (first sentence), pp. 127-130.

Note: This prose piece appears here for the first time in print.

B53 KONRAD OF THE MOUNTAINS 1975

[decorative letters] Junior Ensemble Series | KONRAD OF THE MOUNTAINS | A pageant for voices and instruments | Libretto by Peter Porter | Music by Carey Blyton | Belwin-Mills Music Ltd. | 250 Purley Way, Croydon, CR9 4QD

Collation: $[1]^{16}$ = 16 leaves; 25.3 x 17.5 cm.

Binding: Stapled twice into shiny stiff white wove pictorial paper wrappers printed in black and vivid reddish orange (34); on the front wrapper in vivid reddish orange (34) letters: Junior Ensemble Series | KONRAD OF THE MOUNTAINS | A pageant for voices and instruments | Libretto by Peter Porter | Music by Carey Blyton | Belwin-Mills Music Ltd.; on the rear wrapper in black: JUNIOR ENSEMBLE SERIES | [24 lines on parts of the series] | Belwin-Mills Music Ltd. | 250 Purley Way, Croydon, CR9 4QD | 60p; white wove paper; all edges trimmed.

Publication date: April 1975

Price: 60p

Number of copies: 3,000; second printing, April 1976, 2,000 copies

Contents: "Konrad of the Mountains"

Note: "Konrad of the Mountains . . . was especially commissioned for the BBC's 'Music Workshop' series for children of 9-10, and was produced by William Murphy and broadcast during the Summer Term of 1967, being repeated in the Summer Term of 1970." "Copyright © 1969 Carey Blyton and Peter Porter Copyright assigned 1974 to Belwin-Mills Music Ltd."

B54 NEW POETRY I 1975

a. First edition, hardcover issue:

New poetry I | An anthology edited by | Peter Porter and Charles Osborne | The Arts Council of Great Britain

Collation: $[1\text{-}18]^{8}$ = 144 leaves; 21 x 13 cm.

Binding: Bound in light gray (264) paper-covered boards and lettered down the spine in black: New poetry I Arts Council; on the upper right-hand corner of the front cover in black: 1; white wove paper; all edges trimmed; black wove endpapers; dust wrapper of white wove paper printed in light gray (264), black and white.

Publication date: 24 July 1975

Price: £3.50

Number of copies: 1,000

Contents: "Introduction" (with Charles Osborne), pp. 15-16.

b. First edition, paperback issue:

New poetry I | An anthology edited by | Peter Porter and Charles Osborne | The Arts Council of Great Britain

Collation: $[1\text{-}18]^{8}$ = 144 leaves; 21 x 13 cm.

Binding: Glued in stiff white wove paper wrappers, of which the exterior is shiny and printed in light gray (264) and lettered down the spine: [in white] New Poetry I [black] Arts Council; on the front wrapper: [white fancy letters] New | Poetry | [white] 1; [in black letters to the left] An anthology | edited by | Peter Porter & | Charles Osborne | The Arts Council | of Great Britain; on the rear wrapper in black: [11 lines on the book] | [black] *Distributed by Carcanet Press Ltd £1.80* | ISBN 0 7287 0053 0 | Arts Council Poetry Library | [11 lines on the library] | [black] *Literature Director: Charles Osborne* | [black] *Poetry Librarian: Jonathan Barker*; white wove paper; all edges trimmed; white wove front endpaper.

Publication date: 24 July 1975

Price: £1.80

Number of copies: 1,500

Contents: Same as B54a

B55 POETRY DIMENSION ANNUAL 3 1975

a. First edition, hardcover issue:

Edited by DANNIE ABSE | POETRY DIMENSION | ANNUAL 3 | The Best of the Poetry Year | [publisher's logo: two books] Robson Books

Collation: $[1\text{-}7]^{16}$ = 112 leaves; 19.2 x 12.7 cm.

Binding: Bound in textured medium reddish orange (37) and lettered down the spine in gold: *Poetry Dimension Annual 3* [across the base of the spine in gold: publisher's logo] | Robson Books; white wove paper; all edges trimmed; white wove endpapers; dust wrapper of white wove paper printed in deep orange yellow (72), vivid reddish orange (34) and white.

Publication date: September 1975

Price: £3.25

Number of copies: 1,500

Contents: "Old Fashioned Wedding," p. 167, collected in TCOS and CP.

b. First edition, paperback issue:

Edited by DANNIE ABSE | POETRY DIMENSION | ANNUAL 3 | The Best of the Poetry Year | [publisher's logo: two books] Robson Books

Collation: 112 single leaves; 19.7 x 12.7 cm.

Binding: A perfect binding glued into stiff white card wrappers, of which the exterior is shiny; the front wrapper and spine are printed in deep orange yellow (72) and the rear wrapper is white; printed down the spine in white: *Poetry Dimension Annual 3* [publisher's logo] Robson Books; printed on the front wrapper: [in vivid reddish orange (34) *Poetry* | [in vivid reddish orange (34)] *Dimension* | [in vivid reddish orange (34)] *Annual 3* | [in white] *The Best of the* | [in white] *Poetry Year* | [in vivid reddish orange (34)] *Edited by* | [in vivid reddish orange (34)] *Dannie Abse*; on the rear wrapper in deep orange yellow (72) letters: POETRY DIMENSION ANNUAL 3 | *The Best of the Poetry Year* | EDITED BY DANNIE ABSE | [24 lines on the book and reviews of Poetry Dimension Annual 1 and 2] | [single rule] | [in two columns] [publisher's logo] ROBSON BOOKS LTD | 28 Poland Street, | London WIV 3DB *Cover design by Timothy Jaques, FSIA* | ISBN 0 903895 8 | £1.60 net; white wove paper; all edges trimmed.

Publication date: September 1975

Price: £1.60

Number of copies: 3,000

Contents: Same as B55a

B56 NEW POEMS 1975 1975

[decorative floral device] | NEW POEMS | 1975 | A P.E.N. Anthology | of Contemporary Poetry | [decorative floral device] | *Edited by* | PATRICIA BEER | HUTCHINSON OF LONDON

Collation: $[A]^{14}$ + B-F ^{16} = 94 leaves; 19.2 x 12.4 cm.

Binding: Bound in dark reddish orange (38) imitation cloth paper-covered boards and lettered down the spine in gold: [in two lines]: NEW POEMS 1975 Edited by Patricia Beer | A P.E.N. Anthology of Contemporary Poetry [across the base of the spine: publisher's logo] | HUTCHINSON; white wove paper; all edges trimmed; white wove endpapers; dust wrapper of strong yellowish green (131) wove paper printed in black.

Publication date: 17 November 1975

Price: £3.25

Number of copies: 1,750

Contents: "The Scene of the Crime," p. 61.

Note: The contents also includes "The Descent into Avernus" which was previously collected.

B57 CITY POEMS & CITY MUSIC 1975

[cover title] [in black] Whitechapel Art Gallery, Whitechapel High Street, London E1 7QX | [single rule] | City poems & City music | [single rule] | Ideas gallery, 29 May - 6 July 1975 | [single rule] | [16th century illustration of a plan of London] | St. Paul's and Neighbourhood (from Aggas' Plan, 1563 | [on the left side of the front cover] With the exception of Sir John Betjeman, the sixteen | poets represented here were commissioned in April 1974 | to write a poem about the City of London | [paragraph] These poems were to be part of a large exhibition | about the City of London, which has had to be postponed | for the time being. | [paragraph] In this leaflet the poems are followed by biographies | edited by Patrick Fetherston. [on the right hand side of the cover] John Betjeman, John Birthwhistle, Edwin Brock, Alan | Brownjohn, Jeni Couzyn, Ivor Cutler, Patrick Fetherston, | W S Graham, Harry Guest, John Heath-Stubbs, Adrian | Henri, Edward Lucie-Smith, Roger McGough, Adrian | Mitchell, Peter Porter, Peter Redgrove, John Roberts; [on the rear wrapper an illustration in black and white of "Detail from *Long View of London* from Bankside, 1647, by Wencelaus Hollar]

Collation: $[1]^{8}$ = 8 leaves; 29.5 x 21 cm.

Binding: Stapled twice into heavy shiny, white wove paper wrappers; shiny, white wove paper; all edges trimmed

Publication date: 1975 (details unavailable from publisher)

Price: Data unavailable from publisher

Number of copies: Data unavailable from publisher.

Contents: "London," p. 3

Note: This is the first time this poem appears in print.

B58 NEW POETRY 2 1976

a. First edition, hardcover issue:

New Poetry 2 | An anthology edited by | Patricia Beer & Kevin Crossley-Holland | The Arts Council of Great Britain

Collation: $[1\text{-}18]^8$ = 144 leaves; 21 x 13 cm.

Binding: Bound in light gray (264) paper-covered boards and lettered down the spine in black: New Poetry 2 Arts Council; on the right top corner of the front cover printed in black: 2; white wove paper; all edges trimmed; black wove endpapers; dust wrapper of white wove paper printed in deep pink (3), black and white.

Publication date: 18 November 1976

Price: £3.80

Number of copies: 1,000

Contents: "My old cat dances," p. 189, collected in ES and CP; "An angel in Blythburgh church," pp. 189-190, collected in TCOS and CP

b. First edition, paperback issue:

New Poetry 2 | An anthology edited by | Patricia Beer & Kevin Crossley-Holland | The Arts Council of Great Britain

Collation: $[1\text{-}18]^8$ = 144 leaves; 21 x 13 cm.

Binding: Glued in stiff white wove paper wrappers, of which the exterior is shiny and printed in deep pink (3) and lettered down the spine: [in white] New poetry 2 [in black] Arts Council; on the front wrapper: [in fancy white letters] New | Poetry | 2; [in black letters to the left] An anthology edited by | Patricia Beer and | Kevin Crossley-Holland | The Arts Council | of Great Britain; on the rear wrapper in black: [2 lines on the book] ISBN 0 7287 0109 X £2.00 | Arts Council Poetry Library | [10 lines on the Library] | [black] *Literature Director: Charles Osborne* | [black] *Poetry Librarian: Jonathan Barker;* white wove paper; all edges trimmed

Publication date: 18 November 1976

Price: £2.00

Number of copies: 1,500

Contents: Same as 58a

B59 JOHN BARNICOAT. WORKS ON PAPER 1977

JOHN BARNICOAT | WORKS ON PAPER | TARANMAN | 236 Brompton Road, London SW 3 | Telephone 589 7838 | 26 OCTOBER - 5 NOVEMBER 1977

Collation: $[1]^{10}$ = 10 leaves; 24 x 15.5 cm.

Binding: Stapled twice into heavy white wove paper wrappers [Strothmore Super White]; [on the front wrapper, printed (Monotype Ehrhardt) in black letters]: JOHN BARNICOAT | [reproduction of the artist's gouache, "Hidden White" printed in medium pink (5), light reddish brown (42), light grayish brown (60), black and white]; [the rear wrapper is blank]; white wove paper [125 gsm Mellotext Super White]; all edges trimmed.

Publication date: 26 October 1977

Price: £4

Number of copies: 250

Contents: An untitled introduction, pp. [5-7].

Note: The introduction also contains stanzas of Porter's "The Painters' Banquet," pp. [6-7].

B60 NEW POEMS 1977-78 1977

[decorative floral device] | NEW POEMS | 1977-78 | A P.E.N. Anthology | of Contemporary Poetry | [decorative floral device] *Edited by* | GAVIN EWART | HUTCHINSON OF LONDON.

Collation: $[A]^{16}$ + B-F ^{16} = 96 leaves; 19.7 x 12.5 cm.

Binding: Bound in black textured cloth and lettered down the spine in silver in two lines: NEW POEMS 1977-78 Edited by Gavin Ewart | A P.E.N. Anthology of Contemporary Poetry | [across the base of the spine: publisher's logo] | HUTCHINSON; white wove paper; all edges trimmed; white wove endpapers; dust wrapper of brownish pink (33) wove paper and printed in black.

Publication date: 21 November 1977

Price: £4.95

Number of copies: 1,500

Contents: "Short Mad Poems," pp. 138-140

B61 POET'S CHOICE 1977

77 | POET'S | CHOICE | [publisher's logo: an open book with blank pages backed by wavy lines enclosed within an oval] | AN ANTHOLOGY OF NEW AUSTRALIAN POETRY | EDITED BY PHILIP ROBERTS

Collation: $[1\text{-}3]^{8} + [4]^{6} + [5\text{-}8]^{8}$ = 62 leaves; 19.9 x 14.3 cm.

Binding: Bound in gray reddish orange (39) paper-covered boards and lettered down the spine in black: POET'S CHOICE 1977 ISLAND; white wove paper; all edges trimmed; white wove endpapers.

Publication date: 1977

Price: $6.50

Number of copies: 750

Contents: "Day Mysteries," p. 24.

Note: This poem appears here for the first time in print.

B62 POETRY DIMENSION ANNUAL 5 1978

a. First hardcover edition:

Edited by DANNIE ABSE | POETRY DIMENSION | ANNUAL 5 | *The Best of the Poetry Year* | [publisher's logo] Robson Books

Collation: $[1\text{-}11]^{8}$ = 88 leaves; 19.2 x 12.5

Binding: Glued into light orange (52) textured paper-covered boards and lettered down the spine in gold: *Poetry Dimension Annual 5* [across the spine: publisher's logo] | [across the spine] Robson | [across the spine] Books; white wove paper, all edges trimmed; white wove endpapers; the dust wrapper is of white wove paper, of which the exterior is shiny, printed in vivid red (11), deep reddish orange (36) and white.

Publication date: February 1978

Price: £4.25

Number of copies: Data unavailable from publisher

Contents: "An Exequy," pp. 137-140 and "The Easiest Room in Hell," pp. 141-142, both collected in TCOS and CP.

Note: The contents also includes "An Angel in Blythburgh Church" which was previously collected.

b. First paperback edition

[The transcription of the title page is identical with that of the hardcover issue.]

Collation: $[1\text{-}11]^{8}$ = 88 leaves; 19.9 x 12.7 cm.

Binding: Glued into stiff white wove paper wrappers, of which the exterior is shiny printed in vivid reddish orange (34), deep reddish orange (36) and white; lettered down the spine in white: *Poetry Dimension Annual 5* [publisher's device] Robson Books; lettered on the front wrapper in italics: [deep reddish orange (36)] *Poetry* | *Dimension* | *Annual 5* | [white] *The Best of the* | *Poetry Year* [deep reddish orange (36)] *Edited by* | *Dannie Abse*; on the rear wrapper printed in vivid red (11): POETRY DIMENSIONAL ANNUAL 5 | *The Best of the Poetry Year* | EDITED BY DANNIE ABSE | [13 lines of text on the book] | [single rule] | *From the reviews of previous volumes in the* | POETRY DIMENSION ANNUAL *series:* | [15 lines of reviews] | [single rule] | [publisher's device] ROBSON BOOKS LTD | 28 Poland Street, | London WIV 3DB; [to the right] *Cover designed by* | *Timothy Jacques* | FSIA | ISBN 0 903895 72 2 | £2.25 net; white wove paper; all edges trimmed.

Publication date: February 1978

Price: £2.25

Number of copies: Data unavailable from publisher

Contents: Same as B62a

B63 NIGHT RIDE AND SUNRISE 1978

a. First edition, hardcover issue

Night Ride and Sunrise | An Anthology of New Poems | Edited | and introduced | by | EDWARD LOWBURY | CELTION POETRY

Collation: $[1\text{-}3]^{8} + [4]^{4} + [5]^{8}$ = 36 leaves; 20.4 x 14.6 cm.

Binding: Bound in black paper-covered boards and lettered down the spine in gold: NIGHT RIDE AND SUNRISE Poetry anthology ed. Edward Lowbury

CELTION; white wove paper; all edges trimmed; white wove endpapers; dust wrapper of shiny white wove paper printed in deep yellowish pink (27) and in black and white.

Publication date: 1 May 1978

Price: £3.99

Number of copies: 1,500

Contents: "Cap and Bells," pp. 40-41

Note: This poem appears here for the first time in print.

b. First edition, paperback issue:

Night Ride and Sunrise | An Anthology of New Poems | Edited | and introduced | by | EDWARD LOWBURY | CELTION POETRY

Collation: A perfect binding of 36 leaves: 29.9 x 15 cm.

Binding: Glued into stiff white card wrappers, of which the exterior is shiny, and printed in deep yellowish pink (27) and printed down the spine in white: NIGHT RIDE AND SUNRISE Poetry anthology [in black] CELTION; on the front wrapper: [in white] NIGHT RIDE | [in white] AND | [in white] SUNRISE | [horizontal rule in black] | [in white] edited by Edward Lowbury | [in black] an anthology of new and | [in black] previously unpublished poems | [in black] by some of Britain's most | [in black] distinguished poets | [abstract drawing of sun coming up behind a mountain]; on the rear wrapper in black: [21 lines of information on the book] | [in black] Celtion Publishing Company | Aberystwyth, Wales | ISBN 086053 019 1 | cover design by Kate Russell | £1.99; white wove paper; all edges trimmed.

Publication date: 1 May 1978

Price: £1.99

Number of copies: 3,500

Contents: Same as B63a

B64 NEW POETRY 4 1978

New Poetry 4 | an anthology edited by Fleur Adcock | and Anthony Thwaite | Hutchinson of London | in association with the Arts Council | of Great Britain and PEN

Collation: $[1\text{-} 6]^{16}$ = 96 leaves; 21.4 x 13.6 cm.

Binding: Bound in strong reddish orange (35) imitation cloth and lettered down the spine in gold: [in two lines] NEW POETRY 4 | An Arts Council Anthology | Edited by Fleur Adcock and Anthony Thwaite | [across the base of the spine: publisher's logo] | HUTCHINSON; white wove paper; all edges trimmed; white wove endpapers; dust wrapper of white wove paper, of which the exterior is shiny, printed in vivid red (11), black and white.

Publication date: 20 November 1978

Price: £4.50

Number of copies: 1,000

Contents: "Caspar Hauser Far Out," p. 128; "Country and Cemetery, Macdonald River," p. 129; "Stocktaking," pp. 130-131.

Note: These poems appear here for the first time in print.

B65 POETRY SUPPLEMENT 1978

Poetry Supplement | COMPILED BY | PATRICIA BEER | FOR THE | POETRY BOOK | SOCIETY | *CHRISTMAS* | 1978

Collation: $[1\text{-}2]^{8} + [3]^{4}$ = 20 leaves; 21.4 x 13.9 cm.

Binding: Glued into stiff medium greenish yellow (102) wove paper wrappers; on the front wrapper at the top is the publisher's logo: [in black fancy letters 'P|BS' in a laurel wreath surrounded by a rectangle printed in strong yellowish green (131)] | [in black] POETRY | [in black] SUPPLEMENT | [in strong yellowish green (131)] COMPILED BY | [in black] PATRICIA BEER | [in strong yellowish green (131)] for the POETRY | [in strong yellowish green (131)] BOOK SOCIETY | [in black] CHRISTMAS '78; on the rear wrapper at the lower left-hand corner in black: 50p; white wove paper, all edges trimmed.

Publication date: November 1978

Price: 50p

Number of copies: 1,500

Contents: "Addio Senza Rancor," pp. [33-34], collected in ES and CP.

B66 BEST OF THE POETRY YEAR. POETRY DIMENSION ANNUAL 6 1979

a. First edition, hardcover issue:

Selected by DANNIE ABSE | BEST OF THE POETRY YEAR | Poetry Dimension Annual 6 | [publisher's logo] Robson Books

Collation: $[1\text{-}6]^{16} + [7]^{8}$ = 104 leaves; 19.5 x 12.5 cm.

Binding: Bound in deep red (16) paper-covered boards and printed down the spine in gold: *Best of the Poetry Year 6* [across the base of the spine: publisher's logo] | Robson | Books; white wove paper; all edges trimmed; white wove endpapers; dust wrapper of white wove paper, of which the exterior is shiny, printed in strong blue (178), strong yellowish green (117), deep yellowish green (118) and white.

Publication date: 17 May 1979

Price: £4.95

Number of copies: Data unavailable from publisher

Contents: "Auden's Profession" (Prose), pp. 23-30.

Note: The contents also include "Non Piangere, Liù," and "Scream and Variation" which were previously collected.

b. First edition, paperback issue:

Selected by DANNIE ABSE | BEST OF THE POETRY YEAR | Poetry Dimension Annual 6 | [publisher's logo] | Robson Books

Collation: $[1\text{-}6]^{16} + [7]^{8}$ = 104 leaves; 19.5 x 12.5 cm.

Binding: Glued into stiff white card wrappers, of which the exterior is shiny; the top half of the front wrapper and the spine are printed in strong blue (178) and the lower half of the front wrapper and spine are printed in strong yellowish green (117); a wavy band in deep yellowish green (118) separates the two halves; printed on the front wrapper: [white] *Best of the* | [white] *Poetry Year 6* | [white] *Selected by* | [white] *Dannie Abse* | [in deep yellowish green (118) on the lower half of the wrapper] PETER PORTER Auden's Profession | J P WARD Edward Thomas and Modernism | DONALD DAVIE English and American in Briggflatts | ANDREW WATERMAN Ulsterectomy | A ALVAREZ Back in 1956 and | HOWARD SERGEANT The Movement - an agreed Fiction? | MICHAEL MEYER John Heath-Stubbs in the Forties | PATRICIA BEER Finding a Voice | VERNON SCANNELL Does He look like a poet? | and new poems by | SEAMUS HEANEY WS GRAHAM | PHILIP LARKIN FLEUR ADCOCK | TED HUGHES

ANTHONY THWAITE | PETER REDGROVE CHARLES TOMLINSON | GEORGE MACBETH MICHAEL HAMBURGER | ...and many others; the rear wrapper is white and printed in strong blue (178): Best of the Poetry Year | *Poetry Dimension Annual 6* | SELECTED BY DANNIE ABSE | [13 lines of text] [single rule] | *The previous volume in this series* | Best of the Poetry Year | *Poetry Dimension Annual 5* | [8 lines of text] | ISBN 0 86051 013 1 | [single rule] [in two columns] [publisher's logo] ROBSON Books LTD | 28 Poland Street, | London WIV 3DB [to the right] *Cover designed by* | *Timothy Jaques, FSIA* | ISBN 0 86051 062X | £2.75 net; white wove paper; all edges trimmed.

Publication date: 17 May 1979

Price: £2.75

Number of copies: Data unavailable from publisher

Contents: Same as B66a

B67 POETRY BOOK SOCIETY: THE FIRST TWENTY-FIVE YEARS 1979

Poetry | Book Society | THE FIRST | TWENTY-FIVE | YEARS | *edited by* | Eric W. White | *for members of* | *the Society* | LONDON | Poetry Book Society | 1979

Collation: $[1]^4 + [2\text{-}5]^8$ = 36 leaves; 21.5 x 13.6 cm.

Binding: Bound in deep reddish orange (38) cloth and lettered down the spine in gold: POETRY BOOK SOCIETY 1954-1978; dust wrapper of light gray (264) wove paper printed in dark brown (59) and very deep red (14); white wove paper; all edges trimmed; white wove endpapers.

Publication date: May 1979

Price: £1.00

Number of copies: 2,000

Contents: "Spring 1978. The Cost of Seriousness," 61-62.

B68 THE ENGLISH POETS 1979

[cover title] [within a rectangle at the upper right hand corner printed in deep grayish blue (187) and lettered in white] 1 | Geoffrey Chaucer | Anonymous Medieval Lyrics; [to the left of the rectangle, a feather encircled by a flowering vine in white] | *The* | *English Poets*

Collation: $[1]^{14}$ = 14 leaves; 18.5 x 12 cm.

Binding: Stapled twice into stiff white wove paper wrappers printed in deep grayish blue (187) and white; front wrapper as above; on the rear wrapper within a rectangle at the upper right hand corner printed in deep grayish blue (187): [publisher's logo: a sailing ship] | [in deep grayish blue (187)] Longman | [in deep grayish blue (187)] ISBN 0 582 37378 6 L 37855 9; white wove paper; all edges trimmed.

Price: £45 for 13 cassettes with texts

Publication date: 10 September 1979

Number of copies: 500

Contents: "Introduction to THE ENGLISH POETS" (with Anthony Thwaite), pp. 4-5

Note: The "Introduction" is dated October 1978.

B69 KITES FREE 1979

KITES FREE | HIGHGATE POETS | With an introduction by | PETER PORTER | LONDON | November 1979

Collation: $[1\text{-}4]^{6}$ = 24 leaves; 21 x 15 cm.

Binding: Glued into stiff light gray (364) wove paper wrappers and lettered down the spine in black: Kites Free; lettered on the front wrapper: [in the shape of an arc] KITES FREE | 1979 | [drawings of three abstract kites] | [single rule] | [to the left] [drawing of the front facade of the Highgate Society building]; [to the right] The Highgate Society | 10a South Grove Highgate N6 6BS; on the rear wrapper at the bottom left-hand corner: 80p; white wove paper; all edges trimmed.

Publication date: 10 November 1979

Price: 80p

Number of copies: 300

Contents: INTRODUCTION, iv-v.

Note: The "Introduction" contains a facsimile of the holograph signature of Peter Porter in black on p. v.

B70 POETRY SUPPLEMENT 1979

Poetry Supplement | COMPILED BY | DOUGLAS DUNN | FOR THE | POETRY BOOK | SOCIETY | *CHRISTMAS* | 1979 | *The Poetry Book Society received financial assistance* | *from the Arts Council of Great Britain*

Collation: $[1\text{-}4]^8$ = 32 leaves; 21.6 x 14 cm.

Binding: Glued into stiff deep orange yellow (69) wove paper wrappers; on the front wrapper at the top is the publisher's logo: [in black fancy letters 'P|BS' in a laurel wreath surrounded by a rectangle printed in dark gray reddish brown (47)] | [in black] POETRY | [in black] SUPPLEMENT | [in dark gray reddish grown (47)] COMPILED BY | [in black] DOUGLAS DUNN | [in dark gray reddish brown (47)] for the POETRY | [in dark gray reddish brown (47)] BOOK SOCIETY | [in black] CHRISTMAS '79; on the rear wrapper at the lower left-hand corner in black: 75p ISBN 0 9501895 5 3; white wove paper; all edges trimmed.

Publication date: November 1979

Price: 75p

Number of copies: 1,400

Contents: "Timon and Apemantus," p. [45].

Note: This poem appears here for the first time in print.

B71 SYDNEY 1980

[Verticle black rule just off left center of 20 cm.] SYDNEY | By Peter Porter | and the Editors of Time-Life Books | Photographs by Brian Brake | THE GREAT CITIES· TIME-LIFE BOOKS·AMSTERDAM

Collation: $[1\text{-}2]^{12} + [3\text{-}9]^8 + [10]^{12} + [11]^8$ = 100 leaves; 30 x 23.5 cm.

Binding: Bound in shiny textured cloth printed in white, dark gray (266), light medium gray (265), pale yellow (85), light brown (57) and light olive gray (112) and lettered down the spine in white: THE GREAT CITIES / SYDNEY TIME-LIFE BOOKS; pictorial front cover of a foreshortened side-view of 6 of the 10 curving roof-shells of the Sydney Opera House; the rear cover is in light brown (57) and lettered at the base in white: Reinforced Library Binding | Published by | Silver Burdett Company | 87 20L 22; white wove semi-shiny paper; all edges trimmed; white wove pictorial semi-shiny endpapers; pictorial dust wrapper white wove semi-shiny paper printed in vivid red (11) and various shades of red, yellow and brown.

Publication date: July 1980

Price: $14.95

Number of copies: Data unavailable from publisher

Contents: Gifts of Climate and the Sea - Exiles in a Wild New World - Unbinding the Ties to Britain - The Currents of Prosperity - Nature's Pervasive Presence - A Hearty Taste for the Good Life.

B72 POETRY SUPPLEMENT 1980

Poetry Supplement | COMPILED BY | PETER PORTER | FOR THE | POETRY BOOK | SOCIETY | CHRISTMAS | 1980 *The Poetry Book Society receives financial assistance* | *from the Arts Council of Great Britain*

Collation: $[1\text{-}3]^8$ = 24 leaves; 21.5 x 14 cm.

Binding: Glued into stiff grayish yellow (90) wove paper wrappers; on the front wrapper at the top is the publisher's logo: [in black fancy letters 'P|BS' in a laurel wreath surrounded by a rectangle in dark olive green (126)] | [in black] POETRY | [in black] SUPPLEMENT | [in dark olive green (126)] COMPILED BY | [in black] PETER PORTER | [in dark olive green (126)] for the POETRY | [in dark olive green (126)] BOOK SOCIETY | [in black] CHRISTMAS '80; on the rear wrapper at the lower left-hand corner in black: 75p ISBN 0 9501895 6 1; white wove paper; all edges trimmed.

Publication date: November 1980

Price: 75p

Number of copies: 1,400

Contents: "Good Ghost, Gaunt Ghost," p. [25], collected in ES and CP; "Epiphany," p. [26].

Note: "Epiphany" appears here for the first time in print.

B73 G.B.E. 1981

[cover title] G.B.E. | [single rule] | Happy Birthday | 4 February 1981

Collation: 66 photocopied pages (on one side only) of manuscripts and typescripts of poems, etc., offered to Gavin B. Ewart to celebrate his 65th birthday.

Binding: Photocopies fastened together by a black plastic clip running the entire left-hand side of the copy.

Publication date: 4 February 1981

Price: Not offered for sale and privately distributed.

Number of copies: Unknown

Contents: "The Literary World," pp. [44-45]

B74 THE GREGORY AWARDS 1980 1981

The Gregory Awards 1980 | [single rule] | Poems selected by | Peter Porter | and | Howard Sergeant | Secker & Warburg London

Collation: $[1\text{-}2]^{16}$ = 32 leaves; 21.6 x 13.6 cm.

Binding: Bound in black imitation cloth covered boards and lettered down the spine in gold: The Gregory Awards 1980 S & W; white wove paper; all edges trimmed; white wove endpapers; dust wrapper of white wove paper, shiny on the exterior, printed in "metallic" light gray (264) and black.

Publication date: 8 June 1981

Price: £4.50

Number of copies: 750

Contents: "Introduction" (with Howard Sergeant), p. [v].

B75 LANDSCAPE POETS. THOMAS HARDY 1981

Landscape Poets | [single rule] | THOMAS HARDY | *Selected and introduced by Peter Porter* | *Photographs by John Hedgecoe* | Weidenfeld and Nicolson London

Collation: $[1]^{8} + [2\text{-}4]^{12} + [5]^{4} + [6]^{12} + [7]^{4}$ = 64 leaves; 22.8 x 16.2 cm.

Binding: Bound in deep orange (51) cloth and lettered down the spine in gold: THOMAS HARDY *Landscape Poets* [in two lines] Weidenfeld | & Nicolson; white wove paper; all edges trimmed; white wove endpapers; pictorial dust wrapper of white wove paper, of which the exterior is shiny, printed in medium reddish orange (37), black and white.

Publication date: 17 September 1981

Price: £5.95

Number of copies: 6,500

Contents: "Introduction," pp. [9]-17.

B76 POETRY SUPPLEMENT 1981

Poetry Supplement | COMPILED BY | ANDREW MOTION | FOR THE | POETRY BOOK | SOCIETY | CHRISTMAS | 1981 | *The Poetry Book Society is subsidised by* | *the Arts Council of Great Britain*

Collation: $[1\text{-}4]^{8}$ = 32 leaves; 21.2 x 13.8 cm.

Binding: Glued into stiff very pale blue (184) wove paper wrappers; on the front wrapper at the top is the publisher's logo [in black fancy letters 'P|BS' in a laurel wreath surrounded by a rectangle in dark gray (266)] | [in black] POETRY | [in black] SUPPLEMENT | [in dark gray (266)] COMPILED BY | [in black] ANDREW | [in black] MOTION | [in dark gray (266)] for the POETRY | [in dark gray (266)] BOOK SOCIETY | [in black] CHRISTMAS '81; on the rear wrapper at the lower left-hand corner in black: £1.25 ISBN 0 9501895 7 X; white wove paper; all edges trimmed.

Publication date: December 1981

Price: £1.25

Number of copies: 1,500

Note: The publisher reported that this figure was an approximation.

Contents: "A Waste of Time," pp. [35-36]

Note: This poem appears here for the first time in print.

B77 LARKIN AT SIXTY 1982

Larkin at Sixty | [thick rule] | [thin rule] | Edited by | ANTHONY THWAITE | [publisher's logo] | *faber and faber*

Collation: $[1]^{4} + [2\text{-}4]^{16} + [5]^{14}$ = 76 leaves; 21.4 x 13.5 cm.

Binding: Bound in light gray (264) textured cloth and lettered down the spine in shiny vivid red (11): *Larkin at Sixty* | [a thick and a thin vertical rule] | [in two lines] Edited by | ANTHONY THWAITE [across the base of the spine: publisher's logo]; white wove paper; all edges trimmed; white wove endpapers; dust wrapper of yellowish white (92) wove paper printed in strong red (12), light gray (264), black and white.

Publication date: 24 May 1982

Price: £7.95

Number of copies: 4,000

Contents: "Going to Parties," pp. 139-140.

Note: This poem appears here for the first time in print.

B78 THE FABER BOOK OF MODERN VERSE 1982

a. First edition, hardcover issue

THE FABER BOOK OF | Modern Verse | Edited by | MICHAEL ROBERTS | FOURTH EDITION | Revised by | PETER PORTER | [publisher's logo: two small fancy "f"s] | *faber and faber*

Collation: $[1\text{-}27]^{8}$ = 216 leaves; 19.7 x 12.5 cm.

Binding: Bound in dark blue (183) covered boards and lettered down the spine in gold: [in two lines] THE FABER BOOK OF | MODERN VERSE [vertical rule] Edited by MICHAEL ROBERTS | Revised by PETER PORTER [across the base of the spine: publisher's logo as above]; white wove paper; all edges trimmed; white wove endpapers; dust wrapper of white wove paper, shiny on the exterior, printed in black, white and deep blue (179).

Publication date: 24 May 1982

Price: £6.95

Number of copies: 1,000

Contents: "Introduction to the Fourth Edition," pp. 49-51.

b. First edition, paperback issue:

[The transcription of the title page is identical with that of the first edition, hardcover issue]

Collation: 216 leaves; 19.7 x 12.5 cm.

Binding: A perfect binding glued into stiff white wove paper wrappers, of which the exterior is shiny, and printed in black and deep blue (179); lettered down the spine in white on a rectangle of deep blue (179) [in two lines]: [a thin and a thick vertical rule] THE FABER BOOK | OF MODERN VERSE | *edited by Michael Roberts* | *Revised by Peter Porter* [across the base of the rectangle: the publisher's logo] [a thick and a thin vertical rule]; beginning at the left on the rear wrapper and going across to the right of the upper wrapper are rows of the publisher's logo in black letters; on the front wrapper on a rectangle of deep blue (179) and printed in white: enclosed within a rectangle composed of a thin and a thick rule: THE | FABER BOOK | OF | MODERN VERSE | [single rule] *edited by* | *Michael Roberts* | *revised by* | *Peter·Porter* | Fourth Edition; [on the rear wrapper on a rectangle of deep blue (179) and printed in white: enclosed within a rectangle composed of a thin and thick rule]: [publisher's logo] | *faber and faber* | [single rule] | [17 lines of information on the book] | *Also in hard covers* | Cover design by Pentagram/John Gorham | £3.50 net | ISBN 0 571 18017 5; white wove paper, all edges trimmed.

Publication date: 24 May 1982

Price: £3.50

Number of copies: 25,000

Contents: Same as B78a

B79 SPIRIT OF WIT 1982

Spirit of Wit | RECONSIDERATIONS OF ROCHESTER | [decorative device] | *Edited by* | Jeremy Treglown | Basil Blackwell·Oxford

Collation: $[1\text{-}5]^{16} + [6]^{8} + [7]^{16}$ = 104 leaves; 21.5 x 13.5 cm.

Binding: Bound in medium blue (182) cloth and lettered down the spine in silver: *Spirit of Wit* | Edited by Jeremy Treglown | Blackwell; white wove paper; all edges trimmed; white wove endpapers; dust wrapper of white wove paper, of which the exterior is shiny, printed in very light blue (180), medium gray (265) and black.

Publication date: September 1982

Price: £14

Number of copies: 1,750

Contents: "The Professional Amateur" (prose), pp. 58-74.

B80 NEW EDINBURGH REVIEW ANTHOLOGY 1982

a. First edition, hardcover issue

NEW | EDINBURGH | REVIEW | ANTHOLOGY | *Edited by* | JAMES CAMPBELL | POLYGON BOOKS

Collation: $[1\text{-}13]^8$ = 104 leaves; 21.5 x 13.7 cm.

Binding: Bound in black imitation cloth covered boards; white wove paper; all edges trimmed; white wove endpapers; dust wrapper of white wove paper, of which the exterior is shiny, printed in vivid red (11) and black.

Publication date: October 1982

Price: £8.95

Number of copies: 400

Contents: "Canzone," pp. 161-162

b. First edition, paperback issue

[The transcription of the title page is identical with that of the first edition, hardcover issue.]

Collation: $[1\text{-}13]^8$ = 104 leaves; 21.5 x 13.7 cm.

Binding: Glued into stiff white wove paper wrappers, of which the exterior is shiny, and lettered down the spine: [vivid red (11)] N [in black] EW [in vivid red (11)] E [in black] DINBURGH [in vivid red (11)] R [in black] EVIEW [in vivid red (11)] ANTHOLOGY [across the base of the spine in black: publisher's logo] | [in black] Polygon; on the front wrapper [in vivid red (11)] N [in black] EW | [in vivid red (11)] E [in black] DINBURGH | [in vivid red (11)] R [in black] EVIEW | [in vivid red (11)] ANTHOLOGY | [in vivid red (11): a single rule] | [in black] FICTION, ARTICLES | [in black] CRITICISM AND POETRY | [single rule in vivid red (11)] [in black] FROM [single rule in vivid red (11)] | [in black] NEW EDINBURGH | [in black] REVIEW MAGAZINE | [single rule in vivid red (11)] [in black] EDITED BY [single rule in vivid red (11)] | [in black] JAMES CAMPBELL; on the rear wrapper in black letters: NAOMI MITCHISON | RICK CLUCHEY | DON WATSON | GORDON DONALDSON | TOM NAIRN | JAMES YOUNG | JAMES BALDWIN | HENRY MILLER | NORMAL MacCAIG | GERALD MANGAN | SEAN O'BRIEN | NEAL ASCHERSON | DOUGLAS DUNN | ALLAN MASSIE | JOHN FOWLES | CHRISTINE BOLD | GILES GORDON | PETER PORTER | BRIAN McCABE | GEORGE MACKAY BROWN | RON BUTLIN | JACK DEBNEY | JONATHAN STEFFEN | [at the lower left-hand corner of the rear wrapper in black] £4.50; white wove paper; all edges trimmed.

Publication date: October 1982

Price: £4.50

Number of copies: 1,500

Contents: Same as B80a

B81 NEW YEAR POETRY SUPPLEMENT 1982

New Year | *Poetry Supplement* | COMPILED BY | ALAN BROWNJOHN | FOR THE | POETRY BOOK | SOCIETY | *DECEMBER 1982* | *The Poetry Book Society is subsidised by* | *the Arts Council of Great Britain*

Collation: $[1\text{-}4]^8$ = 32 leaves; 21.7 x 14 cm.

Binding: Glued into stiff yellowish gray (93) wove paper wrappers; on the front wrapper in dark red (16): POETRY BOOK SOCIETY | [drawing of a man reading a book in black by George Szirtes] | [in dark red (16)] NEW YEAR | POETRY | SUPPLEMENT | COMPILED BY | ALAN | BROWNJOHN; on the rear wrapper at the top is the publisher's logo: [in black fancy letters 'P|BS' in a laurel leaf surrounded by a rectangle printed in dark red (16)] | [in black] £1.50 ISBN 0 9591895 8 8; off-white wove paper; all edges trimmed.

Publication date: November 1982

Price: £1.50

Number of copies: 1,500

Note: The publisher reports that this is an approximate figure.

Contents: "The Arbitrary Albrolhos," p. [43]; "In the Fast Lane," p. [44].

Note: "In the Fast Lane" appears here for the first time in print.

B82 OTHER PEOPLE'S CLERIHEWS 1983

[solid black decorative letters] Other People's | [broken rule] | [decorative black and white letters] CLERIHEWS | *Chosen by* | GAVIN EWART | *With Illustrations by* | NICOLA JENNINGS | Oxford New York | OXFORD UNIVERSITY PRESS | 1983

Collation: $[1]^6 + [2\text{-}10]^8$ = 78 leaves; 18.2 x 12.5 cm.

Binding: Bound in strong brown (55) imitation cloth and lettered down the spine in gold: EWART Other People's Clerihews OXFORD; white wove paper; all edges trimmed; double white wove endpapers; pictorial dust wrapper of white wove paper, of which the exterior is shiny, printed in light yellowish green (119), pale yellowish green (121) dark blue (183) vivid red (11), dark reddish orange (38), light orange (52), medium brown (58), brilliant yellow (83) and black and white.

Publication date: 22 September 1983

Price: £5.95

Number of copies: 4,000

Contents: "The Literary World. A Collection of Clerihews for Gavin Ewart on His Sixty-Fifth Birthday," pp. 97, 99, 100.

Note: This poem appears here for the first time in a commercially printed form. See B73.

B83 THE THIRD DIMENSION. VOICES FROM RADIO 3 1983

[within a rectangle composed of a thick and thin rule] THE | THIRD DIMENSION | *Voices from Radio 3* | EDITED BY | PHILIP FRENCH | LONDON | THE STOURTON PRESS | MCMLXXXIII

Collation: A-K^8 = 80 leaves; 24.7 x 15.5 cm.

Binding: Bound in strong red (12) cloth (Ordinary Edition) and in strong red (12) cloth and in quarter leather (Special Edition) and lettered down the spine in gold: THE THIRD DIMENSION; printed on Abbey Mills Text Laid Paper with a watermark as follows: [decorative crown] | [in Old English letters] Abbey Mills | [in Old English letters] Greenfield; all edges trimmed; endpapers of Abbey Mills Text Laid paper as above; dust wrapper of yellowish white (92) wove paper printed in deep yellowish pink (27), light green (144) and deep red (16).

Publication date: 10 October 1983

Price: £26 for the Special Edition and £12.95 for the Ordinary Edition.

Number of copies: 1,300 copies; Special Edition of 100 copies of which 50 were offered for sale; Ordinary Edition of 1,200 copies of which 800 were offered for sale.

Contents: "The Cats of Campagnatico," pp. 134-135.

B84 PETER GRIMES GLORIANA 1983

[open decorative figure in black] 24 | [single rule] | Peter Grimes | Gloriana | [single rule] | Benjamin Britten | *Opera Guide Series Editor: Nicholas John* | *Published in association with* | English National Opera and the Royal Opera | and sponsored by | the Friends of ENO and the US Friends of ENO Inc | [publisher's logo] | John Calder. London | Riverrun Press New York

Collation: 64 leaves; 21.5 x 13.5 cm.

Binding: A perfect binding glued into stiff white wove wrappers, of which the exterior is shiny and printed down the spine in black: Peter Grimes | Gloriana | Britten | Opera Guide 24 | [across the base of the spine] Riverrun | [publisher's logo] | John | Calder; [on the front wrapper is a photograph of B. Britten reproduced in gray reddish brown (46); printed across the front wrapper in black]: Peter Grimes | [single rule] | Gloriana | Britten | [single rule] | English | National | Opera | [within a rectangle] Opera Guide 24 | [within two single rules] The | Royal | Opera; [on the rear wrapper, 48 lines of information on the series, the volume itself, a list of Opera Guides and the publishers' addresses] | U.K. £3.00 | U.S. $5.95 | Can. $6.95 | Cover Design by Roger Davis | ISBN 0 7145 3856 6; white wove paper; all edges trimmed.

Publication date: 27 October 1983

Price: £3 and $5.95

Number of copies: 10,000

Contents: "Benjamin Britten's Librettos" (prose), pp. 7-14.

Note: The prose statement appears here for the first time in print.

B85 WINTER POETRY SUPPLEMENT 1983

Winter | *Poetry Supplement* | COMPILED BY | DAVID HARSENT | FOR THE | POETRY BOOK | SOCIETY | DECEMBER | 1983 | *The Poetry Book Society is subsidised by* | *the Arts Council of Great Britain.*

Collation: $[1\text{-}3]^8 + [4]^4$ = 28 leaves; 21.4 x 14 cm.

Binding: Glued into stiff white wove paper wrappers; [on the front wrapper] [in black] POETRY BOOK SOCIETY | [in black] [drawing of a man reading a book by George Szirtes] | [in very dark green (147)] WINTER | [in very dark green (147)] POETRY | [in very dark green (147)] SUPPLEMENT | [in black] COMPILED BY | [in very dark green (147)] DAVID | [in very dark green (147)] HARSENT; [on the rear wrapper at the top is the publisher's logo: (in black) fancy letters 'P|BS' in a laurel wreath surrounded by a rectangle printed in very dark green (147)] | [at the lower left-hand corner in black] £1.50 ISBN 0 9501895 9 6; white wove paper; all edges trimmed.

Publication date: November 1983

Price: £1.50

Number of copies: 2,400

Contents: "Spectator Sport," pp. [31-2]; "Try a Triolet," pp. [33-34].

Note: These poems appear here for the first time in print.

B86 POEMS FOR POETRY 84

Poems for | Poetry 84 | [decorative reversed "p"] *the* Poetry Society | *at the* National Poetry Centre

Collation: $[1]^{16}$ = 16 leaves; 20.3 x 12.3 cm.

Binding: Stapled twice into heavy gray purplish pink (253) wove paper wrappers; on the front wrapper at the upper right hand corner in dark purplish red (259): Poems for | Poetry 84 | [printed in dark blue (183) italics in two columns are the names of the contributors; above each name is a facsimile signature of the poet printed in dark purplish red; each name and signature is separated by a single rule in dark blue from the next one] | [to the left] Roger McGough | Ian McMillan | D.M. Thomas | Alan Brownjohn | Gavin Ewart | John Heath-Stubbs | Eddie S. Linden | John Mole | Elizabeth Bartlett | Kevin Crossley-Holland | Dannie Abse | Medbh McGuckian | James Berry; [to the right] Peter Porter | Edwin Morgan | Wendy Cope | George MacBeth | John Cotton | Blake Morrison | Jenny Joseph | Charles Causley | Peter Redgrove | John Loveday | Carol Rumens | Jon Silkin | [blank space]; on the rear wrapper: [in dark purplish red] Poems for | [in dark purplish red] Poetry 84 | [next 7 lines in dark blue] Poems for 84 is a collection of | previously unpublished work from 25 | poets and is produced as part of the | Poetry Society's 75th Anniversary | celebrations 'Poetry 84.' | This is a collection purely for enjoyment | and in this spirit it is offered to you. | [in dark purplish red and dark blue: "Fatman Logo" by Paul Peter Piech]; light green gray (154) wove paper; all edges trimmed.

Publication date: Data unavailable from publisher

Price: Free

Number of copies: Data unavailable from publisher.

Contents: "Charmouth Beach," p. 8.

Note: This poem appears here for the first time in print.

B87 INVITED GUESTS 1986

[in dark brown (59) letters] INVITED | [in dark brown letters] GUESTS | *a festschrift for* | [in dark brown letters] KAY PETRIE | on her retirement from | HITCHIN LIBRARY | *3rd September 1986* | Grand Piano Editions | -1986-

Collation: $[1]^{8}$ = 8 leaves; 24 x 16.2 cm.

Binding: Sewn into heavy textured light brownish gray (63) paper wrappers; on the front wrapper printed in black on a pale yellow (89) rectangle pasted on the front wrapper: INVITED | GUESTS; white wove paper; all edges trimmed; pale yellow endpapers.

Publication date: 3 September 1986

Price: £5.00

Number of copies: Data unavailable from publisher.

Contents: "Throw the book at them," p. 11 .

Note: This poem appears here for the first time in print.

B88 THE POETRY BOOK SOCIETY ANTHOLOGY 1986/87 1986

The | Poetry Book Society | Anthology 1986/87 | *Edited with an Introduction by* | JONATHAN BARKER | Hutchinson | London Melbourne Auckland Johannesburg

Collation: $[1\text{-}3]^{16}$ = 48 leaves; 19.8 x 12.8 cm.

Binding: Glued into stiff card wrappers printed in vivid pinkish purple (226), strong purplish blue (196) and vivid red (11); lettered down the spine in strong purplish blue: The Poetry Book Society Anthology 1986/87 [in black] Edited by Jonathan Barker HUTCHINSON | [across the base of the spine: publisher's logo]; on the front wrapper: [in white on a strong purplish blue band] THE | [in strong purplish blue] Poetry Book Society | [in white on a strong purplish blue band] ANTHOLOGY | [in strong purplish blue] 1986/87 | [in white on a strong purplish blue band] Edited by Jonathan Barker | [on a white rectangle with diamonds formed by strong purplish blue line printed in vivid red] INCLUDING POEMS | UNPUBLISHED IN | BOOK FORM BY | Philip Larkin | Graham Greene | AND MANY | OTHERS; [on the rear wrapper in strong purplish blue: 10 lines on the anthology] | [in vivid red, in 14 lines, list of contributors in double columns] | [in black, 6 lines on the editor of the anthology] | [in black to the left] £4.95 net | IN UK ONLY | ISBN: 0 09 165961 2 | Century Hutchinson Ltd [to the right in black and white: bar code label]; white wove paper; all edges trimmed.

Publication date: 23 October 1986

Price: £4.95

Number of copies: 3,487; there was a second printing of 540 copies on 10 April 1987.

Contents: "Paradise Park," pp. 76-77; "The Vogue for Despair in Manchester, Rusholme," p. 77.

Note: These poems appear here for the first time in print.

C

CONTRIBUTIONS TO PERIODICALS

BY PETER PORTER

In this section an attempt has been made to include all of Peter Porter's contributions, i.e. poems, prose, letters to periodicals or newspapers when they appeared there prior to publication in a book. If the poem is untitled, the first line is used for identification. The items are listed chronologically and then numerically by page number if several poems appear in one issue of a periodical or newspaper. Volume and issue numbers are given in the style of the periodical or newspaper cited. In some cases, e.g. *The Observer*, an individual issue is indicated only by the date. The place of publication of a periodical or newspaper has been listed only in the index. Titles of reviews and letters are given although in most cases the title has been assigned by the editor. Following each entry is a note that indicates where the item was published in
The term "Uncollected" indicates that I have not been able to locate a book in which the item was reprinted. Abbreviations for Peter Porter's books are those previously listed. B. followed by a number is a cross reference to the B section of this bibliography.

1958

C1 SICK-ROOM AT HOME (Poem)
Delta, No. 15 (Summer 1958), 6.
OBTB, CP

C2 ONCE BITTEN, TWICE BITTEN (Poem)
Delta, No. 15 (Summer 1958), 6.
OBTB, CP

C3 ALL OTHER TIME IS PEACE (Poem)
Delta, No. 15 (Summer 1958), 7.
OBTB, CP

1959

C4 A CHRISTMAS RECALLED (Poem)
Delta, No. 19 (October 1959), 20
OBTB, CP

1960

C5 METAMORPHOSIS (Poem)
The Times Literary Supplement, No. 3021 (22 January 1960), 52.
OBTB , CP

C6 IN CONCLUSION (Prose)
Writing Today, No. 8 (April 1960), 12
Review of: Wright, Judith (Comp.). *New Land, New Language. An Anthology of Australian Verse.* Oxford University Press.
Uncollected

C7 CONVENTIONS OF DEATH (Poem)
Delta, No. 21 (June 1960), 14
OBTB, CP

C8 TOBIAS AND THE ANGEL (Poem)
Outposts, No. 46 (Autumn 1960), 9.
OBTB, CP

C9 MR. ROBERTS (Poem)
The Observer, 6 November 1960, 27.
OBTB, CP

C10 IN CONCLUSION (Prose)
Writing Today, No. 10 (December 1960), 12.
Review of: O'Keefe, Timothy (ed.). *Alienation. A Symposium.* MacGibbon & Kee.
Uncollected

1961

C11 SOMME AND FLANDERS (Poem)
The New Statesman, LXII, No. 1586 (4 August 1961), 158.
CP

C12 SASHA SAVED (Prose)
The New Statesman, LXII, No. 1606 (22 December 1961), 964-965.
Reviews of: Vigdorova, F. *Diary of a Russian Schoolteacher.* Grove Press; Almedingen, E.M. *Tomorrow Will Come.* Bodley Head; Pakehan, Simona. *Pigtails and Pernod.* Macmillan; Treat, Ida. *In France It Was Spring.* Faber.
Uncollected

1962

C13 SHOPPING SCENES (Poem)
Ambit, No. 12 (1962), 17.
PAAM, CP

C14 CAMUS (Prose)
Writing Today, No. 12 (March 1962), 9-10.
Review of Camus, Albert. *The Rebel.* A Peregrine Book.
Uncollected

C15 HOLDING COURT (Prose)
The New Statesman, LXIII, No. 1627 (18 May 1962), 731-732.
Uncollected

C16 MADAME DE MERTEUIL ON 'THE LOSS OF AN EYE' (Poem)
The New Statesman, LXIV, No. 1646 (28 September 1962), 415.
PAAM, CP

C17 BOOK REVIEWS (Prose)
The Listener, LXVIII, No. 1750 (11 October, 1962), 579.
Reviews of: Nolan, Cynthia. *Outback.* Methuen; Marshall, Jock and Russel Drysdale. *Journey among Men.* Hodder & Stoughton.
Uncollected

C18 EPIPHANY (Poem)
Outposts, No. 55 (Winter 1962), 2.

1963

C19 AUSTRALIA PROLIX (Prose)
The Listener, LXIX, No. 1763 (10 January 1963), 92, 95.
Reviews of: *Australian Civilization.* Angus & Robertson; Glaskin, G.M. *The Land that Sleeps.* Barrie & Rockliff; Beatty, Bill. *Unique to Australia.* Angus & Robertson; Simpson, Colin. *Adam in*

Ochre. Angus & Robertson; Casey, Maie. *An Australian Story*. Michael Joseph; *Sydney Cove, 1788*. Hodder & Stoughton.

Uncollected

C20 HAPPENING AT SORDID CREEK (Poem)
London Magazine, New Series, Vol. 2, No. 11 (February 1963), [5].
PAAM, CP

C21 HOMAGE TO GAETANO DONIZETTI (Poem)
London Magazine, New Series, Vol. 2, No. 11 (February 1963), 6.
PAAM, CP

C22 ENCOUNTER IN ANTIOCH (Poem)
London Magazine, New Series, Vol. 2, No. 11 (February 1963), 6-7.
PAAM, CP

C23 THE SINS OF THE FATHERS (Poem)
London Magazine, New Series, Vol. 2, No. 11 (February, 1963), 7-8.
PAAM, CP

C24 TWO MERITS OF SUNSHINE (Poem)
London Magazine, New Series, Vol. 2, No. 11 (February 1963), 8-9.
PAAM, CP

C25 STEPPING FROM A FLAT-BOTTOMED BOAT (First line, untitled poem)
The New Statesman, LXV, No. 1673 (5 April 1963), 496.
PAAM, CP

C26 REQUIEM FOR MRS. HAMMELSWANG (Poem)
The New Statesman, LXVI, No. 1693 (23 August 1963), 234.
PAAM, CP

C27 A HUDDLE OF IQ'S (Poem)
Delta (The Cambridge Literary Magazine), No. 30 (Summer 1963), 25.
PAAM, CP

C28 SYDNEY COVE, 1788 (Poem)
Delta (The Cambridge Literary Magazine), No. 30 (Summer 1963), 26.
PAAM, CP

C29 AN ADVERTISING MAN IN THE POLERMO CATACOMBS (Poem)
Delta (The Cambridge Literary Magazine), No. 30 (Summer 1963), 27
Uncollected

C30 PUNIC PROBLEMS (Poems)
Lines Review (Scotland's Magazine of Poetry), No. 20 (Summer, 1963), 45-47.
Parts 1-4 of an unfinished work
PAAM

C31 THE CATALOGUE (Poem)
Phoenix, No. 9 (Summer 1963), 9-10.
Uncollected

C32 THE VIEW FROM MISFORTUNE'S BACK (Poem)
Phoenix, No. 9 (Summer 1963), 10-11.
PAAM, CP

C33 AN ANTHROPOLOGIST'S CONFESSION (Poem)
Phoenix, No. 9 (Summer 1963), 11-13.
PAAM, CP

C34 MUSIC IN HISTORY (Poem)
Phoenix, No. 9 (Summer 1963), 13.
Uncollected

C35 BURKE AND WILLS (Prose)
The Listener, LXX, No. 1806 (7 November 1963), 754-755.
Review of: Moorehead, Alan. *Cooper's Creek*. Hamish.
Uncollected

C36 CHANGED FROM MARTIAL'S EPIGRAMS (Book XIII, No. XVIII) (Poem)
Poetry and Audience, Vol. 11, No. 6 (15 November 1963) 5-6.
PAAM

C37 VIENNA (Poem)
The New Statesman, LXVI, No. 1707 (29 November 1963), 784.
PAAM, CP

C38 FOUR HOME POEMS
Ambit, No. 18 (1963/64), 25-26.
Uncollected

1964

C39 BUSHED (Prose)
The Listener, LXXI, No. 1815 (9 January 1964), 81-82.
Reviews of: Mussen, Sarah. *Beating About the Bush*. Jarrolds; Lubbock, Adelaide. *Australian Roundabout*. Heinemann; Attenborough, David. *Quest Under Capricorn*. Lutterworth [sic.]; Millington, Rosemary. *A Nation of Trees*. Hutchinson New Authors; Trollope, Anthony. *Harry Heathcote of Gangoil*. Angus and Robertson.
Uncollected

C40 INSPECTOR CHRISTOPHER SMART CALLS (Poem)
The Listener, LXXI, No. 1822 (27 February 1964), 352-353.
PAAM, CP

C41 PIG IN THE MIDDLE (Poem)
The Listener, LXXI, No. 1822 (27 February 1964), 353.
APF, CP

C42 THE GREAT POET COMES HERE IN WINTER (Poem)
The Listener, LXXI, No. 1822 (27 February 1964), 353.
PAAM, CP

C43 CHANGED FROM MARTIAL'S EPIGRAMS (Book XII, No. XVII) (Poem)
The Listener, LXXI, No. 1822 (27 February 1964), 353.
AM, CP

C44 BOOK REVIEWS (Prose)
The Listener, LXXI, No. 1829 (16 April 1964), 641.
Review of: Brophy, Brigid. *Mozart the Dramatist*. Faber.
Uncollected

C45 STORY FROM A TIME OF DISTURBANCE (Poem)
London Magazine, New Series, Vol. 4, No. 2 (May 1964), [31]-32.
PAAM, CP

C46 SHAMES (Poem)
Phoenix, No. 10 (Spring 1964), 2-3.
PAAM

C47 CHANGED FROM MARTIAL'S EPIGRAMS. (Book IX, No. LIV) (Poem)
Phoenix, No. 10 (Spring 1964), 3.
PAAM, AM, CP

C48 MIRACLES (Poem)
Phoenix, No. 10 (Spring 1964), 3-4.
Uncollected

C49 ONE DIED IN METAPHOR AND ONE IN SONG (Poem)
Phoenix, No. 10 (Spring 1964), 4.
APF, CP

C50 FIRE ON A BUILDING LOT IN WINTER (Poem)
Outpost (*sic*), No. 61 (Summer 1964), 13.
(Note: Cover has correct title - *Outposts*)
Uncollected

C51 FUTURITY (Poem)
The New Statesman, LXVII, No. 1736 (19 June 1964), 957.
APF, CP

C52 HOW TO GET A GIRL FRIEND (Poem)
Encounter, XXIII, No. 3 (September 1964), [48-49].

C53 THREE POEMS OF POSSESSION
London Magazine, New Series, Vol. 4, No. 6 (September 1964), 39-41.
Uncollected

C54 THE ECLIPSE OF LADY SILVERTAIL (Poem)
The New Statesman, LXVIII, No. 1755 (30 October 1964), 666.
APF, CP

C55 [ONE OF] TEN COMMENTS ON A QUESTIONNAIRE (Prose)
London Magazine, New Series, Vol. 4, No. 8 (November 1964), [28]-40.
Uncollected

C56 TWO BOLD WAYS (Poem)
Phoenix, No. 11 (Winter 1964), 6.
Note: Sections I and II
Uncollected

C57 WHITE WEDDING (Poem)
Phoenix, No. 11 (Winter 1964), 7.
APF, CP

C58 HUGO WOLF'S DEATH MASK (Poem)
Phoenix, No. 11 (Winter 1964), 7.
Uncollected

C59 HOMILY IN THE ENGLISH READING ROOMS (Poem)
The Listener, LXXII, No. 1858 (5 November 1964), 717.
APF, CP

C60 SEAHORSES (Poem)
The Listener, LXXII, No. 1858 (5 November 1964), 717
APF, CP

C61 TWO ST. CECILIA"S DAY EPIGRAMS (Poem)
The New Statesman, LXVIII, No. 1758 (20 November 1964), 791.
Uncollected

C62 THREE POEMS FROM A LONGER WORK (Poem)
The Listener, LXXII, No. 1866 (31 December 1964), 1055.
Contents: Lyric 5, Lyric 7, Lyric 8.
Uncollected.

1965

C63 STEPS ON THE WAY (Poem)
The New Statesman, LXIX, No. 1768 (29 January 1965), 167.
APF, CP

C64 SYDNEYSIDE (Prose)
The New Statesman, LXIX, No. 1768 (29 January 1965), 171.
Uncollected

C65 RUDYARD KIPLING: A REASSESSMENT (Prose)
The Listener, LXXIII, No. 1880 (8 April 1965), 513-515.
Uncollected

C66 A HOPLITE'S HELMET (Poem)
London Magazine, New Series, Vol. 5, No. 2 (May 1965), [3].
APF, CP

C67 COMPETITION IS HEALTHY (Poem)
London Magazine, New Series, Vol. 5, No. 2 (May 1965), 4.
APF, CP

C68 AN UNIMPORTANT TRAGEDY (Poem)
London Magazine, New Series, Vol. 5, No. 2 (May 1965), 5-6.
APF

C69 IN A SUFFOLK GARDEN (Poem)
London Magazine, New Series, Vol. 5, No. 2 (May 1965), 6.

C70 BOOK REVIEWS (Prose)
The Listener, LXXIII, No. 1884 (6 May 1965), 676.
Review of: Mellers, Wilfred. *Harmonius Meeting*. Dobson.
Uncollected

C71 ST. JOHN ON PATMOS (Poem)
The Times Literary Supplement, No. 3309 (29 July 1965), 648.
APF, CP

C72 GENIUS LOCI (Poem)
The New Statesman, LXX, No. 1803 (1 October 1965), 486.
APF, CP

C73 IN HORA ULTIMA (Poem)
The New Statesman, LXX, No. 1803 (1 October 1965), 486.
APF, CP

C74 MOANING IN MIDSTREAM (Poem)
The New Statesman, LXX, No. 1810 (19 November 1965), 793.
APF, CP

C75 MY KERLONIAL OATH! (Prose)
Encounter, XXV, No. 5 (November 1965), 87-89
Review of: Ward, Russel, ed. *The Penguin Book of Australian Ballads.*
Uncollected

C76 RECITATIVE AND ARIA (Poem)
Ambit, No. 23 (1965), 3-4.
Uncollected

C77 THE NEXT HUNDRED YEARS WILL BE RELIGIOUS (Poem)
Ambit, No. 23 (1965), 5-6.
APF, CP

C78 ANNUNCIATION IN W.2 (Poem)
Ambit, No. 23 (1965), 6.
Uncollected

1966

C79 THE ASSENT OF '36. AN ENCOMIUM OF AUDEN AND MACNEICE'S 'LETTERS FROM ICELAND' (Prose)
Ambit, No. 27 (1966), 18-23
Uncollected

C80 SIBYLLINE STUTTERINGS (Poem)
The Sunday Times, 16 January 1966, 46
APF, CP

C81 WHERE A GENIUS TROD (Prose)
The Listener, LXXV, No. 1923 (3 February 1966), 180.
Review of: Moorehead, Alan. *The Fatal Impact*. Hamish Hamilton.
Uncollected

C82 WHY WE GET DRUNK (Poem)
The Listener, LXXV, No. 1927 (3 March 1966), 318.
APF, CP

C83 THREE POEMS FOR MUSIC
The Listener, LXXV, No. 1929 (17 March 1966), 409.
APF, CP

C84 OLD GREY CONTINENT (Prose)
The New Statesman, Vol. 71, No. 1830 (8 April 1966), 504
Reviews of: McInnes, Graham, *Humping My Bluey*. Hamish Hamilton; Davies, A.F. and S. Encel, eds. *Australian Society*. Pall Mall.
Uncollected

C85 POETRY (Prose)
London Magazine, New Series, Vol. 6, No. 2 (May 1966), 86-90.
Review of: Ewart, Gavin. *Pleasures of the Flesh*. Alan Ross, Ltd.
Uncollected

C86 ANGLO-JEWISH POETRY. WHAT IS DIFFERENT ABOUT IT? (Prose)
The Jewish Quarterly, Vol. 14, No. 2 (50) (Summer 1966), 27-28.
Uncollected

C87 LOWELL'S KINSMEN (Prose)
The Listener, LXXVI, No. 1954 (8 September 1966), 359.
Review of: Lowell, Robert. *The Old Glory*. Faber.
Uncollected

C88 LYRIC FOUND IN A BOTTLE (Poem)
The Transatlantic Review, No. 22 (Autumn 1966), 82.
APF, CP

C89 LATE LYRIC (Poem)
Encounter, XXVII, No. 4 (October 1966), [16].
APF, CP

C90 THE SHINING GOD AND THE GOD OF CORRECTION (Poem)
London Magazine, New Series, Vol. 6, No. 7 (October 1966), 24-25.
APF, CP

C91 A FEW WORDS OF GREEK (Poem)
London Magazine, New Series, Vol. 6, No. 7 (October 1966), 26.
Uncollected

C92 TWENTY-FOUR LINES (Poem)
London Magazine, New Series, Vol. 6, No. 7 (October 1966), 26-27.
APF, CP

C93 SCENES FROM DOSTOIEVSKY (Poem)
London Magazine, New Series, Vol. 6, No. 7 (October 1966), 27-28.
Scene I: APF, CP
Scene II: Uncollected

C94 THE THIRTEEN COUPLETS (Poem)
Ambit, No. 30 (1966-67), 4
APF, CP

C95 THE RETURN OF INSPECTOR CHRISTOPHER SMART (Poem)
Ambit, No. 30 (1966-67), 5-7.
APF, CP

C96 ADDENDUM TO QUARLES' EMBLEMS (Poem)
Micromegas (British Issue), III, No. 1 (1967), 36-37.
TLOE

C97 BOSWELL IN SEARCH OF A POEM (Poem)
Micromegas (British Issue), No. 1 (1967), 38-40
Uncollected

C98 SO MANY LONDONS (Prose)
The Listener, LXXVII, No. 1972 (12 January 1967), 61-62.
Reviews of: Davies, Henter, ed. *The New London Spy: a Discreet Guide to the City's Pleasures.* Blond Church, Richard. *London, Flower of Cities All.* Heinemann. Colby, Richard. *Mayfair: a Town within London.* Country Life. *The Parish of St. Anne, Soho.* Athlone Press. Norman, Frank and Jeffrey Bernard. *Soho Night and Day.* Secker and Warburg. Clarke, Basil. *Parish Churches of London.* Batsford. Herbert, A.P. *The Thames.* Weidenfeld and Nicolson.
Uncollected

C99 METAMORPHOSES (Poem)
Oz, March, 1967, 14-15.
APF

C100 COCK LINNETS (Prose)
The Listener, LXXVII, No. 1993 (8 June 1967), 758, 760.
Review of: MacInnes, Colin. *Sweet Saturday Night.* MacGibbon and Kee.
Uncollected

C101 THE BATTLE OF CANNAE (Poem)
The Listener, LXXVIII, No. 1999 (20 July 1967), 83.
APF, CP

C102 FANTASIA ON A LINE OF STEFAN GEORGE (Poem)
The Listener, Vol. 78, No. 2001 (3 August 1967), 136.
APF, CP

C103 THE BIRD DREAM (Poem)
The New Statesman, Vol. 74, No. 1900 (11 August 1967), 178.
APF, CP

C104 THE EGG DREAM (Poem)
The New Statesman, Vol. 74, No. 1900 (11 August 1967), 179.
APF, CP

C105 THE POEM DREAM (Poem)
The New Statesman, Vol. 74, No. 1900 (11 August 1967), 179.
APF, CP

C106 THE RECIPE (Poem)
London Magazine, New Series, Vol. 7, No. 6 (September 1967) [17]-18.
APF, CP

C107 MY LATE T'ANG PHASE (Poem)
London Magazine, New Series, Vol. 7, No. 6 (September 1967), 18-19.
APF, CP

C108 QUICK FROZEN POEM (Poem)
London Magazine, New Series, Vol. 7, No. 6 (September 1967), 19.
APF, CP

C109 JOURNAL ENTRY (Poem)
London Magazine, New Series, Vol. 7, No. 6 (September 1967), 19.
APF, CP

C110 THE WAY WE THINK OF IT (Poem)
The New Statesman, Vol. 74, No. 1907 (29 September 1967), 408.

1968

C111 SHORT STORY (Poem)
Ambit, No. 35 (1968), 2-3.
TLOE, CP

C112 FAREWELL TO THEOPHRASTUS (Poem)
Ambit, No. 35 (1968), 3-4.
CP

C113 POEM OF IMPOSSIBLES (Poem)
Australian Letters, Vol. 8, No. 1 (January 1968), 7.
Uncollected

C114 WHAT THE GUIDE BOOK SAID (Poem)
Australian Letters, Vol. 8, No. 1 (January 1968), 9.
APF, CP

C115 A WARNING (Poem)
Australian Letters, Vol. 8, No. 1 (January 1968), 13.
Uncollected

C116 AT THE TRATTORIA TOSCANA (Poem)
Australian Letters, Vol. 8, No. 1 (January 1968), 15.
Uncollected

C117 JEALOUS AND BADGER-LIKE (Prose)
The New Statesman, Vol. 75, No. 1931 (15 March 1968), 348-349.
Review of: *The Penguin Book of Satirical Verse*. Introduced and edited by Edward Lucie-Smith. Penguin.
Uncollected

C118 LET ME BORE YOU WITH MY SLIDES (Poem)
The New Statesman, Vol. 75, No. 1935 (12 April 1968), 490.
TLOE, CP

C119 APPROACHES TO A LINE BY AUDEN AND KALLMAN (Poem)
Phoenix, [No.] 3 (Spring 1968), 2.
APF, CP

C120 ONTOLOGY (Poem)
Phoenix, (No.) 3 (Spring 1968), 2-3.
Uncollected

C121 A TRIBUTE TO FRANCESCO MARIA PIAVE (Poem)
Phoenix, (No.) 3 (Spring 1968), 4-6.
Uncollected

C122 ONE...TWO...THRE...LYRIC (Poem)
Phoenix, (No.) 3 (Spring 1968), 6.
APF

C123 ST CECILIA'S DAY, 1710 (Poem)
The Poetry Review, LIX, No. 1 (Spring 1968), 6.
APF, CP

C124 A CONSUMER'S REPORT (Poem)
The Poetry Review, LIX, No. 1 (Spring 1968), 7-8.
TLOE, CP

C125 THE LAST OF THE DINOSAURS (Poem)
Transatlantic Review, No. 28 (Spring 1968), 29-30.
APF, CP

C126 OLD ENGLAND (Prose)
The New Statesman, Vol. 75, No. 1943 (7 June 1968), 767
Review of: McInnes, Graham. *Goodbye Melbourne Town*. Hamish Hamilton.
Uncollected

C127 POETRY (Prose)
London Magazine, New Series, Vol. 8, No. 4 (July 1968) 80-82
Reviews of: Jones, Brian. *A Family Album*. London Magazine Editions; Normanton, John. *The Window Game*. London Magazine Editions.
Uncollected

C128 INVOLVEMENT: WRITERS REPLY (Prose)
London Magazine, New Series, Vol. 8, No. 5 (August 1968) 5-19.
Porter's comments on pages 17-18.
Uncollected

C129 AT WHITECHURCH CANONICORUM (Poem)
London Magazine, New Series, Vol. 8, No. 6 (September 1968) 74-75.
TLOE, CP

C130 TELEVISION. CONFRONTATIONS. (Prose)
The New Statesman, Vol. 76, No. 1959 (27 September 1968), 405.
Uncollected

C131 TELEVISION. MUSICAL BOX (Prose)
The New Statesman, Vol. 76, No. 1940 (4 October 1968), 439-440.
Uncollected

C132 TELEVISION. SERIES-MINDED (Prose)
The New Statesman, Vol. 76, No. 1962 (18 October 1968), 508.
Uncollected

C133 EUROPE. AN ODE (Poem)
Quarry, Vol. 18, No. 1 (Fall 1968), [6-8]
TLOE, CP

C134 WRITING HOME (Poem)
Quarry, Vol. 18, No. 1 (Fall, 1968), [8].
Uncollected

C135 BABEL (Poem)
Oyster, November 1968, [25].
Uncollected

C136 TELEVISION. MASONIC (Prose)
The New Statesman, Vol. 76, No. 1965 (8 November 1968), 644.
Uncollected

C137 LOVE, POLITICS, DRINKING (Prose)
The New Statesman, Vol. 76, No. 1968 (29 November 1968), 756-757.
Review of: Love, Harold, ed. *The Penguin Book of Restoration Verse*. Penguin.
Uncollected

C138 WE'RE HERE TO MAKE A FILM (Poem)
Poetry and Audience, Vol. 16, No. 7 (Friday, December 13, 1968), [3].
Uncollected

C139 SUNDAY (Poem)
The New Statesman, Vol. 76, No. 1972 (27 December 1968), 909.
TLOE, CP

1969

C140 PRESS TO DESCEND (Poem)
Ambit, No. 38 (1969), 28-33.
Uncollected

C141 CHORUS AT THE END OF THE FIRST ACT (Poem)
Second Aeon, No. 10, (1969), 34.
PTTC, CP

C142 RADIO. WORDS AND MUSIC (Prose)
The New Statesman, Vol. 77, No. 1975 (17 January 1969), 93.
Uncollected

C143 ON STONEBARROW HILL (Poem)
The New Statesman, Vol. 77, No. 1976 (24 January 1969), 125.
TLOE, CP

C144 RADIO. PAPAL POLEMICS (Prose)
The New Statesman, Vol. 77, No. 1977 (31 January 1969), 165.
Uncollected

C145 RADIO. DIRGE FOR CRITICS (Prose)
The New Statesman, Vol. 77, No. 1979 (14 February 1969), 232-233.
Uncollected

C146 RADIO. SHREDDED PIPPA (Prose)
The New Statesman, Vol. 77, No. 1981 (28 February 1969) 305-306.
Uncollected

C147 POETRY: DIVORCE AND AFTER (Prose)
London Magazine, New Series, Vol. 8, No. 12 (March 1969), 85-89.
Reviews of: Snodgrass, W.D. *After Experience*. Oxford University Press; Eberhart, Richard. *Shifts of Being*. Chatto & Windus; Thomas, R.S. *Not That He Brought Flowers*. Hart Davis. Beresford, Anne. *The Lair*. Rapp & Whiting.
Uncollected

C148 CRYPTICS (Poem)
Oyster II, March 1969, [8].
Note: Title of Oyster reads *Oyster* replacing *Paperway*
Oyster II (replacing *Paperway*)
Uncollected

C149 RADIO. INTERROGATIONS (Prose)
The New Statesman, Vol. 77, No. 1983 (14 March 1969), 383-384.
Uncollected

C150 RADIO. THEOPHRASTIAN (Prose)
The New Statesman, Vol. 77, No. 1985 (28 March 1969), 456-457.
Uncollected

C151 CHRISTENINGS (Poem)
The New Statesman, Vol. 77, No. 1986 (4 April 1969), 482.
TLOE, CP

C152 A MEREDITHIAN TREATMENT (Poem)
The New Statesman, Vol. 77, No. 1986 (4 April 1969), 482.
TLOE, CP

C153 RADIO. NEW ARTS (Prose)
The New Statesman, Vol. 77, No. 1987 (11 April 1969), 526.
Uncollected

C154 RADIO. BUDGETEERING (Prose)
The New Statesman, Vol. 77, No. 1989 (25 April 1969), 597-598.
Uncollected

C155 RADIO. IN PROGRESS (Prose)
The New Statesman, Vol. 77, No. 1991 (9 May 1969), 669-670.
Uncollected

C156 RADIO. BULL SESSION (Prose)
The New Statesman, Vol. 77, No. 1993 (23 May 1969), 743.
Uncollected

C157 NOTES ON A RELATED SPECIES (Poem)
Form, No. 1 (Summer 1969), 6.
Uncollected

C158 KEEPING IN TOUCH (Poem)
The Occasional Windhover, Summer, 1969, 24.
TLOE

C159 THIS NIGHT (Poem)
The Occasional Windhover, Summer 1969, 25.
Uncollected

C160 POETRY (Prose)
London Magazine, New Series, Vol. 9, No. 3 (June 1969), 76-80.
Reviews of: Bunting, Basil. *Collected Poems*. Fulcrum Press; Morgan, Pete. *A Big Hat or What?* Kervin Press; Hoffman, Daniel. *Stricking the Stones*. Oxford University Press.
Uncollected

C161 STROKING THE CHIN (SOME POSSIBILITIES) (Poem)
The Poetry Review, Vol. 60, No. 2 (Summer 1969), 72-74.
TLOE, CP

C162 ON THIS DAY I COMPLETE MY FORTIETH YEAR (Poem)
The Listener, Vol. 81, No. 2097 (5 June 1969), 783.
TLOE, CP

C163 ARTS. SHUTTING OFF THE STEAM? (Prose)
The New Statesman, Vol. 77, No. 1995 (6 June 1969), 810.
Uncollected

C164 RADIO. PRESSURE GROUPS (Prose)
The New Statesman, Vol. 77, No. 1997 (20 June 1969), 884.
Uncollected

C165 SPRING IN LLAREGGYB (Prose)
The New Statesman, Vol. 77, No. 1998 (27 June 1969), 911.
Review of: Cleverdon, Douglas. *The Growth of Milk Wood*. Dent.
Uncollected

C166 RADIO. BALZAC PLAIN (Prose)
The New Statesman, Vol. 78, No. 1999 (4 July 1969), 25.
Uncollected

C167 RADIO. FORTRES BBC (Prose)
The New Statesman, Vol. 78, No. 2001 (18 July 1969), 92-93.
Uncollected

C168 THE MANUSCRIPT MARKET (Prose)
The Times Literary Supplement, No. 3518 (31 July 1969), 859.
Uncollected

C169 THE SADNESS OF THE CREATURES (Poem)
London Magazine, New Series 100 [Vol. 9, Nos. 4-5 (July-August 1969)], 55-57.
TLOE, CP

C170 HUTS OF WORDS (Prose)
London Magazine, New Series 100 [Vol. 9, Nos. 4-5 (July-August 1969)], 194-200.
Reviews of: Duncan, Robert. *The First Decade*. Fulcrum Press; Duncan, Robert. *Derivations*. Fulcrum Press; Olson, Charles. *Maximus IV, V, VI*. Cape Goliard; McClure, Michael. *Hymns to St. Geryon and Dark Brown*. Cape Goliard; *Penguin Modern Poets 13 - Charles Bukowski, Philip Lamantia, Harold Norse;* Holden, Molly. *To Make Me Grieve*. Chatto & Windus; Campbell, David. *Selected Poems 1942-1968*. Angus & Robertson
Uncollected

C171 RADIO. GRAND MONARCHS (Prose)
The New Statesman, Vol. 78, No. 2003 (1 August 1969), 158.
Uncollected

C172 RADIO. SPEECH UMBRELLA (Prose)
The New Statesman, Vol. 78, No. 2005 (15 August 1969), 223.
Uncollected

C173 RADIO. GENTLEMAN PLAYER (Prose)
The New Statesman, Vol. 78, No. 2007 (29 August 1969), 286-287.
Uncollected

C174 RADIO. LATHER (Prose)
The New Statesman, Vol. 78, No. 2009 (12 September 1969), 351-352.
Uncollected

C175 THE WORKERS (Poem)
The Listener, Vol. 82, No. 2113 (25 September, 1969), 404.
TLOE, CP

C176 APPLAUSE FOR DEATH (Poem)
The New Statesman, Vol. 78, No. 2011 (26 September 1969), 430.
TLOE, CP

C177 FABER & FABER LIMITED (Prose)
London Magazine, New Series, Vol. 9, No. 7 (October 1969) 81-87
Reviews of: Brownjohn, Alan. *Sandgrains on a Tray*. Macmillan; *Penguin Modern Poets 4*; Dunn, Douglas. *Terry Street*. Faber & Faber; Lerner, Laurence. *Selves*. Routledge & Kegan Paul; Levenson, Christopher. *Cairns*. Chatto & Windus.
Uncollected

C178 RADIO. CASETTES (Prose)
The New Statesman, Vol. 78, No. 2012 (3 October 1969), 472.
Uncollected

C179 RADIO. SUMMER DAZE (Prose)
The New Statesman, Vol. 78, No. 2013 (10 October 1969), 507-508.
Uncollected

C180 SPOKEN WORD (Prose)
The New Statesman, Vol. 78, No. 2016 (31 October 1969), 615-616.
Reviews of: Cutforth, Rene. *Order to View*. Faber. May, Derivent, ed. *Good Talk 2: an Anthology from BBC Radio*. Gollancz.
Uncollected

C181 RADIO. D'YE KEN? (Prose)
The New Statesman, Vol. 78, No. 2017 (7 November 1969), 669.
Uncollected

C182 RADIO. OPEN-ENDED (Prose)
The New Statesman, Vol. 78, No. 2019 (21 November 1969), 742.
Uncollected

C183 FROM THE SANITISED SONNETS: 5 (Poem)
The New Statesman, Vol. 78, No. 2020 (28 November 1969), 782.
TLOE, CP

C184 RADIO. SYNGE HIGH (Prose)
The New Statesman, Vol. 78, No. 2021 (5 December 1969), 837.
Uncollected

C185 RADIO. SON OF RUS (Prose)
The New Statesman, Vol. 78, No. 2024 (26 December 1969), 936.
Uncollected

C186 SOME EPIGRAMS FROM MARTIAL (Poems)
Arion. A Journal of Humanities and the Classics, Vol. 8, No. 4 (Winter 1969), [520]-524.
AM, CP

1970

C187 THE SANITIZED SONNETS (Poems)
Ambit, No. 42 (1970), 19-22.
TLOE, CP

C188 MARTIAL (Poems)
Delos. A Journal on & of Translation, No. 5 (1970), 153-155.
Contents: I.43, II.70, III.35, IV.18, V.10, XI.30
AM, CP

C189 POETRY: WARRIORS AND WORRIERS (Prose)
London Magazine, New Series, Vol. 9, No. 10 (January 1970), 95-101.
Reviews of: MacBeth, George. *A War Quartet*. Macmillan; Black, D.B. *The Educators*. Barrie & Rockliff, The Cresset Press; Howell, Anthony. *Inside the Castle*. Barrie & Rockliff, The Cresset Press; Wright, James. *Shall we Gather at the River*. Rapp & Whiting; Kinnell, Galway. *Body Rags*. Rapp & Whiting.
Uncollected

C190 RADIO. VERSE & PLAYS (Prose)
The New Statesman, Vol. 79, No. 2025 (2 January 1970), 26-27.
Uncollected

C191 DEATH AS KEY (Prose)
The New Statesman, Vol. 79, No. 2026 (9 January 1970), 52-53.
Review of: Newman, Charles. *The Art of Sylvia Plath*. Faber.
Uncollected

C192 RADIO. EPISODIC (Prose)
The New Statesman, Vol. 79, No. 2027 (16 January 1970), 93.
Uncollected

C193 AUDEN ANATOMISED (Prose)
The New Statesman, Vol. 79, No. 2028 (23 January 1970), 120-121.
Reviews of: Fuller, John. *A Reader's Guide to W.H. Auden*. Thames & Hudson; Replogle, Justin. *Auden's Poetry*. Methuen.
Uncollected

C194 RADIO WATERED DOWN (Prose)
The New Statesman, Vol. 79, No. 2029 (30 January 1970), 160-161.
Uncollected

C195 THE KING OF THE CATS IS DEAD (Poem)
London Magazine, New Series, Vol. 9, No. 11 (February 1970), 40-41
PTTC, CP

C196 ELEGY (Poem)
London Magazine, New Series, Vol. 9, No. 11 (February 1970), 41-43.
TLOE, CP

C197 RADIO. PLAYETS (Prose)
The New Statesman, Vol. 79, No. 2031 (13 February 1970), 228.
Uncollected

C198 ARTS. CURRAN DISMISS US (Prose)
The New Statesman, Vol. 79, No. 2033 (27 February 1970), 302.
Uncollected

C199 A PICTURE (Poem)
London Magazine, New Series, Vol. 9, No. 12 (March 1970), 86.
Uncollected

C200 A POSTCARD (Poem)
London Magazine, New Series, Vol. 9, No. 12 (March 1970), 86.
Uncollected

C201 A MAN (Poem)
London Magazine, New Series, Vol. 9, No. 12 (March 1970), 87.
Uncollected.

C202 FROM THE SANITISED SONNETS: 4 (Poem)
The New Statesman, Vol. 79, No. 2034 (9 March 1970), 329.
TLOE, CP

C203 RADIO. TWO FUNNY (Prose)
The New Statesman, Vol. 79, No. 2035 (13 March 1970), 386-387.
Uncollected

C204 PILL-SIZED SENSE (Prose)
The New Statesman, Vol. 79, No. 2036 (20 March 1970), 415-416.
Review of: Mautner, Franz and Henry Hatfield, Trans. *Lichtenberg: Aphorisms and Letters*. Cape.
Uncollected

C205 RADIO. BACKGROUND MUSIC (Prose)
The New Statesman, Vol. 79, No. 2037 (27 March 1970), 456.
Uncollected

C206 RADIO. ARDEN'S DREAM (Prose)
The New Statesman, Vol. 79, No. 2039 (10 April 1970), 525-526.
Uncollected

C207 RADIO. NEWS AND NEWS (Prose)
The New Statesman, Vol. 79, No. 2041 (24 April 1970), 594.
Uncollected

C208 THE BLOOD OF THE UNRIGHTEOUS (Prose)
The New Statesman, Vol. 79, No. 2043 (8 May 1970), 661-662.
Reviews of: Heer, Friedrich. *God's First Love*. Weidenfeld & Nicolson; Cohn, Norman. *The Pursuit of the Millennium*. Temple Smith.
Uncollected

C209 RADIO. SLUGGISH EARS (Prose)
The New Statesman, Vol. 79, No. 2044 (15 May 1970), 711-712.
Uncollected

C210 MORE FROM MARTIAL. (BOOK III, NO. XII) (Poem)
Phoenix, (Nos.) 6 and 7 (Summer 1970), 10.
TLOE, AM, CP

C211 THE CIVIL WAR (Poem)
Phoenix, (Nos.) 6 and 7 (Summer 1970), 10.
TLOE, CP

C212 HYMN (Poem)
Phoenix, (Nos.) 6 and 7 (Summer 1970), 11.
Uncollected

C213 POETRY 1970. A QUESTIONNAIRE (Prose)
Tracks 8, (Summer 1970), 10.
Uncollected

C214 AN OPEN AND SHUT CASE (Poem)
Tracks 8, (Summer 1970), 19-20.
PTTC, CP

C215 OPINION (Prose)
The Review, No. 22 (June 1970), 34-39.

C216 FROM THE SANITISED SONNETS: 2 (Poem)
The New Statesman, Vol. 79, No. 2047 (5 June 1970), 810.
TLOE, CP

C217 RADIO. EGMONT & AFTER (Prose)
The New Statesman, Vol. 79, No. 2048 (12 June 1970), 847-848.
Uncollected

C218 RADIO. AFTERMATH (Prose)
The New Statesman, Vol. 79, No. 2050 (26 June 1970), 926.
Uncollected

C219 RADIO. CLIFF-HANGER (Prose)
The New Statesman, Vol. 80, No. 2051 (10 July 1970), 31-32.
Uncollected

C220 RADIO. TALKING SHOP (Prose)
The New Statesman, Vol. 80, No. 2053 (24 July 1970), 99.
Uncollected

C221 A FORM OF REFRIGERATION (Prose)
London Magazine, New Series, Vol. 10, No. 4 (July/August 1970), 160-166.
Reviews of: Holbrook, David. *Old World, New World*. Rapp & Whiting. Tomlinson, Charles. *The Way of a World*. Oxford University Press. Wain, John. *Letters to Five Artists*. Macmillan. Fraser, G.S. *Conditions*. The Byron Press; Nye, Robert. *Darker ends*. Calder & Boyars; Lomas, Herbert. *Chimpanzees are Blameless Creatures*
Uncollected

C222 RADIO. FOREPLAY (Prose)
The New Statesman, Vol. 80, No. 2055 (7 August 1970), 159-160.
Uncollected

C223 RADIO. COLD THAW (Prose)
The New Statesman, Vol. 80, No. 2057 (21 August 1970), 220.
Uncollected

C224 IN THE BOSOM OF THE FAMILY (Prose)
London Magazine, New Series, Vol. 10, No. 5 (September 1970), 72-78.
Note: Spine of issue reads "Vol. 10, No. 6."
Reviews of: Brock, Edwin. *A Cold Day in the Zoo*. Rapp & Whiting; Harrison, Tony. *The Loiners*. London Magazine Editions; Williams, Hugo. *Sugar Daddy*. Oxford; Dickinson, Patric. *More Than Time*. Chatto & Windus; Dale, Peter. *Mortal Fire*. Macmillan.
Uncollected

C225 RADIO. TALK HOLES (Prose)
The New Statesman, Vol. 80, No. 2059 (4 September 1970), 283.
Uncollected

C226 RADIO. INTERROGATORS (Prose)
The New Statesman, Vol. 80, No. 2061 (18 Spetember 1970), 347.
Uncollected

C227 HISTORY (Poem)
The New Statesman, Vol. 80, No. 2062 (25 September 1970), 380.
Uncollected

C228 ON THE TRAIN BETWEEN WELLINGTON AND SHREWSBURY (Poem)
Wave, No. 1 (Autumn 1970), 23-25.
PTTC, CP

C229 PETER PORTER WRITES... (Prose)
The Poetry Book Society Bulletin, No. 66 (Autumn 1970) [1-2].
Uncollected

C230 RADIO. ART PUBLICS (Prose)
The New Statesman, Vol. 80, No. 2063 (2 October 1970), 430.
Uncollected

C231 RADIO. PARISH PUMPS (Prose)
The New Statesman, Vol. 80, No. 2065 (16 October 1970), 499.
Uncollected

C232 RADIO. MUSICAL GAP (Prose)
The New Statesman, Vol. 80, No. 2067 (30 October 1970), 575.
Uncollected

C233 RADIO. THOUGHT WORLDS (Prose)
The New Statesman, Vol. 80, No. 2069 (13 November 1970), 654-655.
Uncollected

C234 RADIO. FUTURE SHOCK (Prose)
The New Statesman, Vol. 80, No. 2971 (27 November 1970), 734-735.
Uncollected

C235 RADIO. BBC PUBLICATIONS (Prose)
The New Statesman, Vol. 80, No. 2073 (11 December 1970), 814.
Uncollected

C236 RECORDS. DONIZETTI LIVES! (Prose)
The New Statesman, Vol. 80, No. 2075 (25 December 1970), 876.
Uncollected

C237 OBJECTIVE CORRELATIVE (Poem)
Second Aeon, No. 12 (1970), 54.
Uncollected

C238 THE POEM OF THE IT (Poem)
Second Aeon, No. 12 (1970), 55-56.
Uncollected

C239 THE THREE SAGES (Poem)
Second Aeon, No. 12 (1970), 56.
Uncollected

1971

C240 RADIO. ON THE LINE (Prose)
The New Statesman, Vol. 81, No. 2076 (1 January 1971), 27-28.
Uncollected

C241 IN THE PET SHOP (Poem)
Second Aeon, No. 14 (1971), 61-62.
Uncollected

C242 THE PICTURE (Poem)
Second Aeon, No. 15 (1971), 118.
Uncollected

C243 JAMES JOYCE SING 'IL MIO TESORO' (Poem)
Second Aeon, No. 15 (1971), 119.
ASOTM, CP

C244 RADIO. UNSOUND (Prose)
The New Statesman, Vol. 81, No. 2078 (15 January 1971), 89-90.
Uncollected

C245 PLAY POWER (Prose)
The New Stateman , Vol. 81, No. 2080 (29 January 1971), 157-158.
Uncollected

C246 THE TOMB OF SCARLATTI (Poem)
The Listener, Vol. 85, No. 2184 (4 February 1971), 139.
PTTC, CP

C247 RECORDS. SCHUBERTIAD (Prose)
The New Statesman, Vol. 81, No. 2081 (5 February 1971), 192.
Uncollected

C248 RADIO. STRAIGHT TALK (Prose)
The New Statesman, Vol. 81, No. 2082 (12 February 1971), 220.
Uncollected

C249 THREE SANITIZED SONNETS (Poem)
Overland, No. 49 (Spring 1971), 14-15.

C250 RADIO. SELF-JUDGING (Prose)
The New Statesman, Vol. 81, No. 2094 (7 May 1971), 647
Uncollected

C251 RADIO. SPEAKING YOUR MIND (Prose)
The New Statesman, Vol. 81, No. 2986 (12 March 1971), 355-356.
Uncollected

C252 RADIO. PRUNING THE ROSES (Prose)
The New Statesman, Vol. 81, No. 2088 (26 March 1971), 438.
Uncollected

C253 VERSIONS FROM MARTIAL (Poems)
Agenda, Vol. 9, Nos. 2-3 (Spring-Summer 1971), 163-166.
AM, CP
Note: V1 XXII listed as V1, XXIII in AM and CP.

C254 THE SCHOOL FOR LOVE (Poem)
The Listener, Vol. 85, No. 2192 (1 April 1971), 413.
PTTC

C255 RECORDS. MOZARTIANA (Prose)
The New Statesman, Vol. 81, No. 2089 (2 April 1971), 472-473.
Uncollected

C256 RADIO. ON YOUR TOD (Prose)
The New Statesman, Vol. 81, No. 2090 (9 April 1971), 506-507.
Uncollected

C257 RADIO. GREAT PLEASURE (Prose)
The New Statesman, Vol. 81, No. 209 (23 April 1971), 574.
Uncollected

C258 DELPHI (Poem)
London Magazine, New Series, Vol. 11, No. 1 (April-May 1971), 77-79
PTTC, CP

C259 RADIO. BT NEWS (Prose)
The New Statesman, Vol. 81, No. 2096 (21 May 1971), 715.
Uncollected

C260 COLLECTION HER STRENGTH (Prose)
The New Statesman, Vol. 81, No. 2098 (4 June 1971), 774-775.
Review of: Plath, Sylvia. *Crossing the Water*. Faber
Uncollected

C261 RECORDS. MAGIC OPERA (Prose)
The New Statesman, Vol. 81, No. 2099 (11 June 1971), 820.
Uncollected

C262 RADIO. PORNBREAKER (Prose)
The New Statesman, Vol. 82, No. 2102 (2 July 1971), 27.
Uncollected

C263 POI LE PAROLE (Prose)
The New Statesman, Vol. 82, No. 2103 (9 July 1971), 51-52.
Review of: Smith, Patrick J. *The Tenth Muse*. Gollancz.
Uncollected

C264 RADIO. HIDDEN MENTORS (Prose)
The New Statesman, Vol. 82, No. 2104 (16 July 1971), 90-91.
Uncollected

C265 RADIO. NEXT PROGRAMME (Prose)
The New Statesman, Vol. 82, No. 2106 (30 July 1971), 158.
Uncollected

C266 A LAND FIT FOR CONSERVATIVES (Prose)
The Times Literary Supplement, No. 3622 (30 July 1971), 891-893.
Uncollected

C267 MORT AUX CHATS (Poem)
Encounter, XXXVII, No. 2 (August 1971), 53.
PTTC, CP
Note: This poem and the following poem appear under the author's collective title "Two Poems with French Titles."

C268 LE THEATRE DE BRUIT (Poem)
Encounter, XXXVII, No. 2 (August 1971), 53.
PTTC, CP

C269 TODAY'S BULLETIN (Poem)
Encounter, XXXVII, No. 2 (August 1971), 74.
Uncollected

C270 RECORDS. SWALLOWING THE WORDS (Prose)
The New Statesman, Vol. 82, No. 2107 (6 August 1971), 188-189.
Uncollected

C271 RADIO. BITS OF GREEK (Prose)
The New Statesman, Vol. 82, No. 2108 (13 August 1971), 215.
Uncollected

C272 RADIO. NEUTRAL TONES (Prose)
The New Statesman, Vol. 82, No. 2110 (27 August 1971), 279-280.
Uncollected

C273 THOMAS HARDY AT WESTBORNE PARK VILLAS (Poem)
Outposts, No. 90 (Augumn 1971), 3.
PTTC, CP

C274 RADIO. ENLIGHTENERS (Prose)
The New Statesman, Vol. 82, No. 2112 (10 September 1971), 344.
Uncollected

C275 AFFAIR OF THE HEART (Poem)
The New Statesman, Vol. 82, No. 2113 (17 September 1971), 370.
PTTC, CP

C276 RADIO. QUICK-CHANGE DRAMA (Prose)
The New Statesman, Vol. 82, No. 2114 (24 September 1971), 416.
Uncollected

C277 RADIO. TALKING BROWN (Prose)
The New Statesman, Vol. 82, No. 2116 (8 October 1971), 488.
Uncollected

C278 RECORDS. VERDI (Prose)
The New Statesman, Vol. 82, No. 2117 (15 October 1971), 519-520.
Uncollected

C279 RADIO. BIRD NOISES (Prose)
The New Statesman, Vol. 82, No. 2118 (22 October 1971), 566.
Uncollected

C280 ALBAN BERG. AN INDEX TO VIENNA (Prose)
Encounter, XXXVII, No. 5 (November 1971), 79-83.

Review of: *Alban Berg: Letters to His Wife*. Edited, translated and annotated by Bernard Brun. Faber & Faber.
Uncollected

C281 RADIO. PICKUP'S HAMLET (Prose)
The New Statesman, Vol. 82, No. 2120 (5 November 1971), 630.
Uncollected

C282 MEMORY TREE (Poem)
Humanist, Vol. 86, No. 11 (November 1971), 337.
Note: Poem divided into 2 sections called "Survey," and "Report."
Uncollected

C283 RADIO. MASON'S MARCH (Prose)
The New Statesman, Vol. 82, No. 2122 (19 November 1971), 711.
Uncollected

C284 HUMAN GENIUS (Prose)
The New Statesman, Vol. 82, No. 2123 (26 November 1971), 742.
Review of: Levey, Michael. *The Life and Death of Mozart*. Weidenfeld & Nicolson.
Uncollected

C285 THE DARLING OF THE FAMILY (Poem)
London Magazine, New Series, Vol. 11, No. 4 (October/November 1971), [58]-60.
Uncollected

C286 RADIO. I AND WE (Prose)
The New Statesman, Vol. 82, No. 2124 (3 December 1971), 800.
Uncollected

C287 FOSSIL GATHERING (Poem)
The New Statesman, Vol. 82, No. 2125 (10 December 1971), 831.
PTTC, CP

C288 RECORDS. MASTERSINGERS (Prose)
The New Statesman, Vol. 82, No. 2125 (10 December 1971), 839.
Uncollected

C289 A SHARE OF THE MARKET (Poem)
Ambit, No. 47 (1971), 2-4.
ASOTM

C290 POSTCARD POEMS (Poem)
Ambit, No. 47 (1971), 4-6.
PTTC, CP

C291 MOZART'S COMPOSING HIS DIVERTIMENTO, K. 186, CONTRASTED WITH ALMOST ANY ANALYTICAL ARTICLE IN ANY AMERICAN JOURNAL OF MUSICOLOGY (Poem)
Workshop, No. 13 (1971), 8.
Uncollected

C292 DREAM RESTAURANT (Poem)
The Review, Nos. 27-28 (Autumn-Winter 1971-72), 39.
PTTC, CP

C293 EVOLUTION (Poem)
The Carleton Miscellany, XII, No. 3 (Fall-Winter 1971-72), 80-81.
PTTC, CP

1972

C294 THE STORM (Poem)
Second Aeon, No. 16/17 (1972), 41-42.
LIACC, CP

C295 THE DUST (Poem)
Decal. Poetry Review, [No. 1, 1972], 34-35.
PTTC, CP

C296 EPIGRAMS OF THE ABBOT BU-SHOU-SE (Poem)
Ambit, No. 52 (1972), 13-16.
LIACC

C297 THE MAGNIFICENT SEVEN (Poem)
Ambit, No. 52 (1972), 14-15.
ASOTM

C298 QUIET ENJOYMENT (Poem)
Ambit, No. 52 (1972), 15-16.
Uncollected

C299 RECORDS. GREAT CORPUS (Prose)
The New Statesman, Vol. 83, No. 2129 (7 January 1972), 27.
Uncollected

C300 THE KING OF LIMERICK'S ARMY (Poem)
The New Statesman, Vol. 83, No. 2132 (28 January 1972), 118.
PTTC, CP

C301 THE TRUE VEIN OF SATIRE (Prose)
The New Statesman, Vol. 83, No. 2135 (18 February 1972), 210-211.
Review of: Farley-Hills, David, ed. *Rochester: The Critical Heritage*. Routledge.
Uncollected

C302 O MONTREAL (Prose)
The New Statesman, Vol. 83, No. 2136 (25 February 1972), 246.
Review of: Richler, Mordecai. *The Street*. Weidenfeld & Nicolson.
Uncollected

C303 A HINT FROM ARIOSTO (Poem)
The Times Literary Supplement, No. 3653 (3 March 1972), 254.
PTTC, CP

C304 RECORDS. KNIGHT & QUEEN (Prose)
The New Statesman, Vol. 83, No. 2137 (3 March 1972), 290.
Uncollected

C305 SEX AND THE OVER-FORTIES (Poem)
The New Statesman, Vol. 84 [sic] 83, No. 2139 (17 March 1972), 364.
PTTC, CP

C306 MUSIC. SHORT SOLUTIONS (Prose)
The New Statesman, Vol. 84 [sic] 83, No. 2140 (24 March 1972), 400
Uncollected

C307 REALLY BLACK (Prose)
The New Statesman, Vol. 84 [sic] 83, No. 2140 (24 March 1972), 397-398.
Review of: Malamud, Bernard. *The Tenants*. Eyre Methuen.
Uncollected

C308 THE WAY AHEAD (Poem)
Poetry and Audience, Vol. 19, No. 7 (April 1972), 4.
Uncollected

C309 THREE SONGS (Poem)
Westerly, No. 1 (April 1972), 54-55.
Note: Poems numbered I, II, III
Uncollected

C310 TRAVEL SICKNESS IN VENICE (Poem)
Encounter, XXXVIII, No. 4 (April 1972), 55.
Uncollected

C311 MUSIC IN CAPTIVITY (Prose)
The New Statesman, Vol. 84 [sic] 83, No. 2142 (7 April 1972), 467-468.
Uncollected

C312 RIMBAUD AND LES ILLUMINATIONS - PETER PORTER WRITES ABOUT THE CREATION OF A SORT OF NATIONAL PARK OF THE EUROPEAN IMAGINATION (Prose)
The Listener, Vol. 87, No. 2245 (13 April 1972), 480-482.
Uncollected

C313 TO ACCOMPANY A SHEAF OF VERSES (Poem)
The Listener, Vol. 87, No. 2245 (13 April 1972), 482.
ASOTM

C314 TENDING TOWARDS THE CONDITION (Poem)
London Magazine, New Series, Vol. 12, No. 1 (April/May 1972), 110.
PTTC, CP

C315 RECORDS. UNIQUE MIXTURE (Prose)
The New Statesman, Vol. 83, No. 2146 (5 May 1972), 615.
Uncollected

C316 VIEWPOINT (Prose)
The Times Literary Supplement, No. 3663 (12 May 1972), 546.
Uncollected

C317 THE STATE OF POETRY - A SYMPOSIUM (Prose)
The Review, Nos. 29-30 (Spring-Summer 1972), 41-44.
Uncollected

C318 LIVING IN A CALM COUNTRY (Poem)
The Critical Quarterly, Vol. 14, No. 2 (Summer 1972), 126.
LIACC, CP

C319 THREE BAGATELLES (Poems)
The Critical Quarterly, Vol. 14, No. 2 (Summer 1972), 125.
LIACC, CP

C320 POETRY: EXPERTS (Prose)
London Magazine, New Series, Vol. 12, No. 2 (June/July 1972), 144-149.
Reviews of: Smith, Stevie. *Scorpion and other Poems*. Longman; Ewart, Gavin. *The Gavin Ewart Show*. Trigram; Plomer, William. *Celebrations*. Cape; Updike, John. *Seventy Poems*. Penguin.
Uncollected

C321 VIEWPOINT (Prose)
The Times Literary Supplement, No. 3671 (7 July 1972), 774.
Uncollected

C322 SELF-COMMUNING THE YEAR THE TUTANKHAMUN EXHIBITION CAME TO LONDON (Poem)
Anthos, No. 1 (September 1972), 39.
Uncollected

C323 METAMORPHOSES (Prose)
The Guardian, 14 September 1972, 9.
Reviews of: Redgrove, Peter. *Dr. Faust's Sea-Spiral Spirit*. Routledge; Tarn, Nathaniel. *A Nowhere For Vallejo*. Cape; Callow, Philip. *Bare Wires*. Chatto & Windus; Kinsella, Thomas. *Notes from the Land of the Dead*. Cuala Press.
Uncollected

C324 VIEWPOINT (Prose)
The Times Literary Supplement, No. 3681 (22 September 1972), 1102.
Uncollected

C325 THE WORLD IS EXPLORED (Poem)
Overland, Nos. 50-51 (Autumn 1972), 37.
Uncollected

C326 LETTER TO AN AUNT (Poem)
The Listener, Vol. 88, No. 2275 (2 November 1972), 603.
Uncollected

C327 VIEWPOINT (Prose)
The Times Literary Supplement, No. 3689 (17 November 1972), 1394.
Uncollected

C328 CAT'S FUGUE (Poem)
The Times Literary Supplement, No. 3693 (15 December 1972), 1536.
LIACC, CP

C329 HAPPY BIRTHDAY, PETER (Poem)
The Times Literary Supplement, No. 3693 (15 December 1972), 1536.
Uncollected

C330 INTERIORS (Poem)
The Times Literary Supplement, No. 3693 (15 December 1972), 1536.
Uncollected

C331 VIEWPOINT (Prose)
The Times Literary Supplement, No. 3695 (29 December 1972), 1580.
Uncollected

C332 GOOD VIBES (Poem)
Pointer, VIII, No. 2 (Winter 1972), 18.
LIACC, CP

C333 MORNING SONG OF A COURT DWARF (Poem)
London Magazine, New Series, Vol. 12, No. 5 (December 1972/ January 1973), 74.
LIACC, CP

1973

C334 AN AMERICAN MILITARY CEMETERY IN TUSCANY (Poem)
The Listener, Vol. 89, No. 2284 (4 January 1973), 15.
ASOTM, LIACC, CP

C335 THE NINE BRIGHT SHINERS (Poem)
The Honest Ulsterman, No. 37 (Jan./Feb. 1973), 4-6.
Uncollected

C336 WILLOW PATTER (Poem)
The Honest Ulsterman, No. 37 (Jan./Feb. 1973), 6-7.
Uncollected

C337 CLEANING MY TYPEWRITER (Poem)
The Honest Ulsterman, No. 37 (Jan./Feb. 1973), 7-8.
Uncollected

C338 A STUDY OF A BIRD (Poem)
Encounter, XL, No. 2 (February 1973), 41.
LIACC, CP

C339 THE DEFINITION OF HAPPINESS (Poem)
Encounter, XL, No. 2 (February 1973), 41.
Uncollected

C340 A POET'S PRESCRIPTIONS (Prose)
The Observer, 18 February 1973, 36.
Reviews of: Abse, Dannie. *Funland*. Hutchinson; MacBeth, George. *Shrapnel*. Macmillan.
Uncollected

C341 THE VANITY OF POETRY (Poem)
Encounter, XL, No. 3 (March 1973), 38.
Uncollected

C342 VIEWPOINT (Prose)
The Times Literary Supplement, No. 3704 (2 March 1973), 238.
Uncollected

C343 THE AUTOMATIC ORACLE (Poem)
Encounter, XL, No. 4 (April 1973), 36.
Uncollected

C344 VIEWPOINT (Prose)
The Times Literary Supplement, No. 3712 (27 April 1973), 470.
Uncollected

C345 CAGED MUSIC HATERS: THE INNOCENT AND THE IGNORANT (Prose)
New Humanist, 89 (May 1973), 525-527.
Uncollected

C346 TO MAKE IT REAL (Poem)
The New Statesman, Vol. 85, No. 2200 (18 May 1973), 742.
LIACC, CP

C347 THAT DEPRESSION IS AN ABSTRACT (Poem)
Overland, No. 57 (Summer 1973-1974), 14.
LIACC, CP

C348 MY THREE AUNTS (Poem)
Overland, No. 57 (Summer 1973-1974), 15.
Uncollected

C349 DURRELL IN DECLINE (Prose)
The Observer, 17 June 1973, 33.
Reviews of: Durrell, Laurence. *Vega*. Faber; Grigson, Geoffrey. *Sad Grove of an Imperial Mongoose*. Macmillan; Walker, Ted. *Gloves to the Hangman*. Cape; Fried, Michael. *Powers*. The Review.
Uncollected

C350 HIS AND HERS (Poem)
The New Statesman, Vol. 85, No. 2206 (29 June 1973), 966.
LIACC, CP

C351 LIVING IN LONDON - XI (Prose)
London Magazine, New Series, Vol. 13, No. 2 (June/July 1973), [57]-64.

C352 VIEWPOINT (Prose)
The Times Literary Supplement, No. 3724 (20 July 1973), 832.
Uncollected

C353 RADIO. POLAR APOPHTHEGMS (Prose)
The Listener, Vol. 90, No. 2313 (26 July 1973), 128.
Uncollected

C354 A POET FROM ULSTER (Prose)
The Observer, 5 August 1973, 28.
Reviews of: Longley, Michael. *An Exploded View*. Gollancz; Brock, Edwin. *The Portraits and the Poses*. Secker; Walcott, Derek. *Another Life*. Cape; Murray, Les A. *Poems Against Economics*. Angus and Robertson.
Uncollected

C355 RADIO. LONG LIVES (Prose)
The Listener, Vol. 90, No. 2317 (23 August 1973), 259-260.
Uncollected

C356 RADIO. LIFE AND DEATH (Prose)
The Listener, Vol. 90, No. 2321 (20 September 1973), 386.
Uncollected

C357 STILL LIFE (Poem)
The Critical Quarterly, Vol. 15, No. 3 (Autumn 1973), [275].
Uncollected

C358 A REBUKE TO THE TIMID. AUDEN'S ESSAYS AND APHORISMS (Prose)
Encounter, XLI, No. 4 (October 1973), 100-103.
Review of: Auden, W.H. *Forewords and Afterwords*. Faber & Faber.
Uncollected

C359 RADIO. LBC (Prose)
The Listener, Vol. 90, No. 2325 (18 October 1973), 531-532.
Uncollected

C360 THE TRANSIT OF VENUS (Prose)
The Observer, (4 November 1973), 39.
Reviews of: Graves, Robert. *Timeless Meeting*. Bertram Rota; Morgan, Edwin. *From Glasgow to Saturn*. Carcanet; Scannell, Vernon. *The Winter Man*. Allison & Busby; Hall, J.C. *A House of Voices*. Chatto & Windus; McGough, Roger. *Gig*. Cape.
Uncollected

C361 COLLABORATORS (Prose)
The New Statesman, Vol. 86, No. 226 (16 November 1973), 741-742.
Reviews of: Skinner, M. L. *The Fifth Sparrow*. Angus & Robertson; Lawrence, D.H. *The Boy in the Bush*. Heinemann.
Uncollected

C362 PRINT OUT: APOCALYPSE (Poem)
The New Statesman, Vol. 86, No. 2226 (16 November 1973), 734.
LIACC, CP.

C363 RADIO. GOD'S ARCHIVES (Prose)
The Listener, Vol. 90, No. 2330 (22 November 1973), 723-724.
Uncollected

C364 ANGER (Poem)
The New Statesman, Vol. 86, No. 2228 (30 November 1973), 818.
LIACC, CP

C365 REMEMBER, REMEMBER (Poem)
Encounter, XLI, No. 5 (November 1973), 48.
Uncollected

C366 VIEWPOINT (Prose)
The Times Literary Supplement, No. 3744 (7 December 1973), 1506.
Uncollected

C367 SHADOWS ON THE GRASS (Prose)
The Observer, 30 December 1973, 22.
Reviews of: Fuller, Roy. *Tiny Tears*. Deutsch; MacBeth, George. *A Poet's Year*. Gollancz; Maclean, Alasdair. *From the Wilderness*. Gollancz; Harsent, David. *After Dark*. Oxford; Harsent, David. *Truce*. Sycamore Press.
Uncollected

C368 RETRIEVAL SYSTEM (Poem)
Antaeus, No. 12 (Winter 1973), 98-99.
Uncollected

C369 BAROQUE QUATRAINS (DEATH OF A COMIC OPERA COMPOSER) (Poem)
Antaeus, No. 12 (Winter 1973), 100.
Uncollected

C370 THE QUEER ASSAYERS OF THE FRONTIER (Poem)
Antaeus, No. 12 (Winter 1973), 101.
Uncollected

C371 EIGHTEEN YEARS AFTER (Poem)
Zemzem, [No. 1], 1973, [14].
Uncollected

C372 PROSE STATEMENT (Prose)
Ambit, No. 54 (1973), 13-14.
Uncollected

373 MEANWHILE (Poem)
Ambit, No. 54 (1973), 15-16.
LIACC, CP

1974

C374 RADIO. DRAGGED-OUT AFFAIRS (Prose)
The Listener, Vol. 91, No. 2336 (3 January 1974), 28.
Uncollected

C375 HEARTS AND SLEEVES (Prose)
The Observer, 27 January 1974), 30
Reviews of: Fuller John. *Epistles to Several Persons*. Secker & Warburg; Sexton, Anne. *The Book of Folly*. Chatto & Windus; Montgomery, Stuart. *Shabby Sunshine*. Fulcrum; Ackroyd, Peter. *London's Lickpenny*. Ferry Press; Leary, Paris. *The Snake at Saffron Walden*. Carcanet.
Uncollected

C376 THE SETTEMBRINI WALTZ (Poem)
Encounter, XLII, No. 2 (February 1974), 70.
LIACC, CP

C377 RADIO. SCIENCE IS NEWS (Prose)
The Listener, Vol. 91, No. 2341 (7 February 1974), 187, 189.
Uncollected

C378 ACROSS TWO GENERATIONS (Prose)
The Observer, 10 March 1974, 33.
Reviews of: D.H. *Trilogy*. Carcanet; Ross, Alan. *The Taj Express*. London Magazine; Oakes, Philip. *Married/Singular*. Deutsch; Feinstein, Elaine. *The Celebrants*. Hutchinson.
Uncollected

C379 BLIGHT IN AUGUST (Poem)
Outposts, No. 100 (Special Centenary Number) (Spring 1974), 18-21.
Uncollected

C380 DREAMTIME (Poem)
Encounter, XLII, No. 4 (April 1974), [48].
LIACC, CP

C381 FROGS AT LAKE BOLSENA (Poem)
Encounter, XLII, No. 5 (May 1974), 56.
LIACC, CP

C382 FROM MISSOLONGHI TO APSLEY HOUSE - A REAPPRAISAL OF BYRON (Prose)
The Listener, Vol. 91, No. 2355 (16 May 1974), 624.
Uncollected

C383 THE AMERICAN WAY OF LOVE (Prose)
The Observer, 23 June 1974, 33.
Reviews of: Stevenson, Anne. *Correspondences*. Oxford; Stevenson, Anne. *Travelling Behind Glass*. Oxford; Jong, Erica. *Half-Lives*. Secker & Warburg; Stallworthy, Jon. *Hand in Hand*. Chatto & Windus; Stallworthy, Jon. *The Apple Barrel*. Oxford.
Uncollected

C384 SCENE OF THE CRIME (Poem)
Encounter, XLIII, No. 1 (July 1974), [88].

C385 OPINION. GRUB STREET VERSUS ACADEME (Prose)
The New Review, Vol. 1, No. 4 (July 1974), 47-52.
Uncollected

C386 BYRON & THE MORAL NORTH: THE ENGLISHNESS OF 'DON JUAN' (Prose)
Encounter, XLIII, No. 2 (August 1974), 65-72.
Uncollected

C387 FAMILY ALBUM (Poem)
The New Review, Vol. 1, No. 5 (August 1974), 58.
LIACC, CP

C388 STORY OF MY CONVERSION (Poem)
The New Review, Vol. 1, No. 5 (August 1974), 59.
LIACC, CP

C389 AN AUSTRALIAN GARDEN (Poem)
The New Review, Vol. 1, No. 5 (August 1974), 60-61.
LIACC, CP

C390 BEFORE THE WAR (Poem)
The New Review, Vol. 1, No. 5 (August 1974), 61.
Uncollected

C391 THE IMPACT OF THE ABORIGINES (Prose)
The Times Literary Supplement, No. 3780 (16 August 1974), 874-875.
Review of: Dutton, Geoffrey. *White on Black. The Australian Aborigine Portrayed in Art.* Macmillan.
Uncollected

C392 IN YEAT'S FOOTSTEPS (Prose)
The Observer, 18 August 1974, 27.
Reviews of: Clarke, Austin. *Collected Poems.* Dolmen Press; Kunitz, Stanley. *The Terrible Threshold.* Secker & Warburg; Connor, Tony. *The Memoirs of Uncle Harry.* Oxford; Connor, Tony. *Last Poems from the Memoirs of Uncle Harry.* Northern House; Randice, William. *Eight Sections.* Secker & Warburg.
Uncollected

C393 THE TEMPTATION OF SAINT ANTHONY (Poem)
Caret, No. 5/6 (Summer/Autumn 1974), 21.
Uncollected

C394 RETURNING FROM BRIGG (Poem)
Encounter, XLIII, No. 3 (September 1974), 91.
Uncollected

C395 OUT WITH IT (Prose)
The New Review, Vol. 1. No. 6 (September 1974), 74-76.
Reviews of: Greene, Graham. *Lord Rochester's Monkey.* Bodley Head; Farley-Hills, David. *The Benevolence of Laughter.* Macmillan.
Uncollected

C396 RETURN TO ARCADIAN AUSTRALIA (Prose)
The Listener, Vol. 92, No. 2372 (12 September 1974), 333-334.
Uncollected

C397 OLD FASHIONED WEDDING (Poem)
Pick, Vol. 1, No. 1 (Autumn 1974), 12.
TCOS, CP

C398 INSPIRATION FROM THE NORTH-EAST (Prose)
The Observer, 20 October 1974, 32.
Reviews of: Dunn, Douglas. *Love or Nothing*. Faber; Kendrick, George. *Bicycle Tyre in a Tall Tree*. Carcanet; Adcock, Fleur. *The Scenic Route*. Oxford; *Treble Poets 1: Stephen Miller, Elizabeth Maslen, Kit Wright*. Chatto & Windus.
Uncollected

C399 BOOM! (Prose)
The New Review, Vol. 1, No. 9 (December 1974), 65-66.
Review of: *Letters of Puccini*. A selection revised and introduced by Mosco Carner. Harrap.
Uncollected

C400 IN SEARCH OF ENGLAND (Prose)
The Observer, 15 December 1974, 27.
Reviews of: Davie, Donald. *The Shires*. Routledge; Tomlinson, Charles. *The Way In*. Oxford; MacCraig, Norman. *The World's Room*. Chatto & Windus.
Uncollected

1975

C401 ON FIRST LOOKING INTO CHAPMAN'S HESIOD (Poem)
Poetry Nation, No. 5 (1975), 12-14.
LIACC, CP

C402 THE SNAILS OF TURIN (Poem)
Poetry Nation, No. 4 (1975), 17-18.
Uncollected

C403 A TOCCATA OF MUFFAT'S (Poem)
Poetry Nation, No. 4 (1975), 18.
LIACC, CP

C404 DOWN CEMETERY ROAD (Poem)
Encounter, XLIV, No. 1 (January 1975), [38].
LIACC, CP

C405 AUTHENTIC VOICES (Prose)
The Observer, 19 January 1975, 30.
Reviews of: Waterman, Andrew. *Living Room*. Marvell Press; Waterman, Andrew. *Last Fruit*. Mandeville Press; Salvesen, Christopher. *Floodsheaf*. Whitenights Press; Reading, Peter. *For the Municipality's Elderly*. Secker & Warburg; Hewitt, John. *Out of My Time*. Blackstaff Press.
Uncollected

C406 THE DESCENT INTO AVERNUS (Poem)
The Listener, Vol. 93, No. 2390 (23 January 1975), 125.
LIACC, CP

C407 THE FEAST OF THE GODS (Poem)
Encounter, XLIV, No. 2 (February 1975), [36].
Uncollected

C408 LIFE STUDIES (Prose)
The New Statesman, Vol. 80, No. 2293 (28 February 1975) 283-284.
Review of: Abbs, Peter, ed. *The Black Rainbow: Essays on the Present Breakdown of Culture*. Heinemann.
Uncollected

C409 PSYCHOPOMPOS'S SONGS (Poem)
London Magazine, New Series, Vol. 14, No. 6 (February/March 1975), [56]-58.
Uncollected

C410 BOOKS (Prose)
Tempo. A Quarterly Review of Modern Music, No. 112 (March 1975), 40-41.
Review of: Britten, Benjamin. *Kinderkreuzzug*. Faber Music.
Uncollected

C411 CON MALINCONIA (Poem)
Pick, Vol. 1, No. 2 (Spring 1975), 4-5.
Uncollected

C412 ELSINOR REVISITED (Prose)
The Observer, 27 April 1975, 34.
Reviews of: Wain, John. *Feng*. Macmillan; Crichton Smith, Iain. *The Notebooks of Robinson Crusoe*, Gollancz; Scupham, Peter. *Prehistories*. Oxford; Jennings, Elizabeth. *Growing Points*. Carcanet; Pitter, Ruth. *End of Drought*. Barraie and Jenkins.
Uncollected

C413 IN THE NEW WORLD, HAPPINESS IS ALLOWED (Poem)
Aspect. Art and Literature, Spring 1975, 13.
TCOS, CP

C414 REMEMBERING THE MASTER: ACCOUNTS OF AUDEN (Prose)
Encounter, XLV, No. 1 (July 1975), 76-79.
Review of: Spender, Stepher, ed. *W. H. Auden: A Tribute.* Weidenfield & Nicolson; Macmillan, N.Y.
Uncollected

C415 PRUDENCE FARMER POETRY PRIZE (Prose)
The New Statesman, Vol. 90, No. 2311 (4 July 1975), 31.
Uncollected

C416 THE ZONE OF VENUS (Poem)
London Magazine, New Series, Vol. 15, No. 3 (August/September 1975), 43-44.
LIACC, CP

C417 DICHTUNG UND WAHRHEIT (Poem)
Encounter, XLV, No. 3 (September 1975), 37.
Uncollected

C418 BRISBANE COMES BACK (Prose)
Quadrant, No. 98. Vol. XIX, No. 6 (September 1975), 54-58.
Uncollected

C419 THE STORY OF U (Poem)
Quadrant, No. 98. Vol. XIX, No. 6 (September 1975), 54.
Uncollected

C420 WHAT PRINCE CALF FOUND IN LOVE (Poem)
Quadrant, No. 98. Vol. XIX, No. 6 (September 1975), 56.
Uncollected

C421 FROM THE GERMAN OF JOACHIM FALANGER (Poem)
Quadrant, No. 98. Vol. XIX, No. 6 (September 1975), 57.
Uncollected

C422 AUDEN: ORTHODOXY AND RETICENCE (Prose)
Nation Review, Sept. 26-Oct. 2, 1975, 1284.
Review of: Spender, Stephen, ed. *W. H. Auden: A Tribute.* Weidenfeld and Nicolson
Uncollected

C423 A LECTURE BY MY BOOKS (Poem)
Quadrant, No. 99. Vol. XIX, No. 7 (October 1975), 21.
TCOS, CP

C424 THE HONEY CAT (Poem)
Overland, No. 60 (Augumn 1975), 64
Uncollected

C425 PETER PORTER WRITES. . . (Prose)
The Poetry Book Society Bulletin, No. 86 (Autumn 1975), [1-2].
Uncollected

C426 ODE TO AFTERNOON (Poem)
Encounter, XLV. No. 5 (November 1975), [50-51].
LIACC, CP

C427 AN EXEQUY (Poem)
Quadrant, No. 100. Vol. XIX, No. 8 (November 1975), 23.
TCOS, CP

C428 IRONY AND INDIGNATION (Prose)
The Observer, 16 November 1975, 31.
Reviews of: Brownjohn, Alan. *A Song of Good Life*. Secker and Warburg; Enright, D.J. *Sad Ires*. Chatto and Windus; Thomas, R.S. *Laboratories of the Spirit*. Macmillan; Peskett, William. *The Night-owl's Dissection*. Secker and Warburg.
Uncollected

C429 PRIVATE AND PASTORAL (Prose)
The Observer, 14 December 1975, 24.
Reviews of: Fuller, John. *The Mountain in the Sea*, Secker and Warburg; Beer, Patricia. *Driving West*. Gollancz; Brock, Edwin. *The Blocked Heart*. Secker and Warburg; Ewart, Gavin. *Be My Guest*. Trigram Press; Scannell, Vernon. *The Loving Game*. Robson.
Uncollected

C430 ARIADNE'S LAMENT (Poem)
The New Statesman, Vol. 90, No. 2336 (26 December 1975), 822.
Uncollected

1976

C431 THE RAISING OF LAZARUS (Poem)
TR, Vol. 1, No. 3 (1976), 39-40.
Uncollected

C432 THE INK THAT WRITES (Poem)
TR, Vol. 1, No. 3 (1976), 41.
Uncollected

C433 WAITING FOR RAIN IN DEVON (Poem)
TR, Vol. 1, No. 3 (1976), 42.
TCOS, CP

C434 TO VENETIA'S SHORES HAVE COME (Poem)
Poetry Australia, XII, Nos. 60/61 (1976), 4-5.
TCOS, CP

C435 SCHUMANN SINGS SCHUBERT (Poem)
Poetry Australia, XII, Nos. 60/61 (1976), 5
TCOS, CP

C436 A DREAM OF HELL (Poem)
Poetry Australia, XII, Nos. 60/61 (1976), 6-7.
Uncollected

C437 NON PIANGERE, LUÌ (Poem)
Poetry Australia, XII, Nos. 60/61 (1976), 7
TCOS, CP

C438 STUDIES OF A GIRL (Poem)
Poetry Nation, No. 5 (1976), 11.
Uncollected

C439 THE DELEGATE (Poem)
Ambit, No. 66 (1976), 2-4.
TCOS, CP

C440 GERTRUDE STEIN AT SNAIL'S BAY (Poem)
Encounter, XLVI, No. 2 (February 1976), 13.
TCOS, CP

C441 TREASURY OF AMBIGUITIES (Prose)
The Observer, 15 February 1976, 27.
Reviews of: Fowler, Alastair. *Catacomb Suburb*. Edinburgh University Press; Mitchell, Adrian. *The Apeman Cometh*. Cape; Day, David. *Brass Rubbings*. Carcanet; David, Dick. *In the Distance*. Anvil Press.
Uncollected

C442 TLS COMMENTARY. BUNYAN'S PROGRESS (Prose)
Times Literary Supplement, No. 3858 (20 February 1976), 194.
Uncollected

C443 UNDER NEW MANAGEMENT (Poem)
The New Review, Vol. 2, No. 24 (March 1976), 54-55.
TCOS, CP

C444 MY OLD CAT DANCES (Poem)
The New Review, Vol. 2, No. 24 (March 1976), 55.
ES, CP

C445 THE BOCCHERINI MUSIC CAMP (Poem)
The New Review, Vol. 2, No. 24 (March 1976), 56.
TCOS, CP

C446 EVENSONG (Poem)
The New Review, Vol. 2, No. 24 (March 1976), 57.
TCOS, CP

C447 THE EASIEST ROOM IN HELL (Poem)
Encounter, XLVI, No. 4 (April 1976), 28.
TCOS, CP

C448 SUNBURNED NEUROSIS? (Prose)
Hemisphere, Vol. 20, No. 4 (April 1976), 14-21.
Uncollected

C449 BREAKING THE TRIBAL BOUNDS (Prose)
The Times Literary Supplement, No. 3865 (9 April 1976), 431-432.
Reviews of: *Poetry Australia. Francis Webb (1925-1973): Commemorative Issue*. South Head Press; Campbell, David. *Deaths and Pretty Cousins*. Australian National University Press; Maloup, David. *Neighbors in a Thicket*. University of Queensland Press; Shapcott, Thomas W. *Shabbytown Calendar*. University of Queensland Press; Roberts, Philip. *Will's Dream*. University of Queensland Press; Hall, Rodney. *Selected Poems*. University of Queensland Press; Gray, Robert. *Creekwater-Journal*. University of Queensland Press.
Uncollected

C450 A WHIFF OF SULPHUR (Prose)
The Observer, 11 April 1976, 32.
Reviews of: Barker, George. *Dialogues Etc*. Faber; Reading, Peter. *The Prison Cell and Barrel Mystery*. Secker and Warburg; Fainlight, Ruth. *Another Full Moon*. Hutchinson; Flynn, Tony. *Separations*. Proem.
Uncollected

C451 THE REPOSE OF THOMAS OTWAY (Poem)
Encounter, XLVI, No. 5 (May 1976), 64.
Uncollected

C452 RADIO. UP NORTH (Prose)
The New Statesman, Vol. 91, No. 2358 (28 May 1976), 725-726.
Uncollected

C453 CAVAFY'S PERMANENT MUSEUM (Prose)
Nation Review, May 28 - June 3, 1976, 812.
Review of: Cavafy, C.P. *Collected Poems*. Hogarth Press.
Uncollected

C454 SHORT MAD POEMS (Poem)
Thames Poetry, Vol. 1, No. 2 (Summer 1976), 1-3.

C455 WHATEVER HAPPENED TO ME? (Poem)
Thames Poetry, Vol. 1, No. 2 (Summer 1976), 4.
Uncollected

C456 THE INNERMOST CHAMBER (Poem)
Thames Poetry, Vol. 1, No. 2 (Summer 1976), 5-6.
Uncollected

C457 THE ORCHID ON THE ROCK (Poem)
Thames Poetry, Vol. 1, No. 2 (Summer 1976), 7.
TCOS, CP

C458 AN ANGEL IN BLYTHBURGH CHURCH (Poem)
Encounter, XLVI, No. 6 (June 1976), 47.
TCOS, CP

C459 THE CORONATION OF POPPEA (Poem)
The New Statesman, Vol. 91, No. 2360 (11 June 1976), 777.
Uncollected

C460 RADIO. TALKIES (Prose)
The New Statesman, Vol. 91, No. 2361 (18 June 1976), 825.
Uncollected

C461 A POET FOR ALL SEASONS (Prose)
The Observer, 4 July 1976, 22.
Reviews of: Hughes, Ted. *Season Songs*. Faber; Mackay Brown, George. *Winterfold*. Chatto; Daryush, Elizabeth. *Collected Poems*. Carcanet; Carson, Ciaran. *The New Estate*. Blackstaff Press; Foley, Michael. *True Life Love Stories*. Blackstaff Press; *Penguin Modern Poets No. 26: Dannie Abse, Michael Longley, D.J. Enright*.
Uncollected

C462 RADIO. TRUST IN US (Prose)
The New Statesman, Vol. 92, No. 2364 (9 July 1976), 58.
Uncollected

C463 RADIO. HOLD THE FORT (Prose)
The New Statesman, Vol. 92, No. 2367 (20 July 1976), 156.
Uncollected

C464 RADIO. KNOT LIKELY (Prose)
The New Statesman, Vol. 92, No. 2370 (20 August 1976), 252-253.
Uncollected

C465 MIRACLES OF METAMORPHOSIS. GUSTAVE MAHLER (Prose)
Encounter, XLVII, No. 2 (August 1976), 55-60.
Reviews of: Holbrook, David. *Gustave Mahler - And the Courage To Be*. Vision Press; Walter, Bruno. *Gustave Mahler*. Severn House; Mitchell, Donald. *Gustave Mahler: The Wunderhorn Years*. Faber & Faber; La Grange, Henry-Louis de. *Mahler: A Biography*. Gollancz.
Uncollected

C466 AWAY FROM THE TROUBLES (Prose)
The Observer, 22 August 1976, 21.
Reviews of: Maxton, Hugh. *The Noise of the Fields*. Dolmen; Longley, Michael. *Man Lying on a Wall*. Gollancz; Silkin, Jon. *The Little Time-Keeper*. MidNag/Carcanet; Guest, Harry. *A House Against the Night*. Anvil; Wells, Gerry. *Obie's War*. Lincolnshire and Humberside Arts; O'Shaughnessy, Patrick. *Poems*. Lincolnshire and Humberside Arts.
Uncollected

C467 RADIO. TSAR DUST (Prose)
The New Statesman, Vol. 92, No. 2374 (16 September 1976), 383-384.
Uncollected

C468 THE COST OF SERIOUSNESS (Poem)
The New Statesman, Vol. 92, No. 2375 (24 September 1976), 426.
TCOS, CP

C469 RADIO. AN ADVENTURE (Prose)
The New Statesman, Vol. 92, No. 2377 (8 October 1976), 489-490.
Uncollected

C470 AT RAMSHOLT (Poem)
The Times Literary Supplement, No. 3891 (8 October 1976), 1279.
TCOS, CP

C471 GUNN METAL (Prose)
The Observer, 17 October 1976, 33.
Review of: Gunn, Thom. *Jack's Straw Castle*. Faber.
Uncollected

C472 LOOKING AT A MELOZZO DA FORLI (Poem)
Outposts, No. 111 (Winter 1976), 6-7.
TCOS, CP

C473 POEM NOT INVOLVING THE INTELLECT (Poem)
Encounter, XLVII, No. 6 (December 1976), 55.
Uncollected

C474 POETRY AND MADNESS (Prose)
Southerly, No. 4 (December 1976), 385-405.
Uncollected

C475 IMPECCABLE BAD TASTE (Prose)
The Observer, 12 December 1976, 27.
Reviews of: Ewart, Gavin. *No Fool Like An Old Fool*. Gollancz; Forrest-Thomson, Veronica. *On the Periphery*. Street Editions; Schwartz, Delmore. *What is to be Given*. Carcanet; Pilinszky, Janos. *Selected Poems*. Translated by Ted Hughes and Janos Czokits, Carcanet.
Uncollected

C476 THE LYING ART (Poem)
The Times Literary Supplement, No. 3901 (17 December 1976), 1575.
TCOS, CP

C477 THE THIRD MAN IN THE BOAT (Poem)
American Scholar, XLVI, No. 1 (Winter 1976-77), 85.
Uncollected

C478 POETS AT LARGE (Prose)
Overland, No. 64 (Winter 1976), 41-46.
Uncollected

1977

C479 TALKING TO YOU AFTERWARDS (Poem)
Poetry Review, Vol. 67, No. 3 (1977), 4-5.
ES, CP

C480 TOWN MOUSE (Prose)
Vole, [No.] 1 (1977), 48.
Uncollected

C481 MYOPIA (Poem)
Poetry Review, Vol. 67, No. 3 (1977), 6-7.
ES, CP

C482 ODES OF AN EASY TALKER (Prose)
The Observer, 23 January 1977, 27.
Reviews of: Maclean, Alasdair. *Walking the Dead*. Gollancz; Sisson, C.H. *Anchises*. Carcanet; Mitchell, Elma. *The Poor Man in the Flesh*. Peterloo Poets; Wright, Edmond Leo. *The Horwich Hennets*. Peterloo Poets.
Uncollected

C483 YOU'RE THE TOP (Prose)
The New Statesman, Vol. 93, No. 2393 (28 January 1977), 126.
Review of: Young, Percy M. *Beethoven: a Victorian Tribute*. Dobson.
Uncollected

C484 MUSIC. REVISED VERSION (Prose)
The New Statesman, Vol. 93, No. 2396 (18 February 1977), 231-232.
Uncollected

C485 JOURNEY INTO ENGLISH (Prose)
The Observer, 27 February 1977, 25.
Reviews of: Morgan, Edwin. *Rites of Passage*. Carcanet; James, John. *Striking the Pavilion of Zero*. Ian McKelvie; Sexton, Anne. *The Awful Rowing Toward God*. Chatto; Nye, Robert. *Divisions of a Ground*. Carcanet.
Uncollected

C486 FREELANCING WITH POETRY (Prose)
The Author, XXXVIII, No. 1 (Spring 1977), 16-19.
Uncollected

C487 FAMILY LIFE - 2. LOCKED OUT OF PARADISE (Prose)
The New Review, Vol. 3, No. 36 (March 1977), 15-20.
Uncollected

C488 CERTAIN ANGUISH (Prose)
The Listener, Vol. 97, No. 2498 (3 March 1977), 272.
Uncollected

C489 ANGELS OVER PECKHAM (Prose)
The Observer, 20 March 1977, 29.
Reviews of: Brock, Edwin. *Here, Now, Always*. Secker and Warburg; Brock, Edwin. *Song of the Battery Hen*. Secker and Warburg; Paulin, Tom. *A State of Justice*. Faber; Carey, Jack. *Woods and Mirrors*. Salamander; Smart, Elizabeth. *A Bonus*. Polytantric Press.
Uncollected

C490 BRAHMS: INTERMEZZO IN E FLAT, OP. 117, No. 1 (Poem)
The New Statesman, Vol. 93, No. 2412 (10 June 1977), 785.
TCOS, CP
Note: This poem and the following three poems appear under the author's collective title "Keyboard Suite."

C491 BEETHOVEN: BAGATELLE IN B. MINOR, OP. 126, No. 4 (Poem)
The New Statesman, Vol. 93, No. 2412 (10 June 1977), 785.
Uncollected

C492 BACH: PRELUDE IN F MINOR, BWV. 881.
The New Statesman, Vol. 93, No. 2412 (10 June 1977), 785.
Uncollected

C493 SCARLATTI: SONATA IN A MAJOR, L238.
The New Statesman, Vol. 93, No. 2412 (10 June 1977), 785.
TCOS, CP

C494 FUNC (Prose)
The New Statesman, Vol. 94, No. 2417 (15 July 1977), 87.
Review of: Durrell, Lawrence. *Sicilian Carousel*. Faber.
Uncollected

C495 ALL THE DIFFERENCE IN THE WORLD (Poem)
The New Statesman, Vol. 94, No. 2420 (5 August 1977), 190.
ES, CP

C496 MEMORABLE SIMPLICITIES (Prose)
The Observer, 21 August 1977, 29.
Reviews of: Abse, Dannie. *Collected Poems*. Hutchinson; Hamburger, Michael. *Real Estate*. Carcanet; Muldoon, Paul. *Mules*. Faber; Downie, Freda. *A Stranger Here*. Secker and Warburg.
Uncollected

C497 IN THE FACT (Prose)
The New Statesman, Vol. 94, No. 2424 (2 September 1977), 309-310.
Review of: *Between Two Worlds: Byron's Letters and Journals*, Vol. 7, edited by Leslie A. Marchand. John Murray.
Uncollected

C498 NEWS FROM SOMEWHERE (Prose)
The Observer, 4 September 1977, 24.
Reviews of: Redgrove, Peter. *From Every Chink of the Ark*. Routledge; Blackburn, Thomas. *Post Mortem*. Rondo; Mole, John. *Our Ship*. Secker and Warburg.
Uncollected

C499 WHAT'S BECOME OF BROWNING (Prose)
The Observer, 2 October 1977, 26.
Reviews of: Ashbery, John. *Self-Portrait in a Convex Mirror*. Carcanet; Hecht, Anthony. *Millions of Strange Shadows*. Oxford; Wilbur, Richard. *The Mind-Reader*. Faber; Bishop, Elizabeth. *Geography III* . Chatto.
Uncollected

C500 THE PAINTER'S BANQUET (Poem)
Encounter, XLIX, No. 5 (November 1977), 23.
TCOS, CP, N

C501 POEM WAITING TO BE TRANSLATED (Poem)
The New Statesman, Vol. 94, No. 2433 (4 November 1977), 635.
TCOS, CP

C502 A FORTIES SURVIVOR (Prose)
The Observer, 18 December 1977, 24.
Reviews of: Graham, W.S. *Implements in Their Places*. Faber; Davie, Donald. *In the Stopping Train*. Carcanet; Elliot, Alistair. *Contentions*. Ceolfrith Press; Smith, Iain Crichton. *In the Middle*. Gollancz.
Uncollected

C503 BOOKS OF THE YEAR (Prose)
The Observer, 18 December 1977, 21.
Uncollected

C504 OBSERVER CONTRIBUTORS MAKE THEIR ANNUAL CHOICE
The Observer, 18 December 1977, 21.
Uncollected

1978

C505 SCRAMBLED MESSAGE (Prose)
The Observer, 15 January 1978, 28.
Reviews of: Holub, Miroslav. *Notes of a Clay Pigeon.* Secker and Warburg; Wright, Kit. *The Bear Looked Over the Mountain.* Salamander; Harsent, David. *Dreams of the Dean*, Oxford.
Uncollected

C506 ARTS & ENTERTAINMENT. REMEMBERS ME BACK (Prose)
The New Statesman, Vol. 95, No. 2444 (20 January 1978) 87-88.
Uncollected

C507 FURIOSO (Prose)
The New Statesman, Vol. 95, No. 2445 (27 January 1978), 121-122.
Review of: Keller, Hans. *1975.* Dobson.
Uncollected

C508 AUDEN'S CORNUCOPIA. THE 1930's TEXTS (Prose)
Encounter, L, No. 2 (February 1978), 64-70.
Review of: *The English Auden: Poems, Essays and Dramatic Writings, 1927-1939.* Edited by Edward Mendelson. Faber.
Uncollected

C509 VISITING CORNISH CHURCHES (Poem)
Encounter, L, No. 2 (February 1978), 85.
ES, CP

C510 RADIO. BRAGGADOCIO (Prose)
The New Statesman, Vol. 95, No. 2447 (10 February 1978), 195-196.
Uncollected

C511 RHYME AND UNREASON (Prose)
The Observer, 12 February 1978, 26.
Reviews of: *English and American Surrealist Poetry.* Ed. by Edward B. Germain. Penguin; Ewart, Gavin. *Or Where a Young Penguin Lies Screaming.* Gollancz; Evans, Stuart. *The Function of the Fool.* Hutchinson; Cleary, A.A. *Men Homeward.* Ceolfrith Press.
Uncollected

C512 RADIO. BOWS AND ARROWS (Prose)
The New Statesman, Vol. 95, No. 2449 (24 February 1978) 266-267.
Uncollected

C513 PETER PORTER WRITES . . . (Prose)
The Poetry Book Society Bulletin, No. 96 (Spring 1978), 1.
Uncollected

C514 THE CHARNEL HOUSE, ST. LEONARD'S, HYTHE (Poem)
Encounter, L. No. 3 (March 1978), 32.
TCOS, CP

C515 THE PISAN CAGE (Prose)
The New Statesman, Vol. 95, No. 2452 (17 March 1978) 368-370.
Review of: *Ezra Pount and Music*. Edited by R. Murray Schafer. Faber.
Uncollected

C516 ARTS & ENTERTAINMENT. BRINGING THE HOUSE DOWN (Prose)
The New Statesman, Vol. 95, No. 2458 (28 April 1978), 575.
Uncollected

C517 FEELINGS IN A LANDSCAPE (Prose)
The Observer, 7 May 1978, 33.
Reviews of: Alvarez, A. *Autumn to Autumn*. Macmillan; Hope, A.D. *A Late Picking*. Angus and Robertson; Wright, Judith. *Alive*. Angus and Robertson; Wright, Judith. *Fourth Quarter*. Angus and Robertson.
Uncollected

C518 RADIO. BETTER PRICTURES (Prose)
The New Statesman, Vol. 95, No. 2461 (19 May 1978), 687-688.
Uncollected

C519 THE EARL AT SPELSBURY (Poem)
Thames Poetry, Vol. 1, No. 5 (June 1978), 26.
Uncollected

C520 SESTINA WITH HOLES (Poem)
Thames Poetry, Vol. 1, No. 5 (June 1978), 27-28.
Uncollected

C521 SONNET AFTER READING MALLARME (Poem)
Thames Poetry, Vol. 1, No. 5 (June 1978), 30.
Uncollected

C522 THE ARTS. A LATE DEVELOPER IN POETRY . . . PETER PORTER SUMS UP (Prose)
Eastern Times, Vol. 1, No. 18 (8 June 1978), 36.
Uncollected

C523 RADIO. SOUND AND FURY (Prose)
The New Statesman, Vol. 95, No. 2465 (16 June 1978), 825-826.
Uncollected

C524 THE METAPHOR MEN (Prose)
The Observer, 25 June 1978, 26.
Reviews of: Raine, Craig. *The Onion, Memory*. Oxford; Enright, D.J. *Paradise Illustrated*. Chatto and Windus; MacBeth, George. *Buying a Heart*. Omphalos Press; Thomas, D.M. *The Honeymoon Voyage*. Secker and Warburg.
Uncollected

C525 RADIO. PSYCHOPOMP (Prose)
The New Statesman, Vol. 96, No. 2468 (7 July 1978), 29-30.
Uncollected

C526 OCCAM'S RAZOR (Poem)
The New Statesman, Vol. 96, No. 2470 (21 July 1978), 99.
ES, CP

C527 RADIO. THE OLD GUARD (Prose)
The New Statesman, Vol. 96, No. 2471 (28 July 1978), 132.
Uncollected

C528 END OF AFFAIR (Poem)
The Honest Ulsterman, No. 60 (Jul/Oct 1978), 24-25.
Uncollected

C529 ALCESTIS AND THE POET (Poem)
The Honest Ulsterman, No. 60 (Jul/Oct 1978), 25-26.
ES, CP

C530 GARLANDS OF ERUDITION. ON CRITICS, WORDS & OPERA (Prose)
Encounter, LI, No. 2 (August, 1978), 75-79.
Reviews of: Schmidgall, Gary. *Literature as Opera*. Oxford University Press; Conrad, Peter. *Romantic Opera and Literary Form*. University of California Press; Swanston, Hamish F.G. *In Defence of Opera*. Penguin
Uncollected

C531 SONATA FORM: THE AUSTRALIAN MAGPIE (Poem)
Vole, No. 11 (August 1978), 41.
ES, CP

C532 ABOUT THE NEW (Poem)
The New Statesman, Vol. 96, No. 2472 (4 August 1978), 162.
ES, CP

C533 RADIO. THE INSIDER (Prose)
The New Statesman, Vol. 96, No. 2474 (18 August 1978), 221-222.
Uncollected

C534 CAPULETS AND MONTAGUS (Poem)
The New Statesman, Vol. 96, No. 2475 (25 August 1978), 244.
Uncollected

C535 EIGHTEENTH CENTURY ECHOES (Prose)
The Observer, (3 September 1978), 26.
Reviews of: Fenton, James. *A Vacant Possession*. TNR Publications; Falck, Colin. *In This Dark Light*. TNR Publications; Tomlinson, Charles. *The Shaft*. Oxford; Holbrook, David. *Chance of a Lifetime*. Anvil Press.
Uncollected

C536 THE KING TIMER (Prose)
The New Statesman, Vol. 96, No. 2477 (8 September 1978), 301-302.
Review of: Marchand, Leslie A. *Born for Opposition: Byron's Letters and Journals*. Vol. VIII. John Murray.
Uncollected

C537 AT THE ADMISSION CENTRE (Poem)
The New Statesman, Vol. 96, No. 2477 (8 September 1978), 304.
Uncollected

C538 RADIO. SALVAGE (Prose)
The New Statesman, Vol. 96, No. 2478 (15 September 1978), 343.
Uncollected

C539 MUSIC AND METAPHOR (Prose)
The Times Literary Supplement, No. 3989 (15 September 1978), 1008.
Review of: Alldritt, Keith. *Eliot's Four Quartets. Poetry as Chamber Music*. Woburn Press.
Uncollected

C540 GRIMM FOR GROWN-UPS (Prose)
The Times Literary Supplement, No. 3989 (15 September 1978), 1016.
Uncollected

C541 RADIO. SCRAPS (Prose)
The New Statesman, Vol. 96, No. 2480 (29 September 1978), 420.
Uncollected

C542 POETRY (Prose)
Encounter, LI, No. 4 (October 1978), 30, 32, 34.
Uncollected

C543 HOW IMPORTANT IS SEX? (Poem)
Encounter, LI, No. 4 (October 1978), 81.
ES, CP

C544 JUDGMENT OF THE BIRDS
The Observer, 1 October 1978, 34.
Review of: Hughes, Ted. *Cave Birds*. Faber.

C545 RADIO. PRIZE BORES (Prose)
The New Statesman, Vol. 96, No. 2481 (8 October 1978), 450-451.
Uncollected

C546 RADIO. ANY OLD IRONY (Prose)
The New Statesman, Vol. 96, No. 2484 (27 October 1978), 558-559.
Uncollected

C547 THE STORY OF JASON (Poem)
Encounter, LI, No. 5 (November 1978), [27].
ES, CP

C548 THE GOD OF PHILOSOPHERS (Poem)
The New Statesman, Vol. 96, No. 2487 (17 November 1978), 674.
Uncollected

C549 SIGNS OF GREATNESS (Prose)
The Observer, 19 November 1978, 39.
Reviews of: Hill, Geoffrey. *Tenebrae*. Deutsch; Grigson, Geoffrey. *The Fiesta*. Secker & Warburg; Kinnell, Galway. *The Book of Nightmares*, Omphalos & JJ Publications; Ackroyd, Peter. *Country Life*. Ferry Press.
Uncollected

C550 ARTS & ENTERTAINMENT. NEW WAVES (Prose)
The New Statesman, Vol. 96, No. 2488 (24 November 1978), 714
Uncollected

C551 A STATEMENT (Poem)
Encounter, LI, No. 6 (December 1978), 19.
Uncollected

C552 RETURNING (Poem)
The New Statesman, Vol. 96, No. 2491 (15 December 1978), 832.
ES, CP

C553 BOOKS OF THE YEAR (Prose)
The Observer, 17 December 1978, 36.
Uncollected

C554 THOSE STAY MOST HAUNTING (Prose)
The New Statesman, Vol. 96, No. 2492/2493 (22/29 December 1978), 880-881.
Review of: Gardner, Philip and Averil. *The God Approached: a Commentary on the Poems of William Empson.* Chatto.
Uncollected

1979

C555 A DOZEN DOZENS (Poem)
Ambit, No. 78 (1979), 2-5.
Uncollected

C556 RADIO. SEEING STARS (Prose)
The New Statesman, Vol. 97, No. 2494 (5 January 1979), 22-23.
Uncollected

C557 CONFLICTING LOYALTIES (Prose)
The Observer, 7 January 1979, 34.
Reviews of: Fisher, Roy. *The Thing About Joe Sullivan.* Carcanet; Harrison, Tony. *The School of Eloquence.* Rex Collings; Ewart, Gavin. *All My Little Ones.* Anvil Press.
Uncollected

C558 A BOXFUL OF MODERN MASTERS (Prose)
The Observer, 28 January 1979, 35.
Review of: *The Poet's Voice.* Selected and edited by Stratis Haviaras. Faber.
Uncollected

C559 THE BOMB WILL NOT DROP (Poem)
The Honest Ulsterman, No. 61 (Jan/Feb 1979), 20-21.
Uncollected

C560 HOMAGE TO WILLIAM SOUTAR (Poem)
Poetry Australia, No. 69 (February 1979), 4.
Uncollected

C561 RADIO. NIGHT LINE (Prose)
The New Statesman, Vol. 97, No. 2498 (2 February 1979), 162-163.
Uncollected

C562 ITALIAN PEAR AND ENGLISH OAK (Prose)
The Observer, 18 February 1979, 37.
Reviews of: Wright, James. *To a Blossoming Pear Tree*. Faber with Farrar, Strauss & Giroux; Stallworthy, Jon. *A Familiar Tree*, Chatto & Oxford; Motion, Andrew. *The Pleasure Steamers*. Carcanet; Vince, Michael. *The Orchard Well*. Carcanet.
Uncollected

C563 RADIO. FEUDS CORNER (Prose)
The New Statesman, Vol. 97, No. 2501 (23 February 1979), 262.
Uncollected

C564 BOOKS (Prose)
Tempo. A Quarterly Review of Modern Music, No. 128 (March 1979), [24]-26.
Review of: Mitchell, Donald and John Evans. *Benjamin Britten: Pictures from a Life*. Faber.
Uncollected

C565 RADIO. TEQUILA TIME (Prose)
The New Statesman, Vol. 97, No. 2504 (14 March 1979), 371-372.
Uncollected

C566 THE ARBITRARY ABROLHOS (Poem)
Poetry Australia, XV, No. 70 (April 1979), 21.
Uncollected

C567 NIGHTS AT THE OPERA (Poem)
Poetry Australia, XV, No. 70 (April 1979), 22-23.
ES, CP

C568 FAREWELL TO THE MUSE (Prose)
The Observer, 1 April 1979, 38.
Reviews of: Tiller, Terence. *That Singing Mesh*. Chatto and Windus; Dunn, Douglas. *Barbarians*. Faber; Wainwright, Jeffrey. *Heart's Desire*. Carcanet; Tranter, John. *Crying in Early Infancy*. Makar Press.
Uncollected

C569 FELINE FINE (Prose)
Vole, Vol. 2, No. 7 (12 April 1979), 46-47.
Review of: MacBeth, George and Martin Booth, eds. *The Book of Cats*. Penguin.
Uncollected

C570 RADIO. TALKING UP (Prose)
The New Statesman, Vol. 97, No. 2510 (27 April 1979), 612-613.
Uncollected

C571 COUNTRY POETRY AND TOWN POETRY: A DEBATE WITH LES MURRAY (Prose)
Australian Literary Studies, Vol. 9, No. 1 (May 1979), 39.
Uncollected

C572 THE EMBATTLED STATE (Prose)
The New Statesman, Vol. 97, No. 2511 (4 May 1979), 650-651.
Review of: Stravinsky, Vera and Robert Craft. *Stravinsky in Pictures and Documents*. Hutchinson.
Uncollected

C573 THE ENGLISH VICE (Poem)
The New Statesman, Vol. 97, No. 2511 (4 May 1979), 653.
Uncollected

C574 POPE'S CARNATIONS KNEW HIM (Poem)
The New Statesman, Vol. 97, No. 2512 (11 May 1979), 692.
ES, CP

C575 THE SENSE OF AN ENDING (Prose)
The Observer, 20 May 1979, 36.
Reviews of: *Collected Poems by Allen Tate, 1919-1976*. Faber. Winters, Yvor. *Collected Poems*. Carcanet; Prince, F.T. *Collected Poems*. Anvil Press; *Collected Poems by Vasko Popa 1943-1976*. Carcanet.
Uncollected

C576 RADIO. BUGGED (Prose)
The New Statesman, Vol. 97, No. 2514 (25 May 1979), 765.
Uncollected

C577 WHY I WON'T WRITE AN AUTOBIOGRAPHY (Poem)
Argo, Vol. 1, No. 1 (Summer 1979), 28-29.
Uncollected

C578 ODE TO THE SCHOLARS (Poem)
Argo, Vol. 1, No. 1 (Summer 1979), 29.
Uncollected

C579 ABOUT ON THE SERCHIO (Poem)
The New Statesman, Vol. 97, No. 2517 (15 June 1979), 881.
ES, CP

C580 RADIO. A GOLDEN AGE? (Prose)
The New Statesman, Vol. 97, No. 2518 (22 June 1979), 928.
Uncollected

C581 AT LAKE MASSACIUCCOLI (Poem)
Encounter, LIII, No. 1 (July 1979), [30-31].
ES, CP

C582 GARDEN OF EARTHLY DELIGHTS (Poem)
Thames Poetry, Vol. 1, No. 7 (July 1979), 59-60.
ES, CP

C583 TWO-TONED GODS (Poem)
Thames Poetry, Vol. 1, No. 7 (July 1979), 61.
Uncollected

C584 A NOTE ADDED TO BERRYMAN (Poem)
Thames Poetry, Vol. 1, No. 7 (July 1979), 62-63.
Uncollected

C585 WEDDING ANNIVERSARY (Poem)
Thames Poetry, Vol. 1, No. 7 (July 1979), 64.
Uncollected

C586 LANDSCAPE WITH POEMS (Prose)
The Observer, 15 July 1979, 37.
Review of: Hughes, Ted. *Remains of Elmet*. Faber.
Uncollected

C587 RADIO. WORDPLAY (Prose)
The New Statesman, Vol. 98, No. 2522 (20 July 1979), 106.
Uncollected

C588 TRANSFORMATION (Prose)
The Observer, 19 August 1979, 37.
Reviews of: Reid, Christopher. *Arcadia*. Oxford; Szirtes, George. *The Slant Door*. Secker & Warburg; Conn, Stewart. *Under the Ice*. Hutchinson; Lowbury, Edward. *Selected Poems*. Celtion.
Uncollected

C589 RADIO. ECHT (Prose)
The New Statesman, Vol. 98, No. 2527 (24 August 1979), 280.
Uncollected

C590 HOME THOUGHTS (Prose)
The New Statesman, Vol. 98, No. 2529 (7 September 1979), 346.
Review of: Marchand, Leslie A., ed. *In the Wind's Eye: Byron's Letters and Journals*. Vol. 9. John Murray.
Uncollected

C591 STUFF THAT DREAMS ARE MADE OF (Prose)
The Observer, 9 September 1979, 37.
Reviews of: Redgrove, Peter. *The Weddings at Nether Powers*. Routledge; Brock, Edwin. *The River and the Train*. Secker; Adcock, Fleur. *The Inner Harbour*. OUP.
Uncollected

C592 THE LONDON POETRY SCENE. THE PERFORMING ARTS (Prose)
What's on in London, 28 September 1979, 46-47.
Uncollected

C593 THE WERTHER LEVEL (Poem)
Encounter, LIII, No. 4 (October 1979), [89].
ES, CP

C594 ARTS & ENTERTAINMENT. RENAISSANCE RADIO (Prose)
The New Statesman, Vol. 98, No. 2533 (5 October 1979), 521.
Uncollected

C595 LIP SERVICE (Poem)
The New Statesman, Vol. 98, No. 2534 (12 October 1979), 560.
ES, CP

C596 A SOVIET ARTIST'S REPLY TO UNJUST CRITICISM. PETER PORTER REVIEWS THE SHOSTAKOVICH MEMOIRS (Prose)
The Guardian, 25 October 1979, [11].
Review of: *Testimony: the Memoirs of Dmitri Shostakovich*. ed. by Solomon Volkov. Hamish Hamilton.
Uncollected

C597 THE FUTURE (Poem)
The New Statesman, Vol. 98, No. 2536 (26 October 1979), 644.
ES, CP

C598 FOR SOPHONISBA ANGUISCIOLA (Poem)
The New Statesman, Vol. 98, No. 2637 (2 November 1979), 682.
ES, CP

C599 IN THE GRAND STYLE (Prose)
The Observer, 4 November 1979, 40.
Reviews of: Heaney, Seamus. *Field Work*. Faber; Joseph, Jenny. *The Thinking Heart*. Secker & Warburg; Morgan, Pete. *The Spring Collection*. Secker & Warburg.
Uncollected

C600 MUSIC. SUPREME CIRCLE (Prose)
The New Statesman, Vol. 98, No. 2540 (23 November 1979), 822.
Review of: *The Operas of Benjamin Britten*. Edited by David Herbert. Hamish Hamilton
Uncollected

C601 BOOKS OF THE YEAR (Prose)
The Observer, 9 December 1979, 35.
Uncollected

C602 MORE GENIUS THAN TALENT (Prose)
The Observer, 16 December 1979, 38.
Reviews of: Ashbery, John. *Houseboat Days*. Penguin; Leale, B.C. *Preludes*. Caligula Books; Williams, Hugo. *Love Life*. Whizzard Press; Seifert, Jaroslav. *The Plague Column*. Trans. by Ewald Osers. Terra Nova.
Uncollected

1980

C603 LAST POEM TO MY WIFE (Poem)
Ambit, No. 82 (1980), [2]-3.
Uncollected

C604 THE KILLING GROUND (Poem)
Ambit, No. 82 (1980), 3-4.
ES, CP

C605 THE UNLUCKY CHRIST (Poem)
Encounter, LIV, No. 1 (January 1980), [47].
ES, CP

C606 BEI EINER TRAUUNG (Poem)
The Times Literary Supplement, No. 4006 (4 January 1980), 13.
ES, CP

C607 THE WORLD UPSIDE DOWN (Prose)
The Observer, 6 January 1980, 36.
Reviews of: Raine, Craig. *A Martian Sends a Postcard Home*. Oxford; Fuller, John. *Lies and Secrets*. Secker and Warburg; Butlin, Ronald. *Creatures Tamed by Cruelty*. Edinburgh University S.P.B.
Uncollected

C608 PIENZA SEEN BY PRUDES (Poem)
The Times Literary Supplement, No. 4009 (25 January 1980), 79
ES, CP

C609 VOICES FROM ULSTER (Prose)
The Observer, 27 January 1980, 39
Reviews of: Mahon, Derek. *Poems 1962-1978*. Oxford; Longley, Michael. *The Echo Gate*. Secker & Warburg;

Hughes, Ted. *Moortown*. Faber; Bartlett, Elizabeth. *A Lifetime of Dying*. Peterloo Poets.
Uncollected

C610 LANDSCAPE WITH ORPHEUS (Poem)
The Bulletin, 29 January 1980, 179.
ES, CP

C611 A BOTTOM OF SENSE (Prose)
Quarto, No. 3 (February 1980), 15.
Review of: Graves, Richard Perceval. *A.E. Hausmann, the Scholar-Poet*. Routledge & Kegan Paul.
Uncollected

C612 AN EASY ESSAY (Poem)
The Times Literary Supplement, No. 4014 (29 February 1980), 245.
Uncollected

C613 SYMPOSIUM: ON REVIEWING (Prose)
New Edinburgh Review, No. 49 (February 1980), 8.
Uncollected

C614 A LITANY (ST. CECILIA'S DAY, 1979) (Poem)
New Edinburgh Review, No. 49 (February 1980), 24.
Uncollected

C615 LES ARRETS DE LA VIE (Poem)
New Edinburgh Review, No. 49 (February 1980), 24.
Uncollected

C616 AN AMERICAN IN VENICE (Prose)
The Observer, 23 March 1980, 39.
Reviews of: Hecht, Anthony. *The Venetian Vespers*. Oxford; Middleton, Christopher. *Carminalenia*. Carcanet; *The Poems of Drummond Allison*. Ed. by Michael Sharp. Whiteknights Press.
Uncollected

C617 COUNTING BLESSINGS (Prose)
Quarto, No. 6 (May 1980), 7.
Reviews of: Matthews, David. *Michael Tippett: an Introductory Study*. Faber; White, Eric Walter. *Tippett and his Operas*. Barrie & Jenkins; *A Verdi Companion*. Edited by William Weaver & Martin Chusid. Gollancz.
Uncollected

C618 THE SHAPE OF MUSIC AND THE SHAPE OF POETRY (Prose)
Quadrant, No. 154, XXXIV, No. 6 (June 1980), 4-12.

C619 LIFE IN THE MUSEUM (Prose)
The Observer, 8 June 1980, 29.
Reviews of: Jones, Brian. *The Island Normal*. Carcanet; Paulin, Tom. *The Strange Museum*, Faber; Scupham, Peter. *Summer Palaces*, Oxford; Whitworth, John. *Unhistorical Fragments*, Secker and Warburg.
Uncollected

C620 THE JEWS IN THE ICE (Poem)
DAM (Netherlands) Poetry International Documents, Vol. 1, No. 1 (Summer 1980), 96.
Note: Translation of a poem from the Yiddish by Abraham Sutzkever.
Uncollected

C621 BETRAYAL (Poem)
The Literary Review, No. 19 (27th June-10th July 1980), 41.
Uncollected

C622 NOTHING BUT THE BEST
The Observer, 27 July 1980, 29.
Reviews of Beer, Patricia. *Selected Poems*. Hutchinson; Scannell, Vernon. *New and Collected*. Robson Books; Ross, Alan. *Death Valley*. London Mag. Books; Keene, Dennis. *Surviving*. Carcanet. *W.S. Graham: Collected Poems 1942-1977*. Faber.
Uncollected

C623 THE PUBLIC DOMAIN (Poem)
Hibernia Weekly, Vol. 44, No. 31 (31 July 1980), 22.
Uncollected

C624 THE LIGHT FANTASTIC (Prose)
The Observer, 24 August 1980, 27.
Reviews of: Lerner, Laurence. *The Man I Killed*. Secker and Warburg; MacBeth, George. *Poems of Love and Death*. Secker and Warburg; Birtwhistle, John. *Tidal Modes*. Anvil Press; Shepherd, W.G. *Evidences*. Anvil Press; McMillan, Ian. *The Changing Problem*. Carcanet.
Uncollected

C625 ABOUT SUCCESS (Poem)
Encounter, LV, Nos. 2-3 (August/September 1980), 87.
Uncollected

C626 THE AMERICAN ARTICULATE (Poem)
Quarto, No. 10 (September 1980), 7.
ES, CP

C627 THE NEED FOR FOREPLAY (Poem)
Quarto, No. 10 (September 1980), 16.
ES, CP

C628 IN THE SPIRIT OF BROWNING (Prose)
The Observer, 19 October 1980, 29.
Reviews of: Thwaite, Anthony. *Victorian Voices*. Oxford; Muldoon, Paul. *Why Brownlee Left*. Faber; Jay, Peter. *Shifting Frontiers*. Carcanet; Simmons, James. *Constantly Singing*. Blackstaff Press.
Uncollected

C629 THE MISSIONARY POSITION (Poem)
The Times Literary Supplement, No. 4049 (7 November 1980), 1248.
Uncollected

C630 THE WINTER CAPITAL (Poem)
Encounter, LV, No. 6 (December 1980), 30.
ES, CP

C631 A ROUND OF APPLAUSE (Prose)
Quarto, No. 13 (December 1980), 18.
Reviews of: *The Letters of John Wilmot the Earl of Rochester*. Edited by Jeremy Treglown. Blackwell. *The Letters of Claudio Monteverdi*. Edited by Denis Stevens. Faber.
Uncollected

C632 BOOKS OF THE YEAR (Prose)
The Observer, 7 December 1980, 27.
Uncollected

C633 SATIRE WITH A HEART (Prose)
The Observer, 14 December 1980, 28.
Reviews of: Brownjohn, Alan. *A Night in the Gazebo*. Secker and Warburg; Shuttle, Penelope. *The Orchard Upstairs*. Oxford; Brodsky, Joseph. *A Part of Speech*. Oxford
Uncollected

1981

C634 ENGLISH SUBTITLES (Poem)
Encounter, LVI, No. 1 (January 1981), [42].
ES, CP

C635 CLEANING THE PICTURE AT THE EDGES (Poem)
The Times Literary Supplement, No. 4057 (2 January 1981), 15.
Uncollected

C636 MEMORIES OF GRIEF AND GUILT (Prose)
The Observer, 18 January 1981, 31.
Reviews of: Fenton, James. *A German Requiem*. Salamander; Lucas, John and Allan Rodway. *Continuities*. Byron Press; Fuller, John. *The Illusionists*. Secker and Warburg.
Uncollected

C637 STRAINS OF COLLABORATION (Prose)
The Observer, 1 February 1981, 28.
Review of: Mitchell, Donald. *Britten and Auden in the Thirties*. Faber.
Uncollected

C638 THE MUSE IN THE NORTH EAST (Prose)
The Observer, 15 March 1981, 33.
Reviews of: *Ten North East Poets*. Neil Astley, ed. Bloodaxe Books; Constantine, David. *A Brightness to Cast Shadows*. Bloodaxe Books; Flynn, Tony. *A Strange Routine*. Bloodaxe Books; Mayer, Gerda. *Monkey on the Analyst's Couch*. Coelfrith Press; Feaver, Vicki. *Close Relatives*. Secker and Warburg; Rumens, Carol. *Unplayed Music*. Secker and Warburg.
Uncollected

C639 POEM EMPLOYING WORDS FROM AN ARTICLE ON COMBAT STRATEGY (Poem)
Scripsi, Vol. 1, No. 2 (Spring 1981), 2.
Uncollected

C640 THE GREATEST POVERTY IS NOT TO LIVE IN A PHYSICAL WORLD (Poem)
Scripsi, Vol. 1, No. 2 (Spring 1981), 3.
Uncollected

C641 RETROSPECTIVE JEALOUSY. DAS IST EIN FALL NON ANDRER ART (Poem)
Scripsi, Vol. 1, No. 2 (Spring 1981), 4-5.
Uncollected

C642 COMEDY LIES (Poem)
Scripsi, Vol. 1, No. 2 (Spring 1981), 6.
Uncollected

C643 TO HIMSELF. A WORKING FROM LEOPARDI (Poem)
Scripsi, Vol. 1, No. 2 (Spring 1981), 7.
Uncollected

C644 A COLONIAL AT COVENT GARDEN (Prose)
The Times Literary Supplement, No. 4070 (3 April 1981), 368.
Review of: *Nellie Melba: Melodies and Memories*. With introduction and notes by John Cargher. Hamish Hamilton.
Uncollected

C645 VENETIAN INCIDENT (Poem)
Encounter, LVI, No. 5 (May 1981), 50-51.
Uncollected

C646 CANZONE (Poem)
New Edinburgh Review, No. 54 (May 1981), 14.

C647 IL PALAZZO DI PARANOIA (Poem)
The Times Literary Supplement, No. 4076 (15 May 1981), 538.
Uncollected

C648 THE MUSE IN THE OUTBACK (Prose)
The Observer, 17 May 1981, 29.
Reviews of: Murray, Les. A. *The Boys Who Stole the Funeral*. Angus & Robertson; Malouf, David. *First Things Last*. Chatto & Windus; Wallace-Crabbe, Chris. *The Emotions Are Not Skilled Workers*. Angus & Robertson.
Uncollected

C649 MOUNTING A CLASSIC (Prose)
The Times Literary Supplement, No. 4078 (29 May 1981), 603.
Review of: *The Satyricon* (Phoenix Theatre).
Uncollected

C650 THE DESIRE TO DISPLEASE (Prose)
The Observer, 31 May 1981, 29.
Reviews of: Ashbery, John. *As We Know*. Carcanet; Schuyler, James. *The Morning of the Poem*. Faber/Farrar, Strauss; Simpson, Louis. *Caviare at the Funeral*. Oxford.
Uncollected

C651 ACTION PAST (Prose)
The New Statesman, Vol. 101, No. 2620 (5 June 1981), 22-23.
Review of: Marchand, Leslie, ed. *"For Freedom's Battle": Byron's Letters and Journals*, Vol. 11. John Murray
Uncollected

C652 ALL IN THE SAME DISASTER-PRONE BOAT (Prose)
The Observer, 28 June 1981, 33.
Reviews of: Magnus-Enzensberger, Hans. *The Sinking of the Titanic*. Carcanet; Lomas, Herbert. *Public Footpath*. Anvil Press; Mahon, Derek. *Courtyards in Delft*. Gallery Press; Raine, Craig. *A Free Translation*. Salamander Press.
Uncollected

C653 THE LAUREATE OF AMBIGUITY (Prose)
The Times Literary Supplement, No. 4083 (3 July 1981), 745-746.
Review of: Carpenter, Humphrey. *W.H. Auden: a Biography*. Allen and Unwin.
Uncollected

C654 MYFANWY PIPER REMEMBERS BENJAMIN BRITTEN. INTERVIEW AND INTRODUCTION (Prose)
Quarto, No. 20 (August 1981), 17-19.
Uncollected

C655 HARKING BACK TO NATURE (Prose)
The Observer, 2 August 1981, 25.
Reviews of: Tomlinson, Charles. *The Flood*. Oxford; Nicholson, Norman. *Sea to the West*. Faber; Abse, Dannie. *Way Out in the Centre*. Hutchinson; Brackenbury, Alison. *Dreams of Power*. Carcanet.
Uncollected

C656 UNFINISHED REQUIEMS (Poem)
The New Statesman, Vol. 102, No. 2631 (21 August 1981), 23.
Uncollected

C657 SANTA CECILIA IN TRASTEVERE (Poem)
London Magazine, New Series, Vol. 21, Nos. 5 & 6 (August/September 1981), 80-81.
Uncollected

C658 ABOUT FAILURE (Poem)
London Magazine, New Series, Vol. 21, Nos. 5 & 6 (August/September 1981), 81-83.
Uncollected

C659 PETER REDGROVE - A BRIEF MEMOIR (Prose)
Poetry Review, Vol. 71, No. 2/3 (September 1981), 9-14.
Uncollected

C660 CRITICAL GIANT (Prose)
The New Statesman, Vol. 102, No. 2635 (18 September 1981), 26-27.
Review of: Shaw, George Bernard. *Shaw's Music*. Bodley Head.
Uncollected

C661 THRENODY FOR A LOST HOMELAND (Prose)
The Observer, 20 September 1981, 27.
Reviews of: Dunn, Douglas. *St. Kilda's Parliament*. Faber; Fraser, G.S. *Collected Poems*. Leicester University Press; Davie, Donald. *Three for Water-Music*. Carcanet.
Uncollected

C662 AFTER THE LECTURE (Poem)
The Times Literary Supplement, No. 4101 (6 November 1981), 1295.
Uncollected

C663 LAUNDROMAT LYRICS (Prose)
The Observer, 22 November 1981, 27.
Reviews of: Redgrove, Peter. *The Apple-Broadcast*. Routledge; *Poetry Review: Peter Redgrove Special Issue*. Poetry Society; Fisher, Roy. *Poems 1955-1980*. Oxford; Thomas, D. M. *Dreaming in Bronze*. Secker and Warburg; Downie, Freda. *Plainsong*. Secker and Warburg.
Uncollected

C664 THE ORPHEUS AVENUE (Poem)
The Honest Ulsterman, No. 70 (Nov./Dec. 1981), 49-50.
Uncollected

C665 ANOTHER MANNERIST ARRIVES (Poem)
The Honest Ulsterman, No. 70 (Nov./Dec. 1981), 50.
Uncollected

C666 MARIANNE NORTH'S SUBMISSION (Poem)
Encounter, LVII, No. 6 (December 1981), [85].
Uncollected

C667 BOOKS OF THE YEAR (Prose)
The Observer, 6 December 1981, 25.
Uncollected

C668 THE POET AS STORYTELLER (Prose)
The Observer, 20 December 1981, 21.
Reviews of: Browning, Robert. *Poems*. Ed. by John Pettigrew and Thomas J. Collins. Penguin; *The Ring and the Book*. Ed. by Richard Altick. Penguin.
Uncollected

1982

C669 LES MURRAY: AN APPRECIATION (Prose)
The Journal of Commonwealth Literature, XVIII, No. 1 (1982) 45–52.
Uncollected

C670 CYPRUS, AESCHULUS, INANITION (Poem)
Ambit, No. 90 (1982), 14-15.
Uncollected

C671 THE PROFESSION OF A JUSTIFIED SINNER (Poem)
Ambit, No. 90 (1982), 15-16.
Uncollected

C672 THE MAN IN THE LUNCHEON-MEAT HAT (Poem)
Ambit, No. 90 (1982), 16-17.
Uncollected

C673 LITTLE HARMONIC LABYRINTH (Poem)
Poetry London/Apple Magazine, No. 2 (1982), 40-41.
Uncollected

C674 PREPAREDNESS IS ALL (Poem)
Poetry London/Apple Magazine, No. 2 (1982), 41.
Uncollected

C675 OLD AND ILL AND TERRIFIED AND TIGHT (Poem)
Poetry London/Apple Magazine, No. 2 (1982), 42.
Uncollected

C676 THE LATINIST OF LEEDS (Prose)
The Observer, 17 January 1982, 31.
Reviews of: Harrison, Tony. *Continuous*. Rex Colling; Harrison, Tony. *A Kumquat for John Keats*. Bloodaxe Books; Harrison, Tony. *U.S. Martial*. Bloodaxe Books; *The Oresteia of Aeschylus*. Trans. by Tony Harrison. Rex Collings.
Uncollected

C677 STUDENT CANTEEN (Poem)
Encounter, LVIII, No. 2 (February 1982), [48].
Uncollected

C678 HOME THOUGHTS FROM ABROAD (Prose)
The Observer, 7 February 1982, 29.
Reviews of: *Collected Poems of Bernard Spencer*. Oxford. Szirtes, George. *November and May*. Secker and Warburg; Reading, Peter. *Tom O'Bedlam's Beauties*. Secker and Warburg; Mole, John. *Feeding the Lake*. Secker and Warburg.
Uncollected

C679 THE CASTLE IN SIGHT (Poem)
Westerly, Vol. 27, No. 1 (March 1982), 57.
Uncollected

C680 WORDS FOR MUSIC, PERHAPS . . . (Prose)
The Observer, 7 March 1982, 33.
Review of: Winn, James Anderson. *Unsuspected Eloquence*. Yale University Press.
Uncollected

C681 LOW THOUGHTS AND HIGH SPIRITS (Prose)
The Observer, 21 March 1982, 31.
Reviews of: Ewart, Gavin. *The New Ewart*. Hutchinson; MacBeth, George. *Poems from Oby*. Secker and Warburg; Motion, Andrew. *Independence*. Salamander Press; *Poetry Introduction 5*. Faber.
Uncollected

C682 THE CATS OF CAMPAGNATICO (Poem)
London Review of Books, Vol. 4, No. 6 (1-14 April 1982), 5.

C683 WHY WE DON'T TELL THE TRUTH (Poem)
Encounter, LVIII, No. 5 (May 1982), 39.
Uncollected

C684 THE VOICE OF PRIVACY (Prose)
The Observer, 2 May 1982, 31.
Reviews of: Ashbery, John. *Shadow Train*. Carcanet; Fowler, Alastair. *From the Domain of Arnheim*. Secker and Warburg; Walcott, Derek. *The Fortunate Traveller*. Faber; Foley, Michael. *The Go-Situation*. Blackstaff.
Uncollected

C685 THE GROANING MOUNTAIN (Poem)
The New Statesman, Vol. 103, No. 2672 (4 June 1982), 20.
Uncollected

C686 ASHBERRY AND OLD LACE (Prose)
The Times Literary Supplement, No. 4131 (4 June 1982), 611.
Review of: Ashberry, John. "The Heroes" and "The Philosopher" [plays]. (Cafe Theatre Upstairs).
Uncollected

C687 UNHEEDED HOWLS (Prose)
The Observer, 6 June 1982, 30.
Reviews of: Mitchell, Adrian. *For Beauty Douglas: Collected Poems 1953-1979*. Allison and Busby; Scannell, Vernon. *Winterlude*. Robson; Fuller, John. *Waiting for the Music*. Salamander; Paulin, Tom. *The Book of Juniper*. Bloodaxe.
Uncollected

C688 THE BOYS IN BLACK LEATHER (Prose)
The Observer, 27 June 1982, 30.
Review of: Gunn, Thom. *The Passages of Joy* and *The Occasions of Poetry*. Faber.
Uncollected

C689 THE PRISONER OF TRENDA (Poem)
The Times Literary Supplement, No. 4136 (9 July 1982), 735.
Uncollected

C690 AT THE PORTA HUMANA (Poem)
The Times Literary Supplement, No. 4137 (16 July 1982), 771.
Uncollected

C691 OUT OF THE ANTEROOM (Prose)
The Observer, 18 July 1982, 31.
Reviews of: Fenton, James. *The Memory of a War*. Salamander Press; McGuckian, Medbh. *The Flower Master*. Oxford; Scovell, E.J. *The Space Between*. Secker and Warburg.
Uncollected

C692 PROVERBIALIST (Prose)
Quarto, No. 30/31 (July/August 1982), 10-11.
Review of: *Di Piero*. Trans. Giacomo Leopardi. Pensieri.
Uncollected

C693 VIEW FROM HUMBERSIDE (Prose)
The Observer, 15 August 1982, 31.
Reviews of: Dunn, Douglas, ed. *A Rumored City: New Poets from Hull*. Bloodaxe; Didsbury, Peter. *The Butchers of Hull*. Bloodaxe; Dunn, Douglas, ed. *To Build a Bridge: A Celebration of Verse in Humberside*. Lincolnshire and Humberside Arts; Disch, Tom. *Burn This*. Hutchinson.
Uncollected

C694 NOVELIST AS COMPOSER (Prose)
The Observer, 12 September 1982, 33.
Review of: Burgess, Anthony. *This Man and Music*. Hutchinson.
Uncollected

C695 KEEP IT WITH KODAK (Poem)
Outposts Poetry Quarterly, No. 134 (Autumn 1982), 4-5.
M

C696 THE HUMAN FACE OF MARS (Prose)
The Observer, 3 October 1982, 32.
Reviews of: Reid, Christopher. *Pea Soup*. Oxford; Ash, John. *The Goodbyes*. Carcanet; Whitworth, John. *Poor Butterflies*. Secker and Warburg.
Uncollected

C697 MELTING MOMENTS. PUCCINI & HIS CRITICS (Prose)
Encounter, LIX, No. 5 (November 1982), 46-52.
Reviews of: Carner, Mosco. *Puccini*. Duckworth; Osborne, Charles. *The Complete Operas of Puccini*. Gollancz; Greenfield, Howard. *Puccini: A Biography*. Hale.
Uncollected

C698 THE MYSTERY OF YOUTH (Prose)
The Observer, 7 November 1982, 28.
Reviews of: Jamie, Kathleen. *Black Spiders*. Salamander; Fainthorpe, U.A. *Standing To*. Peterloo. Elliot, Alastair. *Talking Back*. Secker and Warburg; Greig, Andrew. *Surviving Passages*. Canongate; Butlin, Ron. *The Exquisite Instrument*. Salamander.
Uncollected

C699 BOOKS OF THE YEAR (Prose)
The Observer, 5 December 1982, 25.
Uncollected

C700 THE LUCK OF THE IRISH (Prose)
The Observer, 19 December 1982, 31.
Reviews of: Mahon, Derek. *The Hunt by Night*. Oxford; Rich, Adrienne. *A Wild Patience has Taken Me This Far*. Norton; Burns, Jim. *International Memorandum*. Rivelin Press; Ewart, Gavin. *More Little Ones*. Anvil.
Uncollected

1983

C701 MATUTINAL (Poem)
The Glasgow Magazine, No. 1 (Winter 1982/83), 3
TAP

C702 JUMPING TO CONCLUSIONS (Poem)
The Glasgow Magazine, No. 1 (Winter 1982/83), 4-5.
Uncollected

C703 THE BIOGRAPHER PROMENADES (Poem)
The Glasgow Magazine, No. 1 (Winter 1982/83), 5-6.
Uncollected

C704 WHERE WE CAME IN (Poem)
Poetry Review, Vol. 73, No. 1 (1983), 5.
Uncollected

C705 CLIPBOARD (Poem)
Poetry Review, Vol. 73, No. 1 (1983), 6.
Uncollected

C706 ELEGY AND FANFARE (Poem)
Poetry Review, Vol. 73, No. 1 (1983), 7-8.
Uncollected

C707 LAST YEARS SENTENCES (Poem)
Poetry Review, Vol. 73, No. 1 (1983), 9.
Uncollected

C708 THE MINERAL LINE (Poem)
Poetry Review, Vol. 73, No. 1 (1983), 10-11.
Uncollected

C709 TWO VOICES FOR OUR TIME (Prose)
The Observer, 23 January 1983, 47.
Reviews of: Prynne, J.H. *Poems*. Agneau; Morgan, Edwin. *Poems of Thirty Years*. Carcanet.
Uncollected

C710 PURSUING PLEASURE (Prose)
The Times Literary Supplement, No. 4165 (28 January 1983), 88.
Review of: Griffiths, Paul (Ed.). *Igor Stravinsky: The Rake's Progress*. Cambridge University Press.
Uncollected

C711 WHAT IS EVIL? (Poem)
Encounter, LX, No. 3 (March 1983), [35].
Uncollected

C712 GRAVE SHORTAGE OF APPROACHABLE CATS (Poem)
Thames Poetry, Vol. 11, No. 12 (March 1983), 13-14.
Uncollected

C713 SCHEIN UND SEIN (Poem)
Thames Poetry, Vol. 11, No. 12 (March 1983), 15.
Uncollected

C714 THE STILL SMALL VOICE (Prose)
The Observer, 20 March 1983, 33.
Reviews of: Beer, Patricia. *The Lie of the Land*. Hutchinson; Barker, Sebastian. *A Fire in the Rain*. Martin Brian & O'Keefe; Stevenson, Anne. *Minute by Glass Minute*. Oxford; Rawling, Tom. *Ghost at my back*. Oxford.
Uncollected

C715 A CATECHISM (Poem)
Gallimaufry, No. 10 (Spring 1983), 15.
Uncollected

C716 ANALOGUE OF HELEN (Poem)
Gallimaufry, No. 10 (Spring 1983), 21.
Uncollected

C717 PETER PORTER WRITES (Prose)
The Poetry Book Society Bulletin, No. 116. (Spring 1983), [2-3]
Uncollected

C718 DIGITAL WATCHWORDS (Prose)
The Observer, 10 April 1983, 31.
Reviews of: Fuller, John. *The Beautiful Inventions*. Secker and Warburg; O'Brien, Sean. *The Indoor Park*. Bloodaxe; Joseph, Jenny. *Beyond Descartes*. Secker and Warburg.
Uncollected

C719 BOOKS & WRITERS. THE MYSTERY & THE MUSIC. ON MOZART'S LIFE (Prose)
Encounter, LX, No. 6 (June 1983), 53-58.
Reviews of: Hildesheimer, Wolfgang. *Mozart*. Dent. Robbins Landon, H.C. *Mozart and the Masons: New Light on the Lodge "Crowned Hope"*. Thames and Hudson.
Uncollected

C720 CHARNEL HOUSE CHIC (Prose)
The Observer, 12 June 1983, 29.
Reviews of: Forche, Carolyn. *The Country Between*. Cape; Starbuck, George. *The Argot Merchant Disaster*. Secker and Warburg; Motion, Andrew. *Secret Narratives*. Salamander Press; Smith, Ken. *The Poet Reclining*. Bloodaxe.
Uncollected

C721 A BUMPER BOOK OF HORRORS (Prose)
The Observer, 3 July 1983, 29.
Reviews of: Reading, Peter. *Diplopic*. Secker and Warburg; Paulin, Tom. *Liberty Tree*. Faber; Rumens, Carol. *Star Whisper*. Secker and Warburg; Adcock, Fleur. *The Virgin and the Nightingale*. Bloodaxe; Dunmore. Helen. *The Apple Fall*. Bloodaxe.
Uncollected

C722 A GUIDE TO THE GODS (Poem)
The Times Literary Supplement, No. 4190 (22 July 1983), 768.
Uncollected

C723 A VEIN OF RACINE'S (Poem)
The Times Literary Supplement, No. 4192 (5 August 1983), 839.
Uncollected

C724 MELLOW PHILIPPICS (Prose)
The Observer, 28 August 1983, 24.
Reviews of: Barker, George. *Anno Domini*. Faber; Michie, James. *New and Selected Poems*. Chatto; Brown, George Mackay. *Voyages*. Chatto; Constantine, David. *Watching for Dolphins*. Bloodaxe.
Uncollected

C725 GULLFEST (Poem)
Quadrant, No. 193, Vol. XXVII, No. 9 (September 1983), 30.
Uncollected

C726 FOR THE LIFE OF ME (Poem)
Quadrant, No. 193, Vol. XXVII, No. 9 (September 1983), 30.
Uncollected

C727 THE HEDONISTS REHEARSE THE UPRISING (Poem)
The Times Literary Supplement, No. 4200 (30 September 1983), 1036.
Uncollected

C728 THE DECLINE OF THE NORTH (Poem)
Grampian English Views, Vol. 6, No. 3 (Autumn 1983), 17.
Uncollected

C729 THE FLOCK AND THE STAR (Poem)
Strawberry Fare, (Autumn) 1983, 37.
Uncollected

C730 REDSKINS IN BELFAST (Prose)
The Observer, 16 October 1983, 33.
Reviews of: Muldoon, Paul. *Quoof*. Faber; Curnow, Allen. *You Will Know When You Get There*. Auckland University Press; Piercy, Marge. *Stone, Paper, Knife*. Pandora Press.
Uncollected

C731 JIFFY BAGS OF FICTION (Prose)
The Observer, 30 October 1983, 33.
Uncollected

C732 A POET FOR OUR TIME (Prose)
The Observer, 6 November 1983, 31.
Review of: Fenton, James. *The Memory of War and Children in Exile: Poems 1968-83*. Penguin.
Uncollected

C733 BOOKS OF THE YEAR (Prose)
The Observer, 4 December 1983, 25
Uncollected

C734 CATCHING THE TONE (Prose)
The Observer, 18 December 1983, 29.
Reviews of: Brownjohn, Alan. *Collected Poems 1952-83*. Secker and Warburg; Scupham, Peter. *Winter Quarters*. Oxford; Howell, Anthony. *Notions of a Mirror*. Anvil.

C735 AUSTRALIAN POETRY TODAY (Prose)
Aquarius, 15/16 (1983-84), 11-13.
Uncollected

C736 FAST FORWARD (Poem)
Aquarius, 15/16 (1983-84), 40.
Uncollected

C737 THE LOTTERY (Poem)
Workshop, Issue No. 7 (n.d.), 20-21.
Uncollected

C738 THE AMPUTEE (Poem)
Workshop, Issue No. 7 (n.d.), 22.
Uncollected

C739 FINGERS AND THUMBS (Prose)
The Observer, 15 January 1984, 49.
Review of: Scruton, Roger. *The Aesthetic Understanding*. Carcanet.

Uncollected

C740 THE MUSIC OF IDEAS (Prose)
The Observer, 22 January 1984, 53.
Reviews of: Szirtes, George. *Short Wave*. Secker & Warburg; Hofmann, Michael. *Nights in the Iron Hotel*. Faber; Morgan, Pete. *A Winter Visitor*. Secker & Warburg.
Uncollected

C741 THE PLAYFUL MUSE (Prose)
The Observer, 11 March 1984, 25
Reviews of: Durcan, Paul. *Jumping the Train Tracks With Angela*. Raven/Carcanet; Hollander, John. *Powers of Thirteen*. Secker & Warburg; Ewart, Gavin. *The Ewart Quarto*. Hutchinson; Lerner, Laurence. *Chapter and Verse and Selected Poems*. Secker & Warburg.
Uncollected

C742 DOES A RAKE GO TO A BROTHEL TO SING? (Prose)
About the House, Vol. 6, No. 11 (Spring 1984), 42-43.
Uncollected

C743 SOME CONTEMPORARIES (Poem)
The Glasgow Magazine, No. 4 (Spring 1984), 26-27.
Note: the poem has the following subtitles:
Page 26: *The Schoolmaster*
The Music Critic
The Controversalist
The Nature Poet

Page 27: *The Junior Minister*
The Series Editor
The Boutique Owner
The Metaphor Man
The Eternal Student
Uncollected

C744 VOLLENDET DAS EWIGE WERK! (FOR STEPHEN SPENDER, 1984) (Poem)
Illuminations, [III] (Spring 1984), 2.
Uncollected

C745 FORMS AND INFLUENCES. A SYMPOSIUM (Prose)
The Times Literary Supplement, No. 4230 (27 April 1984), 462-463.
Uncollected

C746 INNOCENCE OF EXPERIENCE (Prose)
The Observer, 29 April 1984, 22.
Reviews of: Bottrall, Ronald. *Against a Setting Sun*. Allison & Busby; Prince, F.T. *Later On*. Anvil Press; Disch, Tom. *Here I Am, There You Are, Where Were We?* Hutchinson.
Uncollected

C747 PAINTING IN WORDS (Prose)
The Observer, 17 June 1984, 22.
Reviews of: Clampitt, Amy. *The Kingfisher*. Faber; Tomlinson, Charles. *Notes from New York*. Oxford; Rennie, Neil. *The Cargo*. TNR Publications; Earle, Jean. *The Intent Look*. Gomer Press.
Uncollected

C748 A TRIBUTE TO MY ENEMIES (Poem)
Encounter, LXIII, No. 1 (June 1984), [28].
Uncollected

C749 CITIES OF LIGHT (Poem)
Scripsi, Vol. 2, No. 4 (June 1984), 59-61.
FF

C750 DEJECTION. AN ODE (Poem)
Scripsi, Vol. 2, No. 4 (June 1984), 63-64.
FF

C751 HORACE'S FOOTSTEPS (Prose)
The Observer, 29 July 1984, 20.
Reviews of: Elliot, Alistair. *On the Appian Way*. Secker & Warburg; Crichton Smith, Iain. *The Exiles*. Carcanet; Leale, B.C. *Leviathan*. Allison & Busby; Hill, Selima. *Saying Hello at the Station*. Chatto & Windus.
Uncollected

C752 PARADIS ARTIFICIEL (Poem)
Encounter, LXIII, No. 2 (July/August 1984), 15.
Uncollected

C753 YOU HEAR IT ALWAYS (Poem by David Rokeah)
Encounter, LXIII, No. 2 (July/August 1984), 37
(Translated from the Hebrew by the author and Peter Porter)
Uncollected

C754 PLEASURES OF OBSCURITY (Prose)
The Observer, 19 August 1984, 19.
Reviews of: McGuckian, Medbh. *Venus and the Rain*. Oxford; Lomas, Herbert. *Fire in the Garden*. Oxford; Walcott, Derek. *Midsummer*. Faber; Kuppner, Frank. *A Bad Day for the Sung Dynasty*. Carcanet.
Uncollected

C755 FROM THE TRANSLATION CONFERENCE (Poem)
The Times Literary Supplement, No. 4255 (19 October 1984), 1193.
Uncollected

C756 BREAKING NEW GROUND (Prose)
The Observer, 25 November 1984, 26.
Reviews of: Ash, John. *The Branching Stairs*. Carcanet; Morrison, Blake. *Dark Glasses*. Chatto & Windus; Nichols, Grace. *The Fat Black Woman's Poems*. Virago; Kazantzis, Judith. *Let's Pretend*. Virago; Fell, Alison. *Kisses for Mayakovsky*. Virago.
Uncollected

C757 BOOKS OF THE YEAR (Prose)
The Observer, 2 December 1984, 19.
Uncollected

C758 THE WORLD'S WEDDING (Poem)
The Times Literary Supplement, No. 4265 (28 December 1984), 1491.
Uncollected

1985

C759 PISA OSCURA (Poem)
London Review of Books, Vol. 6, No. 24 (20 December 1984 to 24 January 1985), 6.
Uncollected

C760 SMALL LATIN, AND LESS GREEK (Poem)
London Review of Books, Vol. 6, No. 24 (20 December 1984 to 24 January 1985), 6.
Uncollected

C761 A BAG OF PRESSMINTS (Poem)
London Review of Books, Vol. 6, No. 24 (20 December 1984 to 24 January 1985), 6.
Uncollected

C762 THE STARS LOOK DOWN (Prose)
The Observer, 27 January 1985, 50.
Reviews of: Keene, Dennis. *Universe*. Carcanet; Motion, Andrew. *Dangerous Play*. Salamander; Mole, John. *In and Out of the Apple*. Secker & Warburg; Elon, Florence. *Self-Made*. Secker & Warburg.
Uncollected

C763 DISTURBING THE AUGUSTAN PEACE (Prose)
The Times Literary Supplement, No. 4273 (22 February 1985), 187-188.
Review of: Lonsdale, Roger (Ed.). *The New Oxford Book of Eighteenth Century Verse*. Oxford.
Uncollected

C764 TRUE VOICE OF FEELING (Prose)
The Observer, 17 March 1985, 24.
Reviews of: Dunn, Douglas. *Elegies*. Faber; Leale, B.C. *The Colours of Ancient Dreams*. Calder; McCarthy, Thomas. *The Non-Aligned Storyteller*. Anvil; Scammell, William. *Jouissance*. Peterloo.
Uncollected

C765 LAST TO THE LAST (Poem)
Hubbub, III, No. 1 (Spring 1985), 51
Uncollected

C766 LAZARUS UPWIND (Poem)
Hubbub, III, No. 1 (Spring 1985), 52-53.
Uncollected

C767 DISC HORSE (Poem)
Hubbub, III, No. 1 (Spring 1985), 54-55.
Uncollected

C768 HOME AND HOSED (Poem)
Encounter, LXIV, No. 4 (April 1985), [37].
Uncollected

C769 BRYLCREEM HALOES (Prose)
The Observer, 12 May 1985, 21.
Reviews of: Redgrove, Peter. *The Man Named East*. Routledge; Price, Jonathan. *Everything Must Go*. Secker & Warburg; Taylor, Brian. *Transit*. London Magazine Editions.
Uncollected

C770 SLEEPING BEAUTIES (Prose)
The Observer, 2 June 1985, 22.
Reviews of: Longley, Michael. *Poems 1963-1983*. Salamander; Causley, Charles. *Secret Destinations*. Macmillan; Hulse, Michael. *Propaganda*. Secker & Warburg; Gohorry, John. *A Voyage Round the Moon*. Peterloo.
Uncollected

C771 CAMBRIDGE SCHOOL (Prose)
The Observer, 7 July 1985, 21.
Reviews of: Crozier, Andrew. *All Where Each Is*. Allardyce, Barnett; Birtwhistle, John. *Our Worst Suspicions*. Anvil; Manhire, Bill. *Zoetropes*. Carcanet.
Uncollected

C772 SUSANNAH AND THE ELDERS (Poem)
Poetry, CXLVI, No. 4 (July 1985), 209-210.
Uncollected.

C773 TO BE ON THE SAFE SIDE (Poem)
Poetry, CXLVI, No. 4 (July 1985), 210-211.
Uncollected

C774 THE REST ON THE FLIGHT (Poem)
The Times Literary Supplement, No. 4296 (2 August 1985), 839
Uncollected

C775 AUSSIE DOOMWATCH (Prose)
The Observer, 11 August 1985, 21
Reviews of: Wallace-Crabbe, Chris. *The Amorous Cannibal*. Oxford; Butlin, Ron. *Ragtime in Unfamiliar Bars*. Secker & Warburg; Berry, James. *Chain of Days*. Oxford; Murphy, Richard. *The Price of Stone*. Faber
Uncollected

C776 CASSETTES OF ATROCITY (Prose)
The Observer, 1 September 1985, 19.
Reviews of: Reading, Peter. *Ukulele Music*. Secker & Warburg; Simmons, James. *From the Irish*. Blackstaff Press; Jennings, Elizabeth. *Extending the Territory*. Carcanet
Uncollected

C777 A BORN-AGAIN GRAMMARIAN (Poem)
Encounter, LXV, No. 3 (September/October 1985), 24
Uncollected

C778 A PERFORMER WAITING IN THE WINGS (Prose)
The Observer, 6 October 1985, 25
Reviews of: Williams, Hugo. *Writing Home*. Oxford; Reynolds, Oliver. *Skevington's Daughter*. Faber; Hope, Christopher. *Englishmen*. Heinemann; Stevenson, Anne. *The Fiction-Makers*. Oxford
Uncollected

C779 NEGLECTED FICTIONS (Prose)
The Times Literary Supplement, No. 4307 (18 October 1985), 1187.
Uncollected

C780 ATTACCA (Poem)
The Times Literary Supplement, No. 4310 (8 November 1985), 1254.
Uncollected

C781 SONGS FROM ANOTHER COUNTRY (Prose)
The Observer, 17 November 1985, 31.
Reviews of: Reid, Christopher. *Katerina Brac*. Faber; Dooley, Tim. *The Interrupted Dream*. Anvil; Whitworth, John. *Lovely Day for a Wedding*. Secker & Warburg; Latham, John. *From the Other Side of the Street*. Peterloo.
Uncollected

C782 BOOKS OF THE YEAR (Prose)
The Observer, 1 December 1985, 17.
Uncollected

C783 THE BOOK OF COMMON FEAR (Poem)
Outposts Poetry Quarterly, No. 147 (Winter 1985), 10.
Uncollected

C784 'THE DULL MAY WAKEN TO A HUMMING-BIRD' (Poem)
Poetry Australia, No. 102 (1985), 56-57.
Uncollected

C785 THE PRINCE OF ANACHRONISMS (Poem)
Poetry Australia, No. 102 (1985), 58.
Uncollected

1986

C786 ALL TOGETHER NOW (Prose)
The Observer, 12 January 1986, 47
Reviews of: Hill, Geoffrey. *Collected Poems*; MacCaig, Norman. *Collected Poems*. Chatto & Windus; Fuller, John. *Selected Poems 1954-1982*. Secker & Warburg; Hall, J.C. *Selected and New Poems*. Secker & Warburg.
Uncollected

C787 THE GRIMMER REACHES (Prose)
The Observer, 26 January 1986, 50
Reviews of: Durcan, Paul. *The Berlin Wall Cafe*. Blackstaff Press; Sweeney, Matthew. *The Lame Waltzer*. Allison & Busby/Raven Arts; St Aubin de Terán, Lisa. *The High Place*. Cape.
Uncollected

C788 ESSAY ON DREAMS (Poem)
London Magazine, New Series, Vol. 25, No. 11 (February 1986) [57]-58.
Uncollected

C789 A NATIVE TRADITION (Prose)
The Times Literary Supplement, No. 4327 (7 March 1986), 248.
Review of: Simon, Neil. *Brighton Beach Memoirs* (play). Lyttleton Theatre.
Uncollected

C790 OVER-EGGING THE PUDDING (Prose)
The Observer, 9 March 1986, 27
Reviews of: Clampitt, Amy. *What the Light Was Like*. Faber; Roberts, Michèle. *The Mirror of the Mother*. Methuen; Davenport, Guy. *Thasos and Ohio*. Carcanet; Barnett, Anthony. *North North I Said*. Allardyce Barnett.
Uncollected

C791 MARS AND VENUS (Poem)
The Poetry Society Newsletter, April 1986, [5].
Uncollected

C792 TO LACEDAEMON DID MY LAND EXTEND (Poem)
The Rialto, No. 5 (Spring 1986), 4.
Uncollected

C793 NEVERTHELESS (Poem)
The Rialto, No. 5 (Spring 1986), 6-7.
Uncollected

C794 LEGS ON WHEELS (Poem)
The Times Literary Supplement, No. 4335 (2 May 1986), 476.
Uncollected

C795 SHADOWS OF BUDAPEST (Prose)
The Observer, 1 June 1986, 22.
Reviews of: Szirtes, George. *The Photographer in Winter*. Secker & Warburg; Lomas, Herbert. *Letters in the Dark*. Oxford; Pitt-Kethley, Fiona. *Sky Ray Lolly*. Chatto & Windus; Ormsby, Frank. *A Northern Spring*. Secker & Warburg.
Uncollected

C796 THE 'SLEEP-OUT' WARS (Poem)
The Times Literary Supplement, No. 4345 (11 July 1986), 754.
Uncollected

C797 RURITANIAN RESIDUALS (Poem)
The Times Literary Supplement, No. 4347 (25 July 1986), 813
Uncollected

C798 DOCTOR'S DILEMMAS (Prose)
The Observer, 27 July 1986, 23.
Reviews of: Abse, Dannie. *Ask the Bloody Horse*. Hutchinson; MacBeth, George. *The Cleaver Garden*. Secker & Warburg; Crossley-Holland, Kevin. *Waterslain*. Hutchinson; Hesketh, Phoebe. *Over the Brook*. Taxus.
Uncollected

C799 MISSING THE MUSIC (Prose)
The Observer, 24 August 1986, 21.
Review of: Raine, Craig. *The Electrification of the Soviet Union*. Faber.
Uncollected

C800 PUTTING BACK THE FIZZ (Prose)
The Observer, 31 August 1986, 21.
Reviews of: Smith, Ken. *Terra*. Bloodaxe; Shuttle, Penelope. *The Lion from Rio*. Oxford Univ. Press; Scupham, Peter. *Out Late*. Oxford Univ. Press; Horowitz, Michael. *Midsummer Morning Jog Log*. Five Seasons Press.
Uncollected

C801 SPIDERWISE (Poem)
London Review of Books, Vol. 8, No. 15 (4 September 1986), 12
Uncollected

C802 A SLICE OF VERISMO (Prose)
The Times Literary Supplement, No. 4353 (5 September 1986), 976.
Review of the film "Ossessione"
Uncollected

C803 STYLE FROM THE STICKS (Prose)
The Observer, 5 October 1986, 25.
Reviews of: Houston, Douglas. *With the Offal Eaters*. Bloodaxe; Howell, Anthony. *Why I May Never See the Walls of China*. Anvil; Moore, Alan. *Opia* . Anvil; *New Chatto Poets*. Chatto.

C804 OVERHEARD AND UNDERPHRASED (Poem)
The Times Literary Supplement, No. 4358 (10 October 1986), 1144.
Uncollected

C805 HEAD ABOVE THE WATER (Prose)
The Observer, 2 November 1986, 31.
Review of: Osborne, Charles. *Giving it Away*. Secker & Warburg.
Uncollected

C806 ENGLISH, THEIR ENGLISH (prose)
The Observer, 9 November 1986, 28.
Reviews of: Adcock, Fleur. *The Incident Book*. Oxford; Reading, Peter. *Stet and Essential Reading*. Secker & Warburg; Hofmann, Michael. *Acrimony*. Faber; Markham, E.A. *Living in Disguise*. Anvil; Markham, E.A. *Lambchops in Papua/New Guinea*. Sow's Ear.
Uncollected

C807 A POPULAR PURGATORY (Prose)
The Times Literary Supplement, No. 4364 (21 November 1986), 1313.
Review of the film, "Ginger and Fred."
Uncollected

C808 BOOKS OF THE YEAR (Prose)
The Observer, 30 November 1986, 21.
Uncollected

C809 ALAS, FLEETING (Poem)
Scripsi, Vol. 4, No. 2 (November 1986), 6-7.
Uncollected

C810 TIPP-EX FOR THE OSCAR (Poem)
Scripsi, Vol. 4, No. 2 (November 1986), 7-9.
Uncollected

C811 THE COMPACT DESK (Poem)
Scripsi, Vol. 4, No. 2 (November 1986), 9-10
Uncollected

C812 A HEADLAND NEAR ADELAIDE (Poem)
Scripsi, Vol. 4, No. 2 (November 1986), 11.
Uncollected

C813 THE MAP OF THE MURRAY (Prose)
Scripsi, Vol. 4, No. 2 (November 1986), 13-18.
Review of: *The New Oxford Book of Australian Verse*. Chosen by Les A. Murray. Oxford University Press.
Uncollected

C814 THINGS AS THEY ARE (Prose)
The Observer, 21 December 1986, 20.
Reviews of: Middleton, Christopher. *Two Horse Wagon Going By*. Carcanet; Adams, Anna. *Trees in Sheep Country*. Peterloo; Feinstein, Elaine. *Badlands*. Hutchinson; Romer, Stephen. *Idols*. Oxford Univ. Press.
Uncollected

C815 TIP-TOEING THROUGH THE PANTHEON (Prose)
The Times Literary Supplement, No. 4369 (26 December 1986), 1441.
Review of: Everett, Barbara. *Poets in Their Time: Essays on English poetry from Donne to Larkin*. Faber.
Uncollected

C816 WHO NEEDS IT? (Poem)
Ambit, No. 103 (1986), 4-5.
Uncollected

C817 THE ONES WHO DO NOT MATTER (Poem)
Verse, Issue 5 (1986), 6.
Uncollected

D

INTERVIEWS

This list of interviews is confined to those interviews in which Peter Porter discusses his poetry or philosophy in direct response to an individual interrogator.

D1 "Peter Porter" in Orr, Peter, ed. *The Poet Speaks*. London: Routledge & Kegan Paul, 1966, 179-184. (The original interview took place on August 25, 1963.)

D2 "Poets on the Vietnam War," *The Review*, No. 18 (April 1968), 39-40.

D3 "Gavin Ewart, Peter Porter and Alan Brownjohn Talking to Some Students at Manresa House," *The Occasional Windhover* (Summer 1969), 5-23.

D4 "Poetry 1970. A Questionnaire," *Tracks 8 & Tamarish* (Summer 1970), 10.

D5 Douglas, Denis. "Conversation with Peter Porter." *Overland*, No. 44 (Winter 1970), 33-34.

D6 "The Poet in the 'Sixties: Vices and Virtues - a recorded conversation with Peter Porter" in Schmidt, Michael and Grevel Lindop. *British Poetry Since 1960. A Critical Survey*. South Hinksey (Oxford): Carcanet Press, 1972, [202]-212.

D7 Martin, Philip. "Interview with Peter Porter," *Quadrant*, No. 87, XVIII, No. 1 (January-February 1974), 9-19.

D8 "Poet...Politics...Apocalypse...," *Aspect. Art and Literature* (Spring 1975), 5-12.

D9 Raymond, Vicki. "Peter Porter visits the University," *University of Tasmania News*, No. 66 (April 1980), [1]-2.

D10 Coleman, Richard. "A man of many places," *Sydney Morning Herald* (April 12, 1980), 15.

D11 MacLeod, Donald. "'Philosopher of captions' who repairs wounded poetry," *The Scotsman* (May 19, 1981), 11.

D12 Bennett, Bruce. "Peter Porter in profile," *Westerly*, Vol. 27, No. 1 (March 1982), 45-46.

D13 Brownjohn, Alan. "Alan Brownjohn talks to Peter Porter," *The Literary Review*, No. 59 (May 1983), 18-22.

D14 Long, Angela. "A Season in Terra Primitivis," *The National Times* (Sydney, Australia) (June 17 to 23, 1983), 29.

D15 Lee, Hermione. "Interview. Peter Porter on the poetry of James Fenton," *Book Four*, Issue 5 (13th November 1983), 2-4.

D16 "What I Have Written...," *Hemisphere*, Vol. 28, No. 3 (Nov/Dec 1983), 150-156.

INTERVIEWS

D17 "Peter Porter. Interviewed by Martin Harrison," *Australian Literary Studies*, Vol. 11, No. 4 (October 1984), 458-467.

D18 Kavanagh, Paul. "Little Harmonic Labyrinths: An Interview with Peter Porter," *Southerly*, No. 1 (March 1985), 12-22.

E

RECORDINGS

In this section is a list of commercially published recordings of Peter Porter reading his own poems either alone or in company with other poets. Each entry includes an abstract of the record label, a description of the recording, a list of the contents, and where possible, the circumstances of the recording and publication. No attempt has been made to list recordings made at readings or on other occasions that are in institutional archives or owned privately.

E1 a. *The Jupiter anthology of 20th century English poetry, part III* edited by Anthony Thwaite.

Jupiter Recordings Ltd., London, 1963, JUR 00A8.

One 12 in., 33 1/3 r.p.m., monaural disc. Matrix: side I: V A V I//420; side 2: V B V I// 421 11.

Contents: Side 2: What a Lying Lot the Writers Are" and "Somme and Flanders."

b. *Anthology of 20th century English poetry, part III* [edited by Anthony Thwaite].

A Jupiter Recording issued by Folkways, Folkways Records & Service Corporation, New York, N.Y., 1967, FL 9879.

One 12 in., 33 1/3 r.p.m., monaural disc. Matrix: side I: FL 9879A; side 2: FL 9879B.

Contents: Same as E1 a.

c. *The Jupiter Anthology Part Three* 00A8 [edited by Anthony Thwaite].

Audio-Visual Productions, 15 Temple Sheen Road, London SW14 7PY, Telephone 01-876 0064 [February 1975], 00A8

One two track standard cassette.

Contents: Same as E1 a.

E2 *The Poet Speaks*. Ted Hughes, Peter Porter, Thom Gunn, Sylvia Plath. Edited by Peter Orr.

Argo Record Company Ltd., London, 1965, RG 455.

One 12 in., 33 1/3 r.p.m., monaural disc. Matrix: side 1: ARG 2713; side 2: ARG 2714.

Note: The above "ARG" numbers are taken from the label of the record; incised on the record itself are: ARG-2713-1A and ARG-2714-1A.

Contents: Side 1: "Beast and the Beauty," "Made in Heaven," "Who Gets the Pope's Nose?." and "Happening at Sordid Creek" read by Peter Porter.

Notes: Recorded 28 August, 1963 and "made by the British Council in association with the Poetry Room in the Lamont Library of Harvard University." The recordings are accompanied by abstracts of interviews which were published in their entirety in *The Poet Speaks*, edited by Peter Orr and published by Routledge & Kegan Paul (see D1).

On the front sleeve of the record is a drawing by Arthur Wragg of three figures in the foreground and outlines of houses in the background.

E3 *Poets on Record 12*. Peter Porter.

University of Queensland Press, St. Lucia, Queensland, 1974.

One 6 3/4 in., 45 r.p.m., monaural disc. Matrix: side 1 C4KB-1529; side 2: C4KA-1530.

Contents: Side 1: "Your Attention Please," "Phar Lap in the Melbourne Museum" "Once Bitten, Twice Bitten; Once Shy, Twice Shy," and "Notes to a Biographer"; Side 2: "The Sadness of the Creatures," "Sex and the Over Forties," "Story Which Should Have Happened," "Mort aux Chats," all read by Peter Porter.

Note: The record is attached to the inside front cover of the book: Peter Porter reads from his own work (See A12)

E4 *British Poets of Our Time*. Peter Redgrove. Peter Porter. Edited by Peter Orr.

Argo Record Company (Argo. The Decca Record Company Limited), 1976, PLP 1204.

One 12 in., 33 1/3 r.p.m., monaural disc. Matrix: Side 1: ARG 4237; side 2: ARG 4238.

Contents: Side 2: "The Last of the Dinosaurs," "Homily in the English Reading Room," "From the Porter Song Book. I, III. The Sanatorium, IV Clairvoyant, VI Genius Loci, XII White Wedding," "The Last of England. Europe," "The Sadness of the Creatures," "Fossil Gathering," "Sex and the Over Forties," "The Dust," "Mort aux Chats," "Print Out: Apocalypse," "Frogs at Lago di Bolsena."

Note: Cover photo: "Kelly, Spring," by Sidney Nolan.

E5 LP. *London Poets*. Fleur Adcock. Gavin Ewart. Richard Freeman. Peter Porter.

London Poets, 144 Great Marlborough Street, London W.1, n.d.

One 12 in., 33 1/3 r.p.m., monaural disc. Matrix: side 1: FGRP 01A; side 2: FGRP 01B.

Contents: Side 2: "Competition is Healthy," "The Sadness of the Creatures," "Thomas Hardy at Westbourne Park Villas," "Tending Towards the Condition," "A Study of a Bird," "On First Looking into Chapman's Hesiod," "His and Hers," and "The Lying Art."

F

ADDENDA

F1 SPRING COLLECTION 1977

[in brilliant blue (177) letters] SPRING COLLECTION | [in black letters] RICHARD CARLILE R.S. THOMAS | KATHARINE MIDDLETON PETER | SCUPHAM DAVID DAY GEORGE | SZIRTES MADGE HALES PATRIC | DICKSON JOHN STALLWORTHY | JOHN ORMOND PATRICIA BEER | LAWRENCE SAIL PAUL HYLAND | ANTHONY THWAITE JOHN MOLE | FREDA DOWNIE PETER PORTER | [in brilliant blue letters] MANDEVILLE PRESS | [in brilliant blue: publisher's logo] | [in brilliant blue] 1977.

Collation: $[1]^{14}$ = 14 leaves; 22 x 14 cm.

Binding: Sewn into off-white heavy laid paper wrappers and lettered on the front wrapper in black: SPRING COLLECTION | RICHARD CARLILE R.S. THOMAS | KATHARINE MIDDLETON PETER | SCUPHAM DAVID DAY GEORGE | SZIRTES MADGE HALES PATRIC | DICKSON JON STALLWORTHY | JOHN ORMOND PATRICIA BEER | LAWRENCE SAIL PAUL HYLAND | ANTHONY THWAIT JOHN MOLE | FREDA DOWNIE PETER PORTER | MANDEVILLE PRESS; the reas wrapper is blank; white wove paper; all edges trimmed.

Publication date: 15 April 1977

Price: 60p

Number of copies: 250. The publisher reports that there were an additional five copies in marbled wrappers for friends of the Press.

Contents: "The Picture of Nobody," pp. 18-91.

Note: This poem appears here for the first time in print.

F2 NEW POETRY 7 1981

New Poetry 7 | an Arts Council anthology | edited by David Harsent | Hutchinson London Melbourne Sydney Auckland Johannesburg | in association with | The Arts Council of Great Britain and PEN.

Collation: $[1-4]^{16}$ = 64 leaves; 21.5 x 13.5 cm.

Binding: Bound in gray purplish blue (204) paper covered boards and lettered down the spine in solve: [in two lines] NEW POETRY 7 An Arts Council Anthology | Edited by David Harsent HUTCHINSON [across the base of the spine: publisher's logo]; white wove paper; all edges trimmed; white wove endpapers; dust wrapper of white wove paper, shiny on the exterior and printed in deep blue (183) and white.

Publication date: 9 November 1981

Price: £6.50

Number of copies: 776

Contents: "Dis Mannibus," pp. 85-86, collected in FF; "A Study of a Sheep," pp. 87-88.

Note: These poems appear here for the first time in print.

F3 SUCKING ROCK AT THE SEASIDE (Poem)
The Poetry Review, LIII, No. 3 (Summer 1962), 163.
Uncollected

F4 THE LAST OF ENGLAND (Poem)
Clare Market Review, Vol. 64, No. ii (Summer 1968), 54.
TLOE, CP

F5 LINES WRITTEN IMMEDIATELY AFTER WAKING (Poem)
Clare Market Review, Vol. 64, No. ii (Summer 1968), 54.

F6 THE GLASS (Poem)
Clare Market Review, Vol. 64, No. ii (Summer 1968), 54.
Uncollected

F7 HALF-MAST POEMS (Poem)
Clare Market Review, Vol. 64, No. ii (Summer 1968), 55.
APF, CP

F8 AN ARROW (Poem by David Rokeah)
Encounter, LX, No. 3 (March 1983), 33.
(Translated from the Hebrew by the author and Peter Porter.)

INDEX

References in this index are to item numbers in the bibliography. The titles of all items written by Peter Porter are capitalized. The titles of books and pamphlets by Porter and all other books, periodicals and newspapers are in italics. Untitled poems are indexed by first lines enclosed by quotation marks, with the note that the reference is a first line and the poem is untitled. The titles of books reviewed by Peter Porter, the authors of books reviewed and the titles of the reviews have not been indexed; however, these reviews are given reference numbers after the titles of the periodical or newspaper in which they appeared. Publishers of books and persons listed in the introduction or acknowledgements sections of this book are not indexed.

INDEX

INDEX

INDEX

INDEX

INDEX

INDEX

INDEX